Common Formative Assessments 2.0

I respectfully dedicate this book to W. James Popham, professor emeritus, UCLA Graduate School of Education, and the author of 30 books, 200 journal articles, 50 research reports, and 175 papers presented to research societies. I credit Dr. Popham with single-handedly extending my thinking on educational assessment beyond what perhaps even he could imagine. He was the first to lead me to the lightbulb realization: "Assessment revolves around inference making."

Two of his many wonderful books, **Test Better, Teach Better** *(2003) and* **Transformative Assessment** *(2008), have profoundly influenced my own published works on effective assessment practices, particularly this present volume in which I cite him repeatedly. His deep insights into the true purpose and function of assessment, coupled with his sincere desire to help educators improve the quality and usefulness of their classroom assessments and related instruction, have created an educational legacy that will surely stand the test of time.*

For your wisdom, intelligence, common sense, sparkling wit and humor, I sincerely thank you, Jim.

Common Formative Assessments 2.0

How to Write Quality Assessment Questions Aligned to the Rigor of the Standards

Larry Ainsworth

ISBN: 9798760058232

Contents

Prominent Endorsements of
Common Formative Assessments 2.0

"Ainsworth spells out how classroom teachers can work together to create formative assessments in order to monitor student learning and adapt teaching. The new material in this book is critical: Ainsworth introduces constructive alignment of learning outcomes, standards, success criteria, and classroom and larger-scale assessments. He emphasizes the *quality* of assessments to enable excellent diagnostic interpretations of data. He does not ask teachers to do all this alone, but as a community of experts led by instructional leaders (the chapter on PLCs in itself is worth buying the book). He does all of this with the intention of maximizing our positive impact on student learning. There have been many who have written about the power of success criteria, growth and progress, and assessment for teachers, but not how to do it. Ainsworth spells it out to perfection...Changing this thinking is the power of this book."

--John Hattie
Professor of Education and
Director of the Melbourne Education Research Institute
University of Melbourne, Australia

"Based on nearly a decade's worth of real-world evidence obtained by watching educators implement his earlier suggestions, (in the original volume of *Common Formative Assessments*) Ainsworth has clearly refined his thinking about group-guided formative assessment."

--W. James Popham
Professor Emeritus
UCLA Graduate School of Education
Los Angeles, California

Acknowledgments

First of all, a sincere thank you to all of the educators and leaders in school systems throughout North America and other parts of the world who have applied the common formative assessment (CFA) process in their own educational settings and found it to be a highly effective professional practice. I appreciate the many enthusiastic comments and valued endorsements of this process I have received since the first edition of this book was published in 2006.

It is important to particularly acknowledge the many thought leaders and researchers cited in these pages, whose contributions to the extensive literature on formative assessments have helped improve the quality of instruction and assessment for all students.

My heartfelt appreciation goes to the longtime champion-advocate for this new edition, Dan Alpert. As Program Director of Equity/Diversity and Professional Learning for the Publishing and Professional Learning Group at Corwin, Dan has patiently and conscientiously overseen the development of this project from inception to publication. Dan's calm perseverance and respectful manner have set the tone for the many conversations needed to bring it to fruition. The completion of this long-awaited volume is due in large part to him.

I would like to especially thank two author-consultants who contributed greatly to this new edition. Jan Christinson and Tracey Shiel created the original examples of math and English language arts (ELA) common formative assessments, respectively, matched to each step of the CFA 2.0 design process. Their concrete examples proved invaluable to communicating to readers a process that might otherwise have remained in the realm of the abstract.

My appreciation goes out to Debbie Higdon, former K–12 Program Manager of English Language Arts in the San Diego Unified School District, San Diego, California, for permission to use the Grade 5 ELA "unwrapping" standards example as the foundation for Tracey Shiel's completed CFA.

Special thanks to Dave Nagel for his thoughtful input and authoring assistance on the collaborative scoring, grading, and analysis of CFA results in Chapter 11. Dave originated the wonderfully specific charts that I adapted to illustrate key parts of the data analysis process.

My gratitude and appreciation also extend to Barb Pitchford, Ainsley Rose, Kara Vandas, Dave Nagel, Mary Jane O'Connell, Tracey Shiel, B. R. Jones, and Laura Besser for their valued feedback on the overall re-envisioning of the CFA 2.0 design steps.

Every professional writer needs a competent copyeditor. Taryn Bigelow conscientiously edited every word in this expanded new edition. Her meticulous attention to detail has proved invaluable in helping me effectively communicate my CFA 2.0 vision in printed form. Thank you, Taryn.

I also want to recognize the behind-the-scenes publishing support I have received from Veronica Stapleton Hooper, Kimberley Greenberg, Cassandra Seibel, Cesar Reyes, Mayan McDermott, and Monique Corridori.

And last but never least, my heartfelt thanks to Corwin's management team: Kristin Anderson, Director of Professional Learning, for her unflagging support and inspiration, and to Lisa Cuevas Shaw, Executive Director of Publishing and Professional Learning; Elena Nikitina, Director of Marketing and Sales; and Mike Soules, President, for their passionate commitment to excellence in professional learning.

I am especially grateful to Jennie Hurley for her expertise and tireless efforts to bring into print this 2021 Amazon KDP publication of *Common Formative Assessments 2.0* for the benefit of all educators looking for an effective, easy-to-follow process for gaining credible assessment evidence of their students' learning.

About the Authors

Larry Ainsworth is the author or coauthor of 15 published books, including this volume, *Common Formative Assessments 2.0* (2015). Among his other works are *Rigorous Curriculum Design, 2nd Edition* (2019) *"Unwrapping" the Common Core* (2014), *Prioritizing the Common Core* (2013), *Rigorous Curriculum Design* (2010), *Common Formative Assessments* (2006), *Five Easy Steps to a Balanced Math Program -- Primary, Elementary, & Secondary Editions* (2006, 2000), *"Unwrapping" the Standards* (2003), *Power Standards* (2003), and *Student Generated Rubrics* (1998).

Currently an independent education consultant, Larry served as the Executive Director of Professional Development at the Leadership and Learning Center in Englewood, Colorado, from 1999 to 2013. He has traveled nationally and internationally to assist school systems in implementing best practices related to standards, assessment, curriculum, and instruction across all grades and content areas. Throughout his career as a professional developer, Larry has delivered keynote addresses and breakout sessions across North America and in Latin America and regularly worked on-site in school systems to assist leaders and educators in understanding and implementing powerful standards-based practices: prioritizing and "unwrapping" state standards and Common Core standards, developing common formative assessments, designing authentic performance tasks, and creating rigorous curricular units of study in all content areas, PreK through Grade 12.

Drawing upon 24 years of experience as an upper elementary and middle school classroom teacher in demographically diverse schools, Larry presents "timeless" educational practices through the lens of the classroom educator so that the information is clear and doable.

Donald J. Viegut, contributing author of chapters 13 and 14, currently serves as superintendent of the Livingston, Montana school district. Don has been a classroom teacher, building principal, director of curriculum, deputy superintendent, and agency director of a regional service delivery agency. Don is past president of the Wisconsin Association for Supervision and Curriculum Development, served on the ASCD board of directors, and chaired the board of North Central Technical College. He also chaired the PreK–18 Council for the University of Wisconsin-Steven's Point. Don coauthored *Common Formative Assessments,* a million-dollar Corwin publication. He presents nationally and networks extensively throughout the world. Don earned his doctorate from Western Michigan University.

Introduction

THE NEED FOR A NEW EDITION

Even a timeless process needs to remain timely. Fifteen years have passed since *Common Formative Assessments: An Assessment Model to Help All Students Succeed* (2006) was first published, and thousands of K–12 educators across North America have successfully implemented the ideas and processes pre-sented in that original volume. Established professional practices will continue to prove effective now and in the future so long as they remain relevant to the prevailing changes and educational demands of the time.

After many years presenting the CFA process to K–12 educators and leaders in districts all over the United States and Canada, I have seen the need for teams of teachers to revisit their initial CFA drafts in order to evaluate their assessment questions for quality. In doing so, they are able to then revise and improve those assessments. Because the inferences educators make about student learning can only be as good as the evidence they collect, the *source* of that evidence—the assessments themselves—must be of high quality.

Even if you have never attended an assessment design course or workshop, by following the new, step-by-step CFA 2.0 process you will be able to successfully create a quality assessment. Those who are already experienced in designing CFAs will find that this updated process will take your CFAs to an even higher level of effectiveness.

INTRODUCTION TO COMMON FORMATIVE ASSESSMENTS 2.0

Common formative assessments are aligned pre- and post-assessments *for* learning that are collaboratively designed by a grade- or course-level team of educators to assess student understanding of the particular learning intentions (learning targets) and success criteria currently in focus within a curricular unit of study.

CFAs afford grade- and course-level teacher teams a clear lens through which to see their instructional impact on student learning. The assessment questions directly match the levels of cognitive rigor within the unit learning intentions (derived from academic content standards or provincial learning outcomes). Accompanying success criteria describe explicitly what students are to demonstrate in their assessment responses to show they have achieved the learning intentions. Knowing what they are to learn and how their understanding will be evaluated, students are empowered to take a more active role in their own learning.

Learning *progressions* are the smaller, sequenced "building blocks" of instruction necessary for students to understand the larger unit learning *intentions.* Shorter formative assessments—*quick progress checks*—occur throughout the unit after learning progressions. These quick checks of student understanding provide immediate feedback that educators use to adjust instruction and that students use to self-regulate their learning strategies. Learning progressions and corresponding quick progress checks are new steps added to the original CFA process.

KEY BENEFITS OF CFAS

- The CFA 2.0 process is not limited to assessment design only. Rather, it is a *system* of intentionally aligned components (standards, instruction, and assessments) that all work together to improve student learning.
- Grade- and course-level teams of educators collaborate to intentionally align their pre- and post-CFAs and write their assessment questions to match the same level of rigor as in the unit's learning intentions (derived from state, provincial, or national standards).
- CFAs include a blend of assessment formats: selected response, constructed response (short and extended), and Essential Questions requiring students' Big Idea responses. This multiple-format assessment makes learning more visible because it affords students more than one way to "show all they know."
- Teacher teams use the resulting student responses as diagnostic feedback to correctly interpret student understanding and differentiate instruction. Students use the same valuable feedback to monitor and adjust their individual learning strategies.
- Educators often write their CFA questions to reflect the formats of state, provincial, and national assessments so students have ongoing opportunities to demonstrate what they are learning in the ways they will be expected to respond on standardized achievement tests.

- CFA questions are evaluated for quality and revised as needed using established criteria. This ensures that the inferences educators make from the assessment results are accurate.
- Educators find great value in collaboratively scoring the CFAs, discussing the results, and planning ways to achieve improvements in student learning on the next common formative assessment they administer.
- Common *formative* assessments can do what large-scale *summative* assessments, by design, cannot—provide classroom educators with timely, credible evidence of their impact on student learning and achievement. Focusing energy and time on the analysis of small-scale, school-based assessments to improve instruction is sure to help educators meet the diverse learning needs of all students.

WHAT'S NEW IN THE 2.0 EDITION?

The original CFA process remains essentially the same, although it has been enhanced to include important aspects absent from the original. Here is a preview of the key points of emphasis in the CFA 2.0 process, organized by category:

Standards and Learning Outcomes

- Applies to all standards (state and Common Core), all learning outcomes (province specific), all grades, all content areas; educators need only insert the unit-specific learning intentions for their grade level or course into the structure provided.
- Targets the specific learning intentions and student success criteria for a multi-week unit of study that are derived from the **Priority Standards**, "unwrapped" concepts, skills, levels of cognitive rigor, **Big Ideas**, and **Essential Questions**.

Intentional Alignment

- Shows how to match assessment questions to the predetermined levels of cognitive rigor, using the revised Bloom's Taxonomy and Webb's Depth of Knowledge matrices.
- Describes how to partner quick progress checks with learning progressions (the incremental building blocks of the larger unit learning intentions).

- Underscores the importance of teacher teams closely aligning their pre-assessments with their post-assessments for each unit of study.

Large-Scale External Assessments

- Emphasizes the need for educators to know how their students will be assessed on standardized achievement tests and then to design their CFAs to reflect the formats, vocabulary, and rigor of those external exams. In this way, students will become familiar with how they will be expected to show what they have learned prior to taking those high-stakes tests.
- Provides links to online examples of questions from the Smarter Balanced Assessment Consortium (SBAC) and Partnership for Assessment of Readiness for College and Careers (PARCC) assessments.

Diagnostic Use of Data

- Allows for timely analysis of formative assessment data to accurately interpret student understanding and plan instructional "next steps" to meet student learning needs.
- Enables educators to continually modify and adjust instruction during the unit based on results from ongoing quick progress checks aligned to the post-CFA.
- Advocates the sharing of assessment results (pre-CFA, quick progress checks, and post-CFA) with students.

Success Criteria

- Informs students at the beginning of the unit of the success criteria they will need to demonstrate by the end of the unit.
- Provides students with detailed scoring guide success criteria to guide their responses when they complete constructed-response assessment questions.

Assessment Quality

- Presents specific criteria to ensure that the assessment questions are of high quality. These criteria include validity, reliability, freedom from bias, alignment, format, vocabulary, and thinking skill rigor.
- Explains and illustrates how to use assessment quality guidelines to critique and revise assessment questions.

Recent Research Support

- Includes important formative assessment research support published after the original 2006 edition of *Common Formative Assessments* (e.g., John Hattie, *Visible Learning* and *Visible Learning for Teachers*; Dylan Wiliam, *Embedded Formative Assessment*; W. James Popham, *Transformative Assessment*; and others).

The Role of Leaders

- Updates information for leaders on how to implement and sustain common formative assessments and create a culture of improvement within a school and school system.

Each chapter opens with the specific learning intentions for that chapter and, beginning in Chapter 3, a diagram showing the ten sequential steps of the CFA 2.0 process, with the current step highlighted. It then describes the rationale for that step, explains how to complete it effectively, and provides accompanying examples to illustrate it. Each chapter concludes with specific success criteria related to the content of the chapter that readers can use for individual reflection and/or team discussion.

THE IMPORTANT ROLE OF LEADERS

School and district leaders who understand the significant potential that common formative assessments have for improving both the quality of instruction and the subsequent learning of all students play a vital role in implementing this process in their schools. For the CFA 2.0 process to truly take root within the culture of a school or district, leaders need to "champion" the process. They can do this by (1) making a commitment to fully understand the CFA 2.0 process through their own professional learning and then by (2) ensuring that the practice is systematically well implemented in each grade level and/or course.

One essential support that leaders can provide educators is to deliberately look for creative ways to rearrange daily teaching schedules to promote more opportunities for grade- and course-level teams to plan together. By freeing participating teachers to meet in grade-level and course/department teams, administrators provide teachers with both the support and structure critical to effectively plan and implement these important standards, instruction, and assessment practices.

Effective administrators know that for any educational practice to yield lasting changes, classroom teachers must invest in and take ownership of the entire process. Educators must be "at the table" in the research, design, implementation, and monitoring of progress on all-important changes that will impact curriculum, instruction, and assessment. When instituting a key change in professional practice, such as the implementation of CFAs, educators and leaders must continually work together to make that change work.

TOWARD A STUDENT-CENTERED ASSESSMENT PROCESS

Before students can be fully at the center of the assessment process, educators need to have the core components of that process firmly in place within the day-to-day practices of their individual classrooms. They can then begin shifting ownership of that process into the hands of the students. As teacher teams continue to increase students' involvement in the effective use of formative assessments, students can truly take charge of their own efforts to reach and exceed personal learning goals. The step-by-step CFA 2.0 process builds the important foundation that can ultimately lead to greater student involvement and ownership.

LET'S GET STARTED!

Common Formative Assessments 2.0 will provide busy educators and leaders with a practical, how-to guide filled with information, examples, and action steps to assist all K–12 grade- and course-level teams in making this completely re-envisioned process their own. My sincere hope is that this new expanded edition will prove to be a doable road map that you and your colleagues can follow to build your own "highway to aligned assessments," one that makes CFAs an indispensable part of your important work of helping all students succeed.

1

A Highway to Aligned Assessments

In This Chapter You Will Learn:

- The standards and assessment components of a quality CFA.
- How formative progress checks, data analysis, and instruction intersect.
- How you can construct, in progressive steps, the CFA 2.0 "highway" of aligned assessments.

DESTINATION: MAXIMUM IMPACT

Sometimes we begin a journey in education without being completely clear as to why we are doing so. The primary goal of this book is to help educators maximize their positive impact on student learning. The pages that follow will focus on describing and illustrating a powerful means for achieving that goal—effectively designed common formative assessments, often referred to simply as CFAs. Why CFAs? If assessment results enable teacher teams to make valid and reliable inferences regarding their students' current learning status, they will then be able to adjust instruction accordingly and see for themselves the positive impact of those instructional adjustments.

So how do you increase the likelihood that educators will be able to accurately infer what students know and can do with regard to the learning intentions in current focus? By ensuring that each assessment question meets all of the established criteria for quality (presented in Chapter 9). If the assessment does *not* meet all of these criteria, educators will be unable to interpret student understanding confidently.

Our conclusions about what students know and can do are only as good as the evidence we collect, and that evidence is only as good as its source—the assessments themselves. If the assessment questions are faulty, then the inferences are bound to be incorrect. Working through the CFA 2.0 process together, teacher teams create the caliber of assessments that make valid and reliable inferences possible.

To reach the desired destination of maximum impact on student learning, we need to concentrate on building and traversing a "highway" that can take us there. But first, we want to see what that highway is going to look like when finished.

SEEING THE ENTIRE HIGHWAY

Do you consider yourself a "big picture" person? Do you like to see the whole before looking at the individual parts? In my many years of leading educators and leaders through the initial design of a common formative assessment, the answer to that two-part question for the vast majority of participants is *yes*. It's about making connections first, and seeing how all of the parts fit together to form one meaningful whole, before investing time, thought, and energy into any one part or step.

Busy educators and leaders rightly want to know up front, "What is this all about, and where are we headed?" Because the CFA 2.0 process contains many moving parts, it is helpful to first see a blueprint of where all those parts fit into the completed design and how those parts must intentionally work together to produce the desired outcome—a quality set of aligned assessments specific to a unit of study.

To illustrate the construction of the CFA highway, the following sections will introduce each sequence of steps in progressive installments, building by chapter's end to a big-picture view of the completed highway.

CFA 2.0 DESIGN FUNDAMENTALS

Let's start with the basics, each of which will be fully described in later chapters. The CFA 2.0 *design fundamentals* focus on explicit standards and related assessments for an individual **unit of study.** A unit of study is a "series of specific lessons, learning experiences, and related assessments based on designated Priority Standards and related supporting standards for an (instructional) focus that may last anywhere from two to six weeks"

(Ainsworth, 2010, p. 324). The duration of a unit of study depends on the number and rigor of the targeted standards for that unit and the length of time educators estimate it will require for students to learn them.

The fundamental standards components within a unit of study are these:

- Priority Standards (grade- or course-specific state, provincial, and/or national standards to emphasize the most)
- "Unwrapped" Priority Standards concepts, skills, and identified levels of cognitive rigor
- Big Ideas and Essential Questions

The two main assessment components within the unit of study are these:

- Unit post-assessment
- Unit pre-assessment

Figure 1.1 shows a visual representation of these standards and assessment components, arranged in a clockwise direction (starting at the top with Priority Standards) to indicate the design sequence.

Figure 1.1 Building the Foundation: Fundamental Design Steps

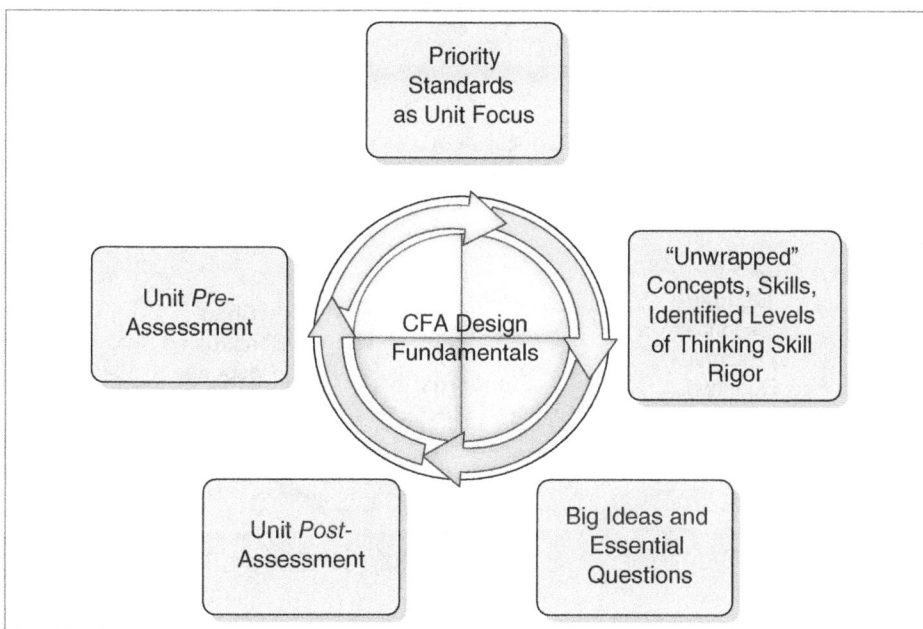

Grade- and course-level teams of educators meet together to "unwrap" selected Priority Standards for a unit of study. Next they create a graphic organizer that includes the "unwrapped" concepts, skills, and levels of cognitive rigor. Then they write Big Ideas and Essential Questions. When these elements are complete, they design the post-CFA followed by an aligned pre-CFA, so they will have an apples-to-apples comparison of student learning from the beginning to the end of the unit.

The post-CFA is a multiple-format assessment directly aligned to the "unwrapped" Priority Standards as shown in Figure 1.2. Note that authentic performance tasks are not part of the on-demand CFA due to the time it takes students to complete them. However, they play a key role in preparing students for success on the post-CFA. Authentic Classroom performance tasks are defined and summarized in Chapter 3.

CFA 2.0—DESIGN FUNDAMENTALS *PLUS*

The CFA 2.0 process incorporates new standards elements into this basic design framework. These new elements are

- Unit learning intentions—the specific learning outcomes or learning targets students are to achieve by the end of the unit

Figure 1.2 A Four-Part Assessment Aligned to Priority Standards

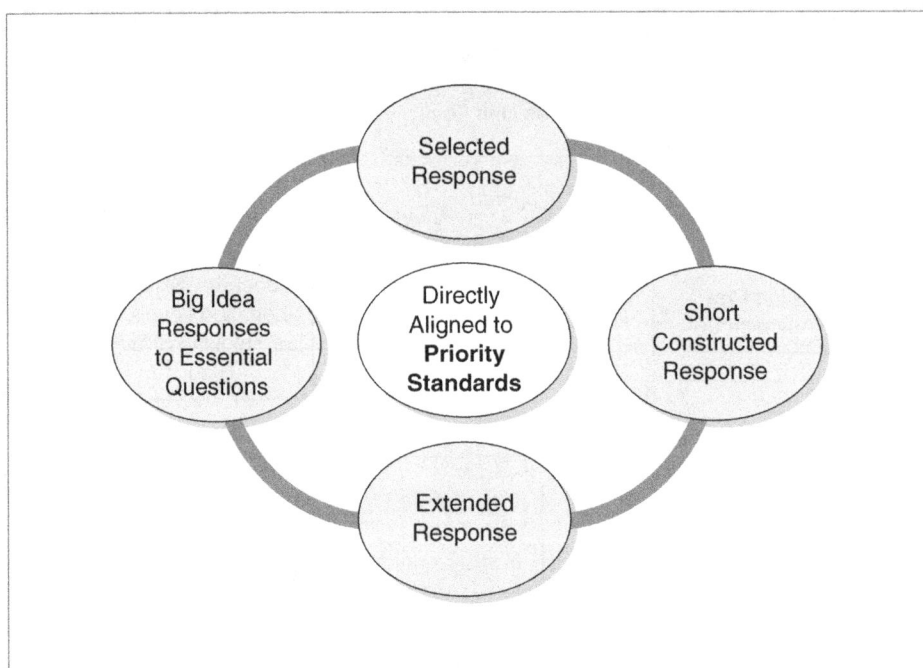

- Student success criteria—performance descriptors that spell out how students will show they have achieved the learning intentions

In the CFA 2.0 process, teacher teams combine their "unwrapped" Priority Standards, targeted vocabulary, Big Ideas, and Essential Questions into unit learning intentions and student success criteria (described and illustrated in Chapter 6). They complete this new step immediately after determining their Essential Questions and *before* designing their post-CFA, as shown in Figure 1.3.

The post-CFA remains a multiple-format assessment but is now directly aligned to the comprehensive list of unit learning intentions and student success criteria, as shown in Figure 1.4.

ANALYZING THE ASSESSMENT RESULTS

After the teachers administer the pre-CFA, they meet to analyze the results, set goals for student improvement, and identify instructional strategies to assist them in achieving these goals. They touch base with one another periodically during the unit to evaluate the effectiveness of their targeted instructional strategies. They meet again as a team at the end of the unit to repeat the data analysis process using the post-CFA results.

Figure 1.3 Strengthening the Foundation: Design Fundamentals *Plus*

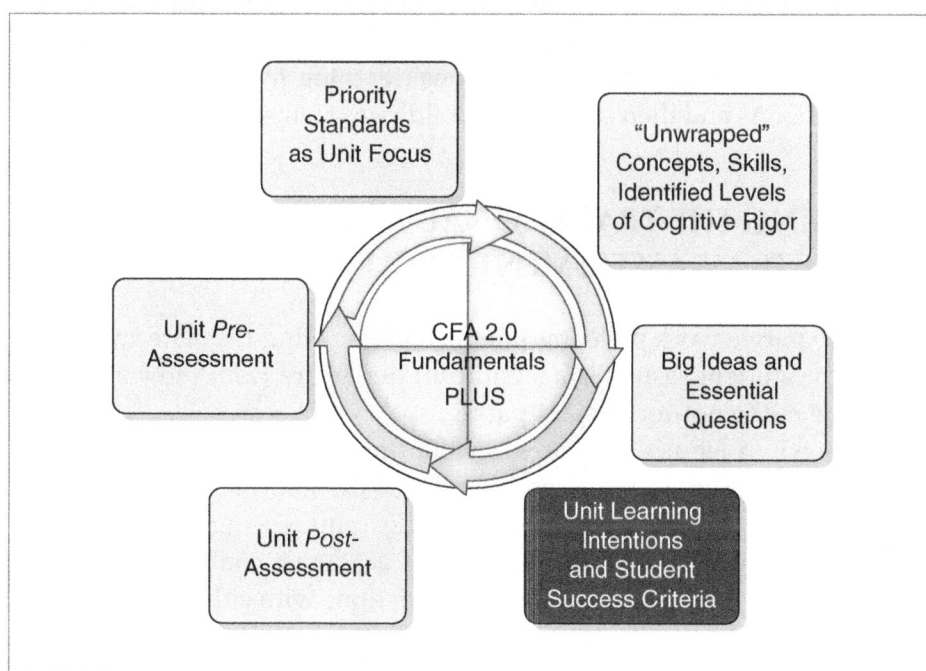

Figure 1.4 From Priority Standards To Unit Learning Intentions

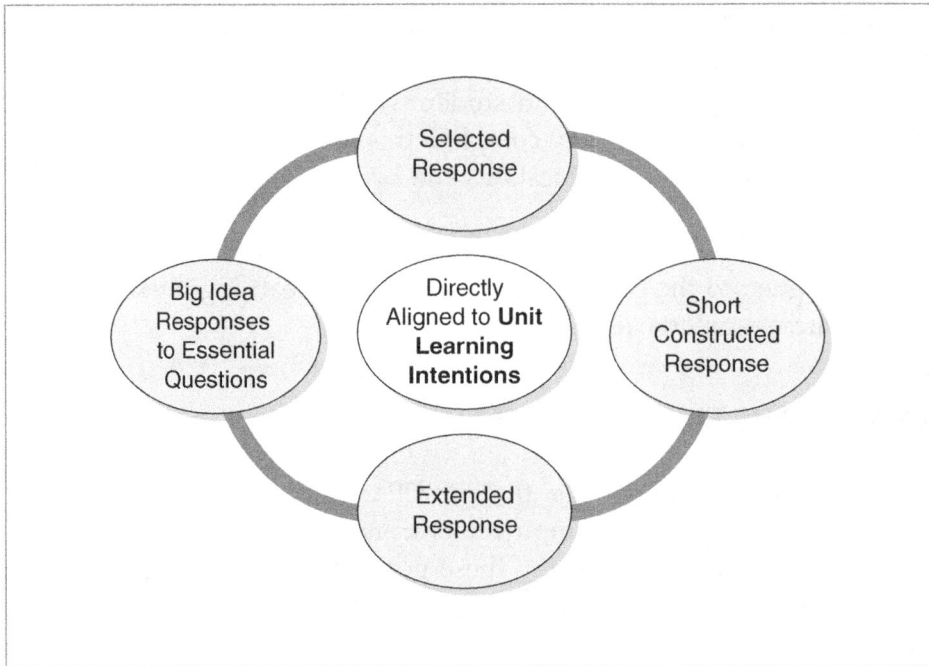

This type of collaboration takes place in what are now widely known as professional learning communities or PLCs. These can include the entire faculty in the broadest sense and/or the smaller, grade- and course-level teacher teams. In the common formative assessment context, educators are part of grade- or course-level professional learning *teams* that design and implement CFAs and then conduct the follow-up analysis of student results.

CHANGING THE TRADITIONAL INSTRUCTION-ASSESSMENT CYCLE

The collaborative work by teams of educators meeting to create a CFA and process the student results is a significant departure from the way things were done in the not-too-distant past.

As shown in Figure 1.5, teachers would pretest (but not always). Then they would teach-teach-teach-teach-teach. At the end of several weeks of instruction, they would posttest, assign grades, and repeat the same process with the next instructional unit or body of academic content. Often there was little, if any, real analysis of student work done with either the formative (pretest) or summative (posttest) results, particularly if the tests had not been deliberately aligned, one to the other.

Figure 1.5 The Traditional Instruction-Assessment Model

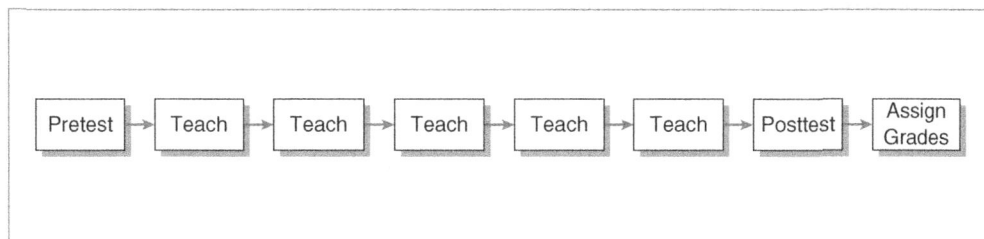

| Pretest | → | Teach | → | Teach | → | Teach | → | Teach | → | Teach | → | Posttest | → | Assign Grades |

Source: Ainsworth & Viegut (2006).

When PLCs began forming with the express purpose of collaboratively looking at student work and planning subsequent instruction, *data analysis* was introduced into the instruction-assessment model, as shown in Figure 1.6.

The emphasis now became more about using the pre- and post-assessment data to determine with more accuracy what students knew going into the unit, analyzing the data to set an improvement goal for all students, selecting instructional strategies to achieve it, and then determining what students had learned by the end of the unit.

At this time, creating *common* formative assessments as a team was still a new professional practice for most educators, so analyzing student assessment data to interpret student learning during PLC meetings was usually limited to the pre- and post-CFA results only. The infrequency of meetings was not necessarily because educators didn't feel they were useful. Teams were simply having trouble finding ways to schedule common planning time. However, enterprising teams with the support of their administrators began scheduling a short meeting around the middle of the unit to determine if their targeted instructional strategies were having the kind of impact they expected, or if those strategies needed to be adjusted or replaced altogether.

Figure 1.6 The Collaborative Data Analysis Process

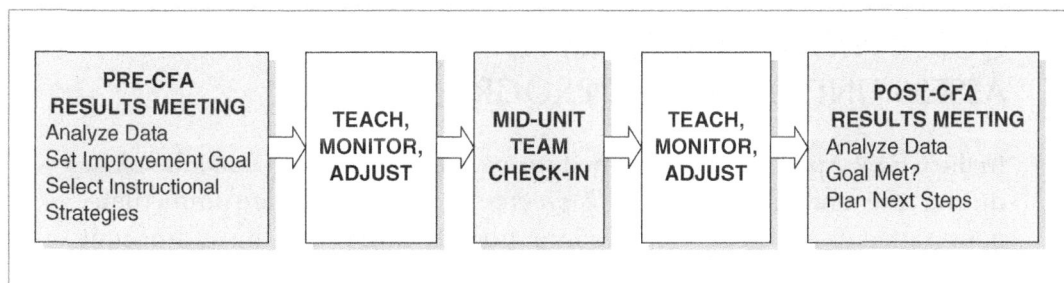

| PRE-CFA RESULTS MEETING
Analyze Data
Set Improvement Goal
Select Instructional Strategies | → | TEACH, MONITOR, ADJUST | → | MID-UNIT TEAM CHECK-IN | → | TEACH, MONITOR, ADJUST | → | POST-CFA RESULTS MEETING
Analyze Data
Goal Met?
Plan Next Steps |

Throughout the unit, teachers were on their own to teach and check for student understanding, as represented by the "teach, monitor, adjust" steps shown in Figure 1.6. During a lesson, they would ask students for a "thumbs up, thumbs down" response as a quick way to check for understanding. Occasionally they might insert a quiz ("pop" or prepared) that they later graded. Older students would turn in "exit slips" at the end of class that teachers read through to informally assess student understanding. Teachers regularly collected homework and daily class work that they checked and/or graded. They would utilize these and other means to determine which students were doing fine and which ones were struggling. Individual professional judgment, experience, and gut instincts were usually the determining factors as to whether or not students were meeting the standards and understanding essential concepts and skills.

PRE-PLAN YOUR "CHECKS FOR UNDERSTANDING"

All teachers—including myself—have used these perfectly legitimate formative assessment methods to gather evidence of student learning and make inference-based instructional decisions. They are a regular part of the ordinary routine of daily classroom instruction.

However, the problem with this smorgasbord approach to formative assessment is that very often those checks for understanding are not deliberately planned. This can lead to incorrect conclusions about what students know and do not know. When teachers rely mainly on their moment-to-moment assumptions to gauge student understanding, sometimes those assumptions are right and sometimes they are wrong.

With regard to team-created CFAs, a loosely structured approach to administering informal checks for understanding during the unit of study can often lead to widely varying student results on the post-CFA. Students in classrooms who receive the benefit of *pre-planned* checks for understanding, followed by instructional adjustments to close their learning gaps, will be much better prepared for the end-of-unit assessment than those students in classrooms who do not receive this benefit.

QUICK PROGRESS CHECKS TO ASSESS UNIT LEARNING PROGRESSIONS

In the CFA 2.0 process, pre-planned formative assessments that take place during the unit are called *quick progress checks.* These are immediate, non-graded assessments that are intentionally aligned to the end-of-unit post-assessment and serve as stepping-stones to student success on the post-CFA. Their purpose is to provide in-the-moment feedback so educators can make timely adjustments in their instruction and students can adjust their learning strategies. Quick progress checks do not happen randomly; they are intentionally planned to coincide with the unit *learning progressions*.

Learning progressions are the sequential building blocks of instruction necessary for students to understand the larger learning intentions of the unit. They provide the instructional pathway students need to traverse in order to arrive at the learning destination. It may be helpful to think of learning progressions as the daily "chunks" of instruction that incrementally build student understanding over time toward a more complex learning outcome.

The use of predetermined learning progressions and quick progress checks are relatively new practices for most educators, so for now just think of them as the specific instructional steps students need to take from the starting point to the ending point during a unit of study, with formative assessment checkpoints along the way.

Figure 1.7 shows the important additions of learning progressions and quick progress checks to the CFA 2.0 design fundamentals. The teacher team plans their learning progressions and quick progress checks *after* they

Figure 1.7   New Design Steps to Improve the Highway

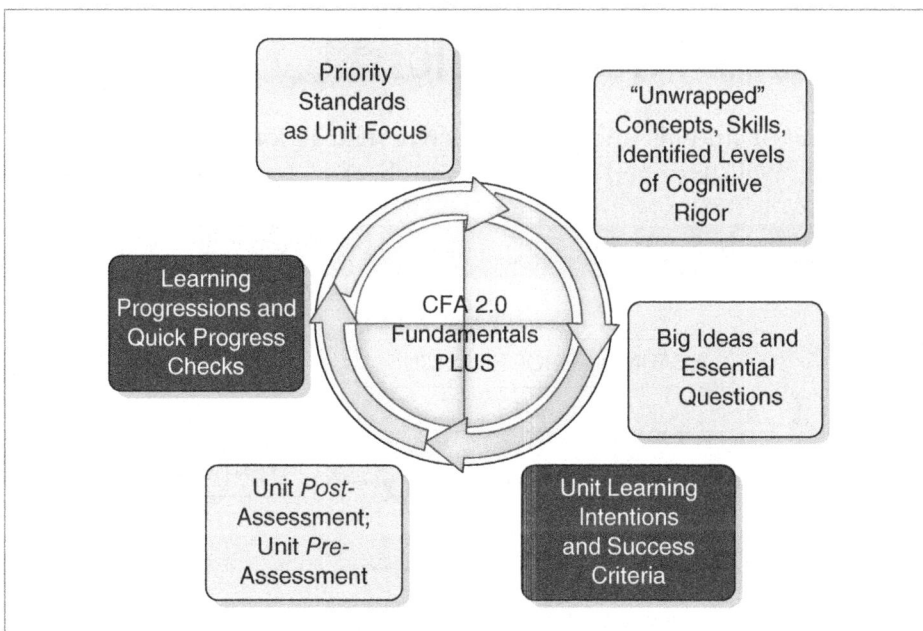

design their post-CFA and pre-CFA. This enables them to "work backwards" to create the instruction-assessment pathway leading to the end-of-unit assessment.

The learning progressions necessary for students to understand a learning intention can be numbered to indicate their instructional sequence. Figure 1.8 shows the sequenced building blocks of learning progressions (labeled LP 1, LP 2, LP 3, LP 4) leading to a unit learning intention. The arrows indicate where the corresponding quick progress checks of student understanding occur. These take place immediately after one or more lessons related to a specific learning progression. Note that the number of learning progressions within a unit of study is not limited to four, a number used here for illustration only.

Quick progress checks are essential to knowing where students currently are relative to the unit learning intentions. Individual teachers often create these from day to day or week to week, depending on where they are instructionally within the unit so that the progress checks match their own pace of instruction.

However, as educators have become more experienced in creating CFAs and meeting regularly to process student feedback together, they are making it a priority to collaboratively plan and create their quick progress checks *in advance.* Teachers find that doing this step together ensures greater consistency of assessment experiences for all students—even if team members use those quick progress checks at slightly different times during the unit of study than their team colleagues do.

TEACH-ASSESS-INTERPRET-ADJUST

When a unit of study is underway, effective instruction naturally precedes assessment. Well-designed quick progress checks—based on the particular

Figure 1.8 How Learning Progressions and Quick Progress Checks Work Together

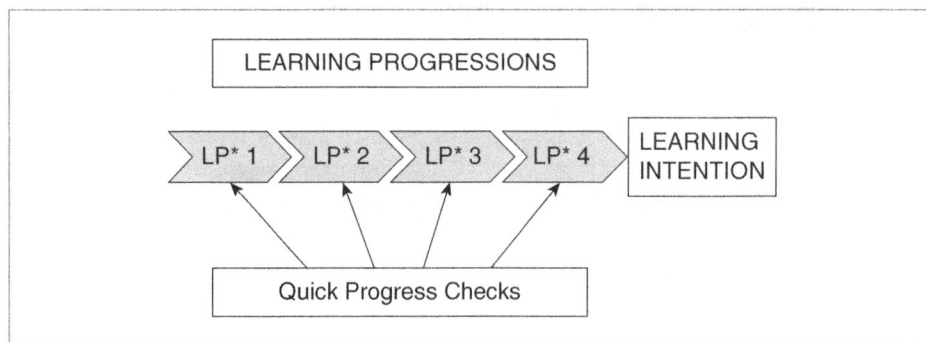

*Learning Progression.

learning progressions in focus—enable educators to accurately *interpret* student understanding and determine instructional next steps. Adjustments to instruction can then take place immediately.

As represented in Figure 1.9, *teach-assess-interpret-adjust* is the quartet of inseparable practices that, keeping with the highway metaphor, transport students down the main road to the post-CFA destination.

Using predetermined, collaboratively planned, quick progress checks to adjust instruction demonstrates a dramatic shift in professional practice. This type of approach moves educators away from the traditional instruction-assessment cycle in which teaching continues on as originally planned from the beginning of the unit to the end with little or no modification. Inserting assessment-driven, inference-based instructional corrections into the cycle may well prove to be the "missing link" to improving student learning.

STUDENT USE OF CFA FEEDBACK

So far in this sequential progression of the CFA 2.0 design blueprint, the emphasis has been on what teachers do. Understandably, teachers need to carry out these design steps first. Yet where does *student use of CFA feedback* come in? When feedback is shared with students, they can be shown how to use it to self-regulate their learning. When teachers are ready to shift the process to include their students, the use of pre-CFA, post-CFA, and quick progress checks expands to include student participation, as indicated within the Student Involvement steps on pages 18–20 (in bold).

Figure 1.9 The Quartet of Instruction and Assessment Practices

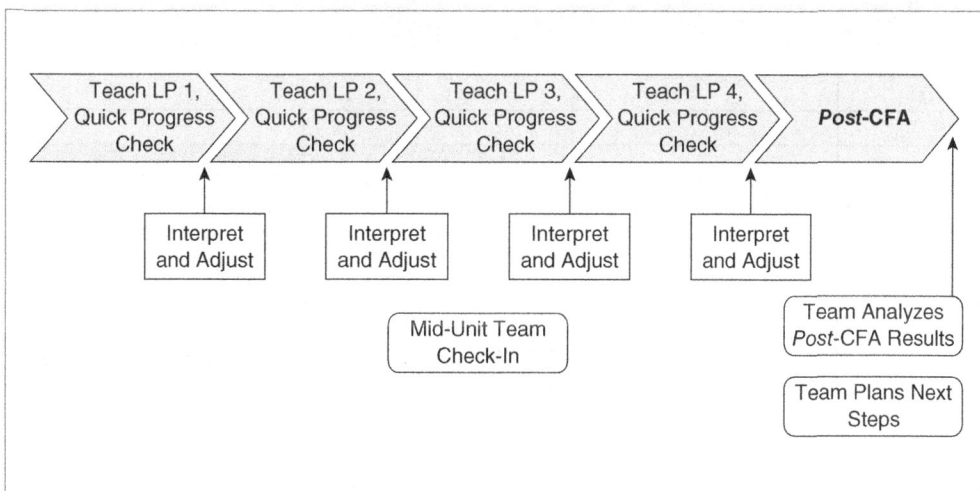

Teacher Actions:

1. Educators begin by analyzing the pre-CFA results to correctly identify student learning strengths and areas of need. Because the unit pre-assessment is intentionally aligned to the post-assessment and the targeted learning intentions for the unit, educators can analyze the pre-CFA results to interpret student learning strengths and areas of need and adjust instruction earlier and more decisively.

2. Team members then set improvement goals for all students in the grade or course based on specific pre-assessment results and desired post-assessment gains. After that they select specific instructional strategies to help students achieve these goals.

Student Involvement:

3. The bar graph shows how students can set specific targets for their learning. For example, Matthew records his pre-assessment results by shading in the corresponding number of items he responded to correctly—two. He then sets a personal goal to score at least eight items correctly on the post-assessment and shades in the corresponding number in the "goal" column. When Matthew receives his post-assessment results at the end of the unit, he shades in his *actual* number of correct answers in the post-CFA results column.

   Note: The number 10 in the graph is used for simplicity of illustration only. It is not a recommendation of how many assessment questions to include on either the pre- or post-CFA. The purpose of the graph is to enable students to record their pre-CFA results, set an achievement goal for their post-CFA, record their actual post-CFA results, and see visible evidence of their improvement in learning.

Pre-/Post-Assessment Results			
10			
9			
8			
7			
6			
5			
4			
3			
2			
1			
Matthew	Pre-CFA Score	Goal Post-CFA Score	Actual Post-CFA Score

4. **With teacher guidance, students create a personal SMART goal (Specific-Measurable-*Ambitious*-Relevant-Timely) with regard to the learning intentions and success criteria for the unit. This goal indicates the quantifiable achievement they want to demonstrate on the end-of-unit post-CFA.**

Student's SMART Goal for Unit

"My learning goal for this unit on adding and subtracting fractions with unlike denominators is to achieve a score of 80 percent or higher on the post-CFA. I only got two problems right on the pre-CFA, so I have a lot of learning to do in this unit."

Teacher Actions:

5. After instruction of each predetermined learning progression, the teachers administer a quick progress check based on that progression.

Student Involvement:

6. **Students receive feedback results from the quick progress check and ask clarifying questions to understand what changes or adjustments in their learning approach they need to make in order to close their understanding gaps.**

7. **Students receive new instruction and guidance from the teacher and apply the information received to continue and/or revise their learning strategies.**

Comment: When teachers use the feedback from quick progress checks to inform next-steps instruction, students are able to correct any misconceptions *while* they are learning. Teachers don't have to wait until the end-of-unit assessment or even the middle of the unit to see the impact their instruction is having or to discover that students didn't learn as much as expected.

8. **At the midpoint of the unit, students complete a short self-reflection to determine whether they think they are on track to achieve the unit learning intentions and success criteria as measured by the post-CFA. Students also clarify what they think they need next in terms**

of instructional support from the teacher(s). They review their self-reflection responses with their teacher.

Teacher Actions:

9. Steps 5–7 repeat throughout the remainder of the unit.

10. At the end of the unit, the teachers administer and score the post-CFA and evaluate the results.

Comment: The post-CFA is a cumulative assessment representing all of the unit learning intentions and student success criteria in focus over a period of several weeks. Because all of the quick progress checks are intentionally aligned to the post-CFA, students have been receiving incremental feedback and adjusting their learning strategies throughout the unit. Thus they are far more prepared to achieve success on the post-CFA because they have been practicing for success all along the way. This enables the teachers' instructional impact and degree of effectiveness to be reliably measured by a body of valid assessment evidence they have gathered during the entire unit of study.

Student Involvement:

11. **Students receive their post-assessment results along with their returned pre- and post-assessment results graph and personal SMART goal that they completed at the start of the unit. They shade in their post-assessment results column to correspond with the number of questions they answered correctly and determine if they did or did not reach their learning goal.**

12. **Finally, students complete the post-unit self-reflection, noting where they did well, what strategies they feel are working best for them, where they need to go next in their learning, and what plan they have to improve while they are on the "Bridge" (described in the next section).**

Comment: Involving students in self-reflection encourages them to "think about their thinking." This metacognitive strategy ranks 14th on the list of practices that influence student learning, producing an overall effect size of 0.69 (Hattie, 2012, p. 251). This research finding certainly makes self-reflection a practice worth incorporating on a regular basis.

Student's End-of-Unit Self-Reflection

"My learning goal for this unit was to achieve a score of 80 percent or higher on the post-CFA. I scored 80 percent on the post-CFA, so I did reach my learning goal!

"I think I did really well on learning how to add and subtract fractions with unlike denominators. It was hard for me to understand at first, but using the manipulatives helped me to make sense of how two or three different denominators can all be changed to equivalent forms. It took me longer to learn that the values of the numerators have to change too.

"I still am kinda slow at converting the numerators correctly whenever there are three fractions I'm adding together. And then to change the large improper fraction to a mixed number is tricky, especially when the fraction part of the mixed number has to be reduced to lowest terms.

"When I'm on the Bridge, I need to practice what I just wrote about so it's easier for me to convert multiple fractions with unlike denominators to like denominators and then correctly complete the rest of the steps."

Now, if only this thoughtful and systematic approach could guarantee that every student would demonstrate competency on every post-CFA in every unit of study throughout the entire school year! So what about those students who do not meet their learning goal and still need further instruction specific to their learning needs, along with a chance to try again for assessment success? The answer to this can be found on the Bridge.

THE "BRIDGE" BETWEEN UNITS

When educators begin implementing a unit of study within their year-long curriculum, they often feel frustration and indecision if and when their students do *not* demonstrate proficiency on the post-CFA. Should they proceed to the next unit of study even though some of their students are not ready to do so? If they delay moving ahead in order to close the learning gaps in their students' understanding through reteaching and reassessing, how will they keep up with the curriculum's preset pacing schedule?

When educators keep moving ahead rather than slowing down to ensure that students master certain aspects of the curriculum, they often do so out of concern they will be unable to complete all of the curricular units before the end of the school year. Any educator confronted with the mounting accountability pressures of today can certainly relate to this feeling of unease. The question lingers: "Will my students have covered enough of the standards in time to be academically prepared for the cognitive demands of the large-scale annual assessments?" Often what happens in response to such uncertainty is a sacrifice of student learning in favor of keeping on pace.

These issues present very real pressures educators continually face when student learning does not happen "right on time." One powerful way to ensure that needed remediation and reassessment can take place for students who need it is to deliberately schedule the inclusion of a **Bridge** between each of the units of study. This Bridge, also known by many educators and leaders as the "buffer" (Ainsworth, 2010, p. 30), can last anywhere from two to five class periods within a week of school. The Bridge provides educators with scheduled breathing room *between* units of study. Its purpose is to give teachers and students additional time to regroup in order to close student learning gaps. During this time, those students who need additional instruction (reteaching, remediation) receive it in a different way than it was initially taught during the unit. They then have the opportunity to be reassessed and show improvement (i.e., achieve the success criteria).

The Bridge also serves those students who demonstrate proficiency or better on the post-CFA. During this time, they have an opportunity to extend their knowledge and further refine their skills by taking part in enrichment learning, engaging in activities that enlarge their understanding of the unit's learning intentions.

One main reason educators have validated and endorsed the idea of scheduling this Bridge between units is its usefulness to *all* students. Often educators understandably devote the bulk of their efforts to assisting struggling learners, but it is at the expense of giving sufficient time and attention to advanced students. The purpose of the Bridge is to help educators equalize that distribution of time and attention. It is just as much about meeting the learning needs of high-performing students as it is about assisting those students who sometimes just need a do-over to succeed. Chapter 11 describes how to effectively plan for the Bridge.

THE COMPLETE HIGHWAY

To recap, the successive construction stages of our CFA 2.0 highway began with the *fundamental standards* and *assessment components* (Figures 1.1–1.4).

Next we included the initial *data analysis* components (Figures 1.5–1.6). Then we added in the *learning progressions* and *quick progress checks* (Figures 1.7–1.8), followed by the *teach-assess-interpret-adjust* quartet of practices (Figure 1.9).

The entire CFA 2.0 process—with arrows indicating the construction sequence—culminates in a completed highway to intentionally aligned standards, instruction, assessments, and data analysis, as shown in Figure 1.10. Appearing on both sides of the figure is the Bridge between units that occurs between all curricular units of study throughout the school year. The dark boxes in the figure represent the "highway improvements" made to the original CFA process. These improvements are now essential segments of the CFA 2.0 highway.

BEYOND THE HIGHWAY

For obvious reasons, educators cannot control the composition of assessments they did not create—particularly the external, high-stakes accountability tests that states, provinces, and national assessment consortia administer to millions of students each year. What educators *can* control, however, is the close alignment between assessments they themselves create for every unit of study: the post-CFA, the pre-CFA, and the quick progress checks that follow learning progressions. But must the aligned assessment highway end where the large-scale assessments begin? Can we build a connecting road between the two?

At the risk of mixing the metaphors, the challenge of being able to extend the highway into the realm of standardized achievement tests is like comparing apples to oranges. Whereas internally created CFAs are specifically designed to gauge student understanding of *unit-specific* Priority Standards, externally created standardized achievement tests can only *sample* all of the standards students are to learn within an entire school year. There are simply too many grade- and course-specific standards in tested content areas to make feasible a full inclusion of related questions. This fact underscores the need for Priority Standards—a carefully selected subset of the entire list of standards at each grade level (described and illustrated in Chapter 4) that includes those particular standards most likely to be assessed on standardized achievement tests.

Another challenge to this extension of alignment is the mismatch between internal assessments that are designed to reveal instructional impact on student learning, and external assessments that are designed to provide a summative report of student attainment of grade- or

Figure 1.10 How Teacher Teams Intentionally Align Standards, Instruction, Assessment, and Data Analysis

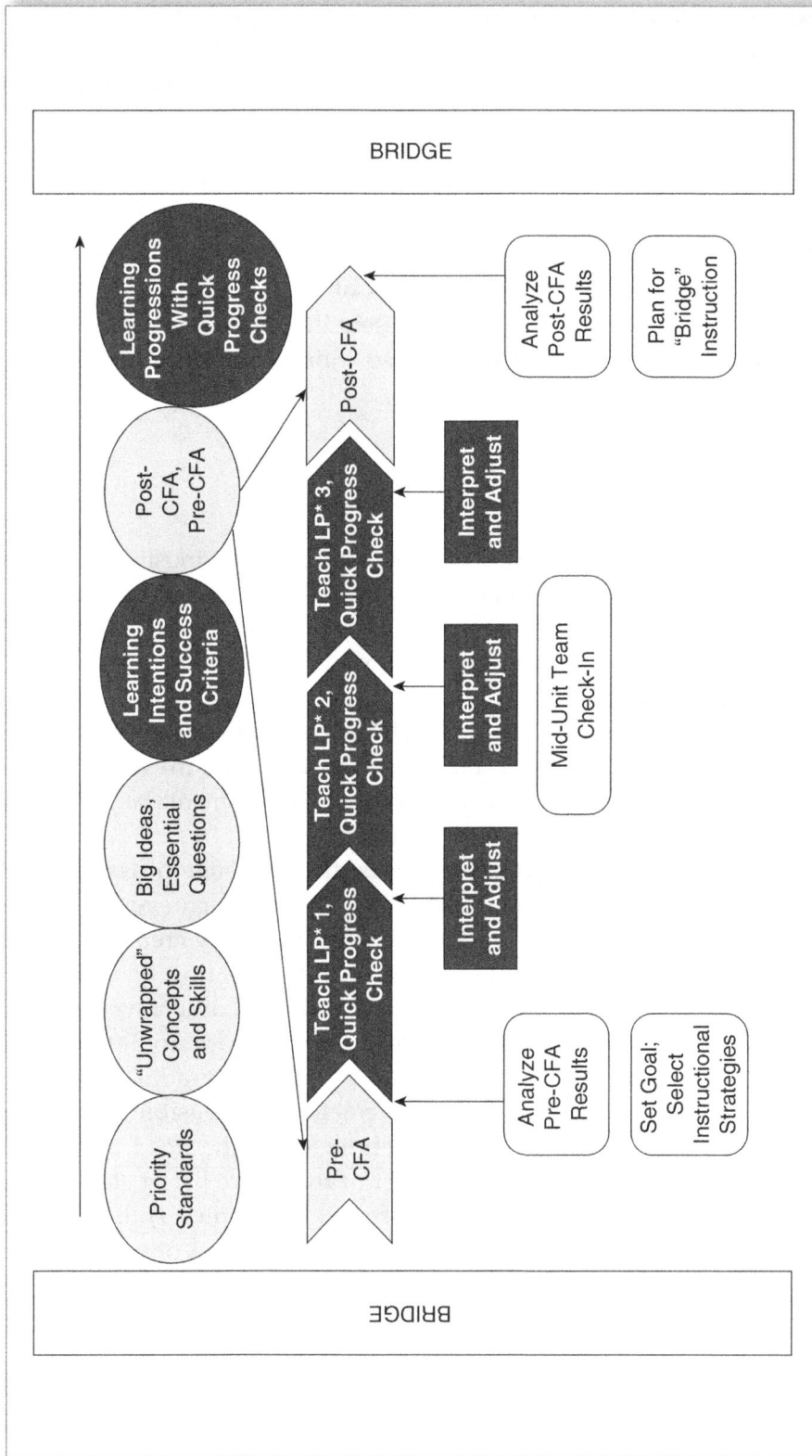

BRIDGE

BRIDGE

Priority Standards

"Unwrapped" Concepts and Skills

Big Ideas, Essential Questions

Learning Intentions and Success Criteria

Post-CFA, Pre-CFA

Learning Progressions With Quick Progress Checks

Pre-CFA

Teach LP* 1, Quick Progress Check

Teach LP* 2, Quick Progress Check

Teach LP* 3, Quick Progress Check

Post-CFA

Interpret and Adjust

Interpret and Adjust

Interpret and Adjust

Analyze Pre-CFA Results

Set Goal; Select Instructional Strategies

Mid-Unit Team Check-In

Analyze Post-CFA Results

Plan for "Bridge" Instruction

*Learning Progression.

course-level standards. This mismatch is well summed up by W. James Popham in Chapter 7 of his book, *Transformative Assessment* (2008):

> Almost all of today's educational accountability tests are *instructionally insensitive,* incapable of detecting the difference between effective and ineffective instruction. . . . When an instructionally insensitive test is used as an accountability test, the bulk of learning benefits from classroom formative assessment simply won't show up in the test results. (p. 123)

However, Siobhan Leahy and Dylan Wiliam (as cited in Hattie, 2012) report high correlations between educators who regularly use formative assessments and improved student performance as measured on large-scale external assessments:

> When formative assessment practices are integrated into the minute-to-minute and day-by-day classroom activities of teachers, substantial increases in student achievement—of the order of a 70 to 80 percent increase in the speed of learning—are possible, even when outcomes are measured with externally mandated standardized tests. (p. 128)

To connect internal and external assessments, educators should craft their CFA questions to align with the format, vocabulary, and rigor of standardized assessment questions. Doing so will help prepare their students to respond to external test questions that might otherwise appear in new or unfamiliar formats.

CONSTRUCTING THE HIGHWAY IN SEGMENTS

The purpose of this chapter was to provide you with a panoramic vision of the completed CFA 2.0 highway (most educators like seeing the big picture first, remember?). However, if this full preview was a bit too much to take in all at once, don't worry. Each component of the completed highway will be covered in detail in subsequent chapters. Beginning in Chapter 3, you will see a flow chart of the ten-step CFA 2.0 design process. This same flow chart appears in each succeeding chapter with the current step (or steps) highlighted as a reminder of where it fits into the overall design process.

SUCCESS CRITERIA

At the start of this chapter, three learning intentions set the stage for the content to follow. Those same learning intentions now reappear here as *success criteria.* The content is the same, but the statements now begin with an action verb that asks you to demonstrate that you were successful in attaining those intentions.

Success Criteria:

- Describe the standards and assessment components of a quality CFA.
- Summarize the connections between quick progress checks, data analysis, and instruction.
- Explain how to construct, in progressive steps, the CFA highway of aligned assessments. (It is perfectly okay to treat this as an "open-book" question and refer back to the content of the chapter.)

To synthesize what you've learned from this chapter, take a few moments to write your responses to these success criteria. If you'd prefer an alternative (and faster) way of responding, evaluate your understanding of each of the success criteria on a scale of one to five, with five representing, "I totally get it and could teach it to others." If you are reading this book as part of a professional study group, share your thoughts and ideas with colleagues.

When finished debriefing this chapter, you're ready to see how your current assessment literacy fares within the context of the CFA 2.0 framework.

2 Assessment Literacy 2.0

In This Chapter You Will Learn:

- How and why assessment literacy can benefit all educators.
- The importance of formative assessment.
- Why a shared understanding of assessment-related terms is necessary.
- The differences between assessments *for* and *of* learning as applied to in-school CFAs, district benchmarks, and standardized achievement tests.

Every educator must understand the principles of sound assessment and must be able to apply those principles as a matter of routine in doing their work. Accurate assessment is not possible unless and until educators are given the opportunity to become assessment literate. [They] must understand student achievement expectations and how to transform those expectations into accurate assessment exercises and scoring procedures.

—National Education Association, 2003, p. 4

THE NEED FOR ASSESSMENT LITERACY

Exactly what is **assessment literacy?** It is the ability to understand the different purposes and types of assessment in order to select the most appropriate type to meet a specific purpose. How can improved assessment literacy benefit educators and students?

When [teachers] know and understand principles of sound assessment, know how to translate those principles into sound assessments and quality information about students, and because they involve students in the assessment process as part of their effective instruction, a range of benefits will accrue to all. (Stiggins, 1997, p. 7)

As educators develop and refine their own assessment literacy, they become more confident in their ability to make use of a greater variety of assessment tools in their assessment toolkit. As they learn the specific attributes of each type of assessment and gain experience creating and using each type, they can more effectively match the right tool to the right job. Learning how to design a variety of effective assessments, rather than over-relying on one particular type, educators become more adept at utilizing multiple measures to reveal student understanding.

Promoting a shared understanding of assessment literacy within a school faculty becomes especially important to grade- and course-level teachers when they design common formative assessments. Together the participating educators can deliberately select the particular type(s) of assessment that will best reveal their students' understanding of the unit learning intentions and student success criteria currently in focus. Should they later discover that the assessment type they first selected proves limited in providing the feedback they need on student progress, they will be better able to collaboratively decide upon a different type of assessment.

A fundamental principle of assessment literacy is rooted in the ability to answer the question, "Why assess?"

THE RATIONALE FOR ASSESSMENT

Why do educators assess? There are a host of reasons. In general, educators want to know if, and to what degree, students are making progress toward mastery of particular concepts or skills in the standards. They use assessment results to determine levels of proficiency, to assign letter grades, and to communicate to parents where students are and where they need to improve.

For their more immediate purposes, educators assess students (1) to evaluate the effectiveness of instructional strategies and make adjustments as needed, (2) to give students feedback about what they currently know and can do, and (3) to show students how to use feedback to determine where they need to go next in their learning.

Educators assess student progress informally through ongoing observations, questioning, dialogue, and anecdotal note taking. When they need a more formal method, they select or design an appropriate assessment matched to their intended purposes and then use the student results to answer their questions about student learning.

The bottom line as to why educators assess is to accurately determine their instructional impact on student learning. The feedback from students' assessment results provides the authentic evidence of the efficacy of educators' efforts.

W. James Popham (2003) asks educators to think deeply about the following four questions during the planning stages of instruction and assessment:

- What am I really trying to teach?
- What do my students need to know and be able to do?
- How can I translate the big curricular goals . . . into specific teachable components?
- What do my students already know about the topic I'm planning to teach? (p. 5)

Each of these questions is addressed within the ten CFA 2.0 design steps. Educators "unwrap" the unit Priority Standards to identify key concepts, skills, and corresponding levels of cognitive rigor in Step 2. This clarifies what they are "really trying to teach" and "what students need to know and be able to do." By deciding the sequenced learning progressions in Step 9, they break down the "big curricular goals into specific teachable components." The pre-CFA for the unit of study, created in Step 7, reveals students' prior knowledge, "what students already know about the topic." From the resulting feedback, educators strive to correctly interpret student understanding in order to appropriately plan their instructional next steps.

No explanation about the purpose of assessments had a greater impact on my own understanding of assessment's essential function than these words of W. James Popham (2003):

Teachers use test [results] in order to make inferences about their students' cognitive status. Once those score-based inferences have been made, the teacher then reaches instructional decisions based (at least in part) on those inferences. *Educational assessment revolves around inference making.* (p. 60; italics added)

This passage again underscores the critical importance of *well-written* assessment questions. If the questions are flawed, the inferences educators derive from the students' feedback will be flawed, and the resulting instructional adjustments will likely not correct students' misunderstandings.

FOUNDATIONS OF ASSESSMENT LITERACY

Assessment literacy is founded upon six sequential steps that inform instructional decision making, reprinted here from *Rigorous Curriculum Design* (Ainsworth, 2010):

1. **Know your purpose.** Determine exactly what it is you want to find out, what it is you want the assessment to do, and why you are administering the assessment in the first place.

2. **Determine the appropriate assessment that will accomplish your identified purpose.** In this context, "appropriate" means the specific type(s) or format(s) most likely to tell you what you want to know (selected response, constructed response, and performance based).

3. **Select or create a quality assessment.** Take great care in choosing questions from an external source and/or crafting the assessment questions yourselves. If a question is faulty in any way, and students answer it incorrectly, educators will later have to determine whether the question itself was the problem or whether students simply did not know the content upon which it was based. Decide whether the planned questions included in the assessment will enable you to make an *accurate* inference as to what students know and can do.

4. **Administer and score the assessment; analyze the assessment results.** Look for evidence of student learning, specific to your purpose, in the student responses. Conduct an item analysis, determining which questions individual students answered correctly and which ones they did not.

5. **Make an accurate inference.** This will be possible only if the assessment questions that you selected or created in Step 3 are of quality and provide valid and reliable data.

6. **Adjust instructional decisions in a timely manner.** Determine instructional next steps for students based on the inferences you have made. (pp. 137–138)

Because no single assessment can fulfill *all* the purposes of assessment or provide comprehensive evidence of student proficiency, Carol Ann Tomlinson (1995) states,

Fruitful assessment often poses the question, 'What is an array of ways I can offer students to demonstrate their understanding and skills?' In this way, assessment becomes a part of teaching for success and a *way to extend rather than merely measure* learning. (italics added)

How then do these assessment *purposes* translate to definable assessment *practices?* Let's start with a well-rounded understanding of what formative assessments are.

FORMATIVE ASSESSMENT DEFINITIONS

There are many definitions and descriptions of **formative assessment**. Here is a sampling of definitions that collectively convey the essence of what formative assessment is and how it should be used:

- "Formative assessment is a planned process in which assessment-elicited evidence of students' status is used by teachers to adjust their ongoing instructional procedures or by students to adjust their current learning tactics" (Popham, 2008, p. 6).
- "Formative assessment is a loop: Students and teachers focus on a learning target, evaluate current student work against the target, act to move the work closer to the target, and repeat" (Brookhart & Nitko, 2007, p. 116).
- "The purpose of formative assessment is to provide feedback to teachers and students during the course of learning about the gap between students' current and desired performance so that action can be taken to close the gap" (Heritage, 2008, p. 2).
- "Assessments *for* learning happen while learning is still underway. These are the assessments that we conduct throughout teaching and learning to diagnose student needs, plan for next steps in instruction, provide students with feedback they can use to improve the quality of their work, and help students see and feel in control of their journey to success" (Stiggins, Arter, Chappuis, & Chappuis, 2006, p. 31).
- "Assessment *for* learning is any practice which provides information to pupils about what to do to improve. Assessment *as* learning is any practice which takes the 'what to improve' into 'how to improve'" (Clarke, 2008, p. 9).
- "An alternative to consider is 'assessment as feedback.' . . . As teachers derive feedback information from assessments that they set (for) their students, there can then be important adjustments to how they teach, how they consider what success looks like, how they recognize students' strengths and gaps, and how they regard their own effects on students" (Hattie, 2012, pp. 125–126).

DRAMATIC RESEARCH SUPPORT

Underscoring the practical reasons for formative assessment is an extensive body of supporting research. The influence of formative assessment associated with student learning gained widespread attention with the publication of the 1998 *Phi Delta Kappan* article by British researchers Paul Black and Dylan Wiliam (1998b) and their extensive review of the research on classroom assessment that same year. Their meta-analysis (1998a) concluded that student learning gains resulting from the use of formative assessment were among "the largest ever reported for educational interventions" (p. 61).

After summarizing a body of research on the impact of formative assessments distilled from four thousand studies spanning 40 years, Dylan Wiliam (2007–2008) concluded, "When well-implemented, formative assessments can effectively *double* the speed of student learning" (p. 36).

In *Rigorous Curriculum Design* (Ainsworth, 2010), I took the liberty of interpreting the opening words of Wiliam's conclusion, *when well implemented:*

> It is not enough just to *administer* formative assessments. To realize their full potential for improving student achievement, such assessments must be carefully constructed, student results must be thoughtfully analyzed, inferences must be accurately made, and subsequent instruction must be differentiated to meet student learning needs accordingly." (p. 41)

Recently published educational research continues to underscore the effects that formative assessment, when effectively implemented, can have on raising student achievement levels. In *Visible Learning* (2009, pp. 2–3), world-renowned educational researcher John Hattie explains that any professional practice that can achieve a 0.40 effect size equates to *approximately one year of growth in student learning*. (See the glossary at the end of this book for a further description of **effect size**.)

Formative evaluation ranks fourth among all positive influences on student learning, producing an overall effect size of 0.90—equivalent to *more than two years* of student gains within a single academic school year. The effective use of feedback ranks tenth, with an effect size of 0.79 and a nearly similar result—*almost two years* of student growth.

Such impressive statistics provide a highly persuasive rationale in support of educators making formative assessment and feedback part of their bread-and-butter staples of educational best practice. Common formative assessments are a great way for educators and students to receive and utilize resulting feedback to correctly interpret student understanding and adjust instruction accordingly.

KEY ASSESSMENT TERMINOLOGY

There are many terms associated with the word *assessment* and as many interpretations of what those terms mean. Often the terms become confusing for educators and result in misinterpretations of meaning that consume valuable collaboration time to clarify, time that could be more productively spent interpreting student learning needs and collaboratively deciding how best to instructionally meet them.

For example, educators often use interchangeably (and incorrectly) these assessment labels: formative, summative, interim, common, performance, diagnostic, progress monitoring, progress checks, and assessments *of, for,* and *as* learning, to name only a few.

Therefore, it is important to strive for a consensus of understanding about what frequently used terms mean, a key component of assessment literacy. It is important to create a printed lexicon or glossary of assessment terminology within a school and school system so that everyone can be on the same vocabulary page.

To help you begin this endeavor, specific terms that apply to the CFA 2.0 process are defined throughout the chapters and appear again in a comprehensive list at the end of the book. This glossary will help inform professional discussions and promote a school- and district-wide consensus of understanding. Let's clarify a few of those terms here.

ASSESSMENTS *FOR* LEARNING: CLASSROOM AND COMMON

Classroom **formative assessments** include pretests or pre-assessments given to students before unit instruction occurs, informal checks to gauge student progress during instruction, and even a comprehensive assessment at the conclusion of the unit—*if* the results are used to inform instruction. Formative assessments are, by name and intention, formative. Thus, they are typically not used to assign grades. These assessments *for* learning yield diagnostic student feedback that educators use solely to inform and adjust instruction.

Common **formative assessments** are closely similar to classroom formative assessments with one exception: they are collaboratively designed by elementary grade-level and secondary course-level *teams* of educators who are all teaching the same unit of study to their students during the same timeframe. Common formative assessments include a pre-/post- design format, wherein students are given the same (or an alternate form of the same) assessment at the start of a unit and again at its conclusion. The results of the pre-CFA help the team members determine students' prior knowledge and current understanding *before* instruction of a standards-based unit begins. The results of the post-CFA provide evidence of students' understanding *after* a unit of instruction has been concluded.

CFA teams collaboratively use assessment results to (1) accurately interpret student learning needs, (2) set individual classroom goals as well as grade- and course-level team goals for student improvement, (3) identify and share effective teaching strategies to accomplish these goals, (4) create appropriate lessons and activities for groups of learners or individual students, (5) plan ways to differentiate instruction and correct student misconceptions, and (6) inform students about their current progress so they can adjust their learning methods and strategies.

The National Education Association (NEA, 2003) explains why formative assessments *for* learning are so vital to students:

> In the context of classroom assessment, however, one key purpose can be to use assessment results to *inform students about themselves.* That is, classroom assessments can inform students about the continuous improvements in their achievement and permit them to feel in control of that growth. Thus, classroom assessments become assessments *for* learning. Teachers involve their students in the classroom assessment process for the [express] purpose of increasing their achievement. (p. 6)

ASSESSMENTS *OF* LEARNING: CLASSROOM AND COMMON

Classroom **summative assessments,** given by individual teachers, or *common* **summative assessments,** given by teacher teams, can occur at the end of a unit, quarter, trimester, semester, course, or an academic school year. Since these assessments take place after all instruction and student learning have ended, they are summative in both design and intent. They report the final results of student learning to the educators, to their students, to students' parents, and to administrators—typically to support the assignment of letter grades and/or levels of proficiency. Thus, they serve as assessments *of* learning.

When all instruction and related learning activities for particular standards have concluded, the results of summative assessments are not often used to improve student understanding for current students. Instead, teachers typically use these assessment results to judge the effectiveness of their teaching practices and to improve instruction of those standards for future students.

These dual purposes of assessment—formative and summative—are well expressed in the following statement from the NEA (2003): "Assessment must be seen as an *instructional tool* for use while learning is occurring and as an *accountability tool* to determine if learning has occurred" (p. 3; italics added).

IS THIS ASSESSMENT FORMATIVE OR SUMMATIVE?

In *Visible Learning for Teachers*, John Hattie (2012) shares Bob Stake's humorous maxim: "When the cook tastes the soup, it is formative; when the guests taste the soup, it is summative" (p. 144).

Confusion can exist in the minds of educators when attempting to classify an assessment given at the end of a unit as anything other than summative. One broad distinction is this: If the results from that assessment are not used to monitor and adjust instruction in order to improve students' learning, the assessment is indeed summative. If those results are so used, the assessment can rightly be classified as formative.

> Practice in a classroom is formative to the extent that evidence about student achievement is elicited, interpreted, and used by teachers, learners, or their peers, to make decisions about the next steps in instruction that are likely to be better, or better founded, than the decisions they would have taken in the absence of the evidence that was elicited. (Black & Wiliam, 2009, p. 9)

Whether to regard an assessment as either formative or summative depends on the assessment's purpose and how the assessment results are to be used. Here are three examples to illustrate:

1. If the assessment is simply a final measure of how students performed on multiple standards taught during the quarter, trimester, semester, or course of study, the assessment is obviously summative.

2. If an educator uses the results from an end-of-unit assessment in any way to inform instruction for the same students before or during the next unit of study, the results are being used formatively, even though the assessment itself is a summative measure used to determine student understanding of the unit learning intentions.

3. If an educator provides students with the opportunity to revise their work during the evaluation process and thus improve their performance on a particular assessment, the assessment should rightly be considered formative. After the students complete their revisions and the final evaluation is determined, the assessment can then be regarded as summative.

Whenever educators use the feedback results of any assessment in a diagnostic way—to correctly interpret student learning needs in order to instructionally meet those needs or to enable students to revise and improve their work—then that assessment is thought of as being formative. It is an *in-process* assessment.

CFAs, by name and purpose, are principally formative assessments, but they can serve a summative function after all of the formative uses of the assessment results are concluded at the end of a unit.

One important point of clarification: Even though educators (myself included) typically refer to an *assessment* as being either formative or summative, it is more accurate to say that educators are *using the results formatively* to adjust ongoing instruction or *using the results summatively* to measure the end of students' learning, rather than to assign those labels to the assessment itself.

Hattie (2012) emphasizes the distinction this way:

> One major mistake is to consider that the notions of "formative" and "summative" have something to do with tests; in fact, there is no such thing called summative or formative tests. "Formative" and "summative" refer to *the time at which* a test is administered and, more importantly to the nature of the interpretations made from the tests. (p. 144)

DISTRICT BENCHMARK ASSESSMENTS

It is a widespread practice for school systems to administer district benchmark assessments to elementary and middle school students at the beginning of the school year and at the end of nine-week marking periods or twelve-week trimesters throughout the rest of the year. The purpose of these assessments is to determine if students are on track for success on the annual large-scale standardized achievement tests. In some districts these assessments are designed to be formative, with results made available quickly so that educators can see how their students are doing and make instructional changes accordingly.

But more typically these assessments are summative, administered to survey student understanding of the grade- or course-level standards taught during an entire quarter or trimester. School and district administrators in particular use this data to see how students in each building and in all schools across the district are progressing prior to the annual standardized achievement tests. However, these assessments can come with a heavy accountability factor if and when the results are used to classify and rank educators, students, and entire schools as underperforming.

Classroom educators do not find benchmark assessments particularly useful unless they inform their current and ongoing instruction to help students improve. Robert Marzano (2010) states that benchmark assessments "frequently violate many of the basic assumptions underlying good formative assessment" (p. 9), and cites James McMillan in support of that assertion:

> These tests, which are typically provided by the district or commercial test publishers, are administered on a regular basis to compare student achievement to "benchmarks" that indicate where student performance should be in relation to what is needed to do well on end-of-year high stakes tests. . . . . Although the term *benchmark* is often used interchangeably with *formative* in the commercial testing market, there are important differences. Benchmark assessments are formal, structured tests that typically do not provide the level of detail needed for appropriate instructional correctives. (2007, pp. 2–3)

POSITIVE WAYS TO USE BENCHMARK ASSESSMENTS

Even though periodic benchmark assessments place additional accountability demands on educators and increased testing demands on students, they can be beneficial *if* educators are able to use the results properly, that is, to improve instructional efficacy. A few of the positive ways educators can use benchmark assessments include

- *Intervening* appropriately for students who are far from proficiency well in advance of the large-scale summative assessments.
- *Accelerating* instruction effectively to help already-proficient students achieve advanced or exemplary levels of performance on the external assessments.
- *Modifying* existing assessments and creating alternative assessments similar to the format and rigor of large-scale assessments to assist English language learners and special needs students.

How closely these district benchmark assessments are aligned to state and provincial assessments in terms of assessment formats (selected response and constructed response), cognitive rigor, and vocabulary varies from one district to another. However, the more closely district assessments are aligned to large-scale assessments in terms of format and wording, the greater the likelihood that students will be familiar with the ways they are being expected to demonstrate their understanding on those external exams.

LARGE-SCALE ASSESSMENTS *OF* LEARNING

The National Education Association refers to the annual assessments developed at the state level and then administered by local school districts as assessments *of* learning. In a report entitled *Balanced Assessment: The Key to Accountability and Improved Student Learning* (2003), the NEA pinpoints the essential purpose of such large-scale, external assessments:

> When standardized tests are administered, they typically are intended to inform various policy-level and programmatic decision makers, as well as teachers, parents and the community, about student achievement. They are assessments *of* learning. Students are not the intended users. Rather, the tests inform others about students. (p. 6)

Large-scale assessments by themselves have minimal impact on an individual child's academic growth. The usual turnaround time it takes to receive results is a significant drawback that greatly limits the assessment's usefulness with regard to informing current instructional decision making. As a rule, in the United States it takes weeks and even months for schools to receive the student results of their annual state tests. By that time, students have moved on to the next grade, rendering useless that data to improve learning for those same students *unless* the next grade's teacher uses the data to identify the learning needs of those incoming students.

This is not to denigrate the administration of large-scale assessments, however. Analysis of large-scale assessment results can lead to broad changes in curriculum content, curricular sequencing, curriculum delivery, and enhancements of individual classroom test items (Sargent, 2004). Although all these changes can be very good, the actual data still will not give educators the specific and timely information they need to impact the learning of individual students they work with each day.

Ask educators, "What data about student achievement are most useful to you on a daily basis?" and their answer is almost always, "The data we collect from informal checks of student understanding—particularly when we use that feedback to determine where students currently are in relation to achieving the unit learning intentions."

Yet, paradoxically, the data that carry the greatest weight in terms of accountability are the data derived from students' performance on large-scale assessments. This is problematic because standardized achievement tests, even those that are aligned to content standards, are *instructionally insensitive.* Here is how Popham (2013) defines that term and describes its relationship to external exams and teacher evaluations:

> **Instructional sensitivity** is the degree to which students' performances on a test accurately reflects the quality of instruction specifically provided to promote students' mastery of what is being assessed. . . . If a standardized test is instructionally *insensitive*, it should have no role at all in evaluating the instructional ability of a teacher. (p. 63, bold and italics added)

A BALANCED ASSESSMENT SYSTEM

Even though large-scale, standardized testing is likely here to stay, at best it can only provide snapshots of what a child knows and can demonstrate during the high-pressure weeks of spring testing each year. Looked at in isolation from other assessments, such on-demand snapshots are insufficient. To maximize their value, they should be presented as part of a "photo album" that shows evidence of student understanding acquired over time—an album that includes the results of formative and summative assessments along with student work products from authentic classroom performance tasks collected throughout a yearlong curriculum of multiple units of study. These "photos," when viewed together as a whole, will show a complete picture of student growth in learning, even when the students have left for the next level of schooling and taken their photo album with them.

DISCONTINUE MINIMAL-IMPACT ASSESSMENTS

As important as it is for educators to be on the same page of understanding regarding assessment terminology, it is even more important for them to take a hard look at the *usefulness* of each in-school assessment and to discontinue administering any assessments that are not yielding valuable information that can impact teaching and learning. This includes careful scrutiny of those assessments that are part of an adopted curricular program.

With so many different types of assessments educators are required to administer, they need to become very critical consumers in their selection of assessments. They can accomplish this by applying the first two steps of assessment literacy presented earlier in this chapter:

1. **Know your purpose.** Determine exactly what it is you want to find out, what it is you want the assessment to do, and why you are administering the assessment in the first place.

2. **Determine the appropriate assessment that will accomplish your identified purpose.**

Considering the amount of valuable time it takes educators to design, administer, score, and analyze assessment results, each assessment needs to be worth that investment of time. If it is not contributing significantly to valid and reliable inferences about what students currently know and can do—and what they need next in their learning —you may want to give serious consideration to dropping it from the assessment roster.

Identify and focus on those assessments that truly have meaning and the potential for producing maximum impact on student learning. School leaders can greatly support classroom educators in this by encouraging them to rely upon their professional judgment and that of their colleagues to judiciously "weed the assessment garden."

CHAPTER SUCCESS CRITERIA

In the next chapter you will have a first look at the complete diagram of sequential steps for designing a quality CFA. As an ongoing reminder, this same diagram will reappear in each succeeding chapter with the particular step in focus highlighted. In this way you will be able to continually reorient yourself as to where you are in the entire CFA 2.0 process.

But first, please take a few moments and write your responses to the success criteria for this chapter, or simply evaluate your understanding of each statement on a scale of one (low) to five (high). If you give yourself a lower score, identify your learning gap and reread the related section(s) for clarification. As suggested at the conclusion of Chapter 1, if you are reading this book as part of a professional study group, share your thoughts and ideas with colleagues.

Success Criteria:

- Explain how and why assessment literacy can benefit all educators.
- Summarize the importance of formative assessment.
- State why a shared understanding of key assessment-related terms is necessary.
- Describe the differences between assessments *for* and *of* learning as applied to in-school CFAs, district benchmarks, and standardized achievement tests.

3 Overview of the CFA 2.0 Design Steps

In This Chapter You Will Learn:

- The sequential steps in designing a quality CFA.
- How to describe each of the CFA 2.0 components.
- The role performance tasks play in assessing student understanding of the unit learning intentions.

To ensure the most effective use of common formative assessments, there are certain design guidelines for grade- and course-level teams to follow. In this chapter, you will see an overview of the step-by-step CFA 2.0 design process and understand the role each of the components plays in that process. Subsequent chapters will describe these components in more detail and provide illustrations of each one using Common Core State Standards (CCSS) in both mathematics and in English language arts and literacy.

Why the Common Core? Rather than selecting representative standards from individual states or learning outcomes from individual Canadian provinces that would only be relevant to educators in those particular states and provinces, it made more sense to illustrate the CFA design steps using standards familiar to readers in the majority of states. But keep in mind, the CFA process preceded the Common Core by several years; it works with <u>all</u> state standards and <u>all</u> provincial learning outcomes in every grade and content area.

Whether you have created many CFAs with your colleagues or have yet to design your first one, the linear steps of the process and the accompanying explanations and illustrations will help you in designing an effective CFA and/or improving an existing one. It takes an investment of several hours and collaborative effort to construct a first-draft assessment. Then that first draft requires a quality critique and subsequent revision. Educators carry out these quality-control tasks to ensure that the finished assessment is fulfilling its chief purpose: making possible *valid* and *reliable* *inferences* about student understanding of the learning intentions in focus. After that, the CFA is ready for its "road test" in the participating classrooms, so the teacher team can see what works, what doesn't, what to keep, and what to change. This naturally leads to further fine-tuning of the assessment questions before the CFA is administered again in the future.

CFA 2.0 DESIGN STEPS AT A GLANCE

In Chapter 1, you learned how to construct, in segments, the "highway" to aligned assessments. Reprinted here from the first edition of this book are the ten planning steps teachers take when designing a CFA and its component parts. One phrase and two sentences that are presented in bold type represent new additions to this design sequence. Note that Steps 1–6 represent the central *purpose* of assessment—what students are to learn. Steps 7–10 refer to the *types* of assessment and instructional pathways needed to meet that purpose.

1. Identify within any content area the particular Priority Standards to emphasize in an upcoming unit of study.

2. Identify other related standards—referred to as *supporting standards*—that connect to the Priority Standards.

3. "Unwrap" the Priority Standards *only* in order to pinpoint the specific concepts and skills students need to learn and then **create a graphic organizer that includes those "unwrapped" concepts and skills.**

4. Determine Big Ideas based on the "unwrapped" Priority Standards that represent the connections or conclusions teachers want students to realize on their own by the end of the unit of study.

5. Write Essential Questions matched to the Big Ideas to focus instruction throughout the unit and to inform students of their learning goals.

6. **Confirm the learning intentions to be assessed (the specifics of what students are to understand and be able to do by the end of**

the unit) and the success criteria (how students will show they have achieved the learning intentions).

7. Select the assessment types (selected response, short and extended constructed response) that will produce credible evidence that students have learned the "unwrapped" concepts and skills.

8. Create the post-assessment questions and scoring guides for the selected assessment type(s).

9. Create the pre-assessment questions to align with the post-assessment ones.

10. **Determine the learning progressions—the building blocks of instruction leading to the learning intentions—and plan quick progress checks to assess student understanding of each one.**

Figure 3.1 shows the updated ten steps for designing a matching set of pre- and post- CFAs followed by a synopsis of each step. The shaded steps are new to the CFA 2.0 design process. Note the addition of a quality control check inserted immediately after the pre-assessment design step. The CFA process is linear and straightforward, so you and your colleagues can

Figure 3.1 The Ten Design Steps of CFA 2.0

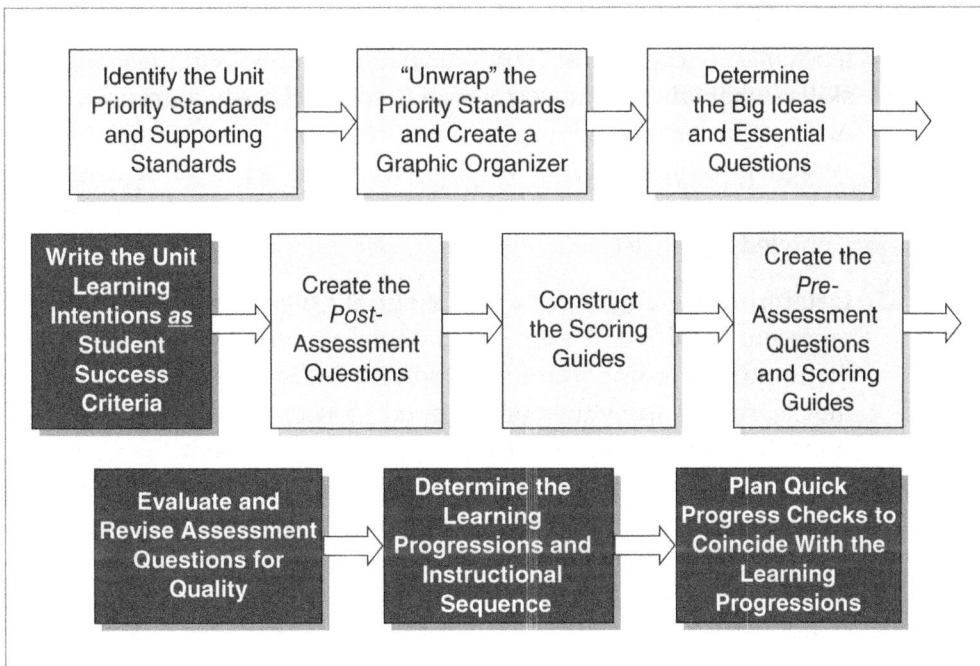

construct a new CFA or revise an existing one by following the directions associated with each of these steps in the coming chapters.

SYNOPSES OF THE TEN DESIGN STEPS

1. **Identify the Priority Standards and Supporting Standards for the Unit.** From the complete list of grade- or course-level Priority Standards, select three to five standards maximum to be the learning focus of the unit. These specific Priority Standards should come from a *combination* of strands or domains within the content area, and not be limited to one strand or domain only. The Priority Standards assigned to the unit are the foundations from which the unit learning intentions will be decided.

   The supporting standards are the standards that connect or relate to the Priority Standards but do not receive the same degree of instructional emphasis. The CFA assesses student understanding of the Priority Standards only, not the supporting standards. However, the supporting standards provide instructional supports, or scaffolds, to help students achieve understanding of those Priority Standards. Select a limited number of supporting standards that directly connect to the unit Priority Standards.

2. **"Unwrap" the Priority Standards and Create a Graphic Organizer.** Deconstruct the Priority Standards *only* in order to identify the teachable concepts (what students need to know) and the assessible skills (what students need to be able to do). Create a graphic organizer representing all of the "unwrapped" concepts and skills. Assign to each concept-skill pair an associated level of cognitive rigor using the revised Bloom's Taxonomy and Webb's Depth of Knowledge matrices.

3. **Determine the Big Ideas and Essential Questions.** The Big Ideas represent the three or four foundational understandings specific to the unit that are important for students to discover on their own as they learn and apply the "unwrapped" concepts and skills. To introduce the unit of study to students, educators present three or four corresponding Essential Questions derived from the "unwrapped" concepts and skills that will guide all instruction and learning activities throughout the unit. The expectation is that students will respond to the Essential Questions with corresponding Big Ideas stated in their own words on the post-CFA at the end of the unit.

4. **Write the Unit Learning Intentions _as_ Student Success Criteria.** The "unwrapped" concepts and skills, the levels of cognitive rigor, the Big Ideas and Essential Questions, and the unit vocabulary terms derived from both the Priority Standards and the supporting standards collectively represent the unit learning intentions that students are to achieve by the end of the unit. In this step, teacher teams write these unit learning intentions in the form of student success criteria—performance statements that describe how students will show they have achieved the learning intentions.

5. **Create the Post-Assessment Questions.** The CFA is a multiple-format assessment that includes a blend of selected-response and short and extended constructed-response questions directly aligned to the unit learning intentions ("unwrapped" concepts, skills, corresponding levels of cognitive rigor, targeted vocabulary, Essential Questions, and Big Ideas). When combined together effectively, these assessment formats help educators determine students' overall understanding of the learning intentions in focus during the unit. Reprinted here from Chapter 1, Figure 3.2 shows this blend of

Figure 3.2 Multiple-Format Assessment Directly Aligned to Learning Intentions

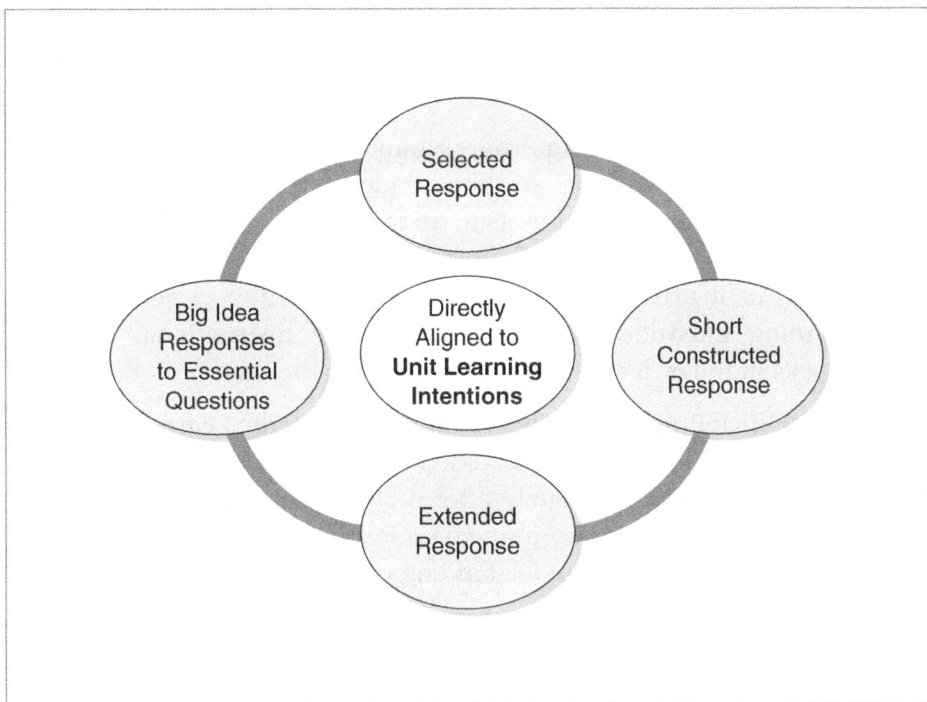

formats. Beginning with the end in mind, educators create the post-CFA *before they plan instruction* so they have a clear picture of what they want their students to show they have learned by the end of the unit.

6. **Construct the Scoring Guides**. Scoring guides provide *detailed* success criteria that make performance expectations *explicit*. They communicate in specific, objective terms exactly what students need to include in their constructed responses. Teams now prepare an answer key for the selected-response questions and scoring guides for the constructed-response questions (short and extended).

7. **Create the Pre-Assessment Questions and Scoring Guides.** The CFA process measures growth in student understanding by comparing results from the pre-assessment to the post-assessment. After designing the post-CFA, educators create a pre-CFA to align with the post-assessment. Then, they prepare an answer key and the specific scoring guides needed for the constructed-response questions.

8. **Evaluate and Revise Assessment Questions for Quality.** The inferences educators make from the student responses to the post- and pre-CFA questions can only be as good as the assessment questions are. After creating the post- and pre-CFA questions and related scoring guides, the grade- or course-level team now uses established guidelines associated with quality assessment questions to evaluate and revise as needed each of their post- and pre-CFA questions, in that order.

9. **Determine the Learning Progressions and Instructional Sequence.** Learning progressions are the sequenced "building blocks" of instruction that lead students to understand the unit learning intentions. Look at each unit learning intention to decide what increments of instruction students will need to fully understand that learning intention. Then sequence these instructional building blocks in the order they will occur during the unit.

10. **Plan Quick Progress Checks to Coincide With the Learning Progressions.** A quick, informal, ungraded check for student understanding needs to occur immediately after each learning progression. Quick progress checks provide immediate feedback to educators and students about students' understanding of the learning progression and where to go next instructionally. The most effective formative progress checks are planned in advance by the teacher team to coincide with the various learning progressions.

ABOUT CLASSROOM PERFORMANCE TASKS

Performance tasks are not included as part of the post-CFAs. The reason is that CFAs are "on-demand" assessments that students complete independently within a single class period (although some secondary-level CFAs may take place over two class periods if the requirements of the extended-response question require more student response time). Performance tasks if sufficiently challenging and rigorous, can typically require two, three, or several class periods for students to complete collaboratively. They serve a critical purpose in helping students develop deep understanding of the learning intentions during the unit so students are better prepared to demonstrate all they have learned on the post-CFA at the end of the unit.

It's important to underscore that performance tasks are not tests, but rather classroom learning tasks that students engage in with peers in order to create a product or performance aligned to the unit learning intentions. Whereas the CFA is aligned to the Priority Standards only, classroom performance tasks are matched to *all* of the targeted standards for the unit—Priority and supporting.

BENEFITS OF CLASSROOM PERFORMANCE TASKS

Performance tasks are often thought of as "mini-culminating events" that educators assign to students, usually three or four times, during an instructional unit. These hands-on, active learning tasks enable students to apply the concepts and skills they are learning by creating a representative product or performance that can be evaluated with a scoring guide.

Interdisciplinary by design, performance tasks require students to write, make connections, and apply the concepts and skills they are learning to real-world situations. Performance tasks become the "learning vehicles" that provide both educators and students with in-process feedback. Educators use this feedback to modify or adjust instruction as the unit proceeds. Students produce and revise work guided by each task's scoring guide criteria in order to provide evidence that they are achieving the unit learning intentions.

Performance tasks are *authentic* in that they require students to apply the concepts and skills they are learning to real-world situations. In completing classroom performance tasks, students exercise what is now referred to in education as 21st-century thinking skills: the ability to think critically, solve problems, communicate effectively both orally and in writing, access and analyze information, and exercise curiosity and imagination (Wagner, 2008, pp. 21–22). The boxed text showcases the key attributes of well-designed performance tasks.

Effective Performance Tasks . . .

- Present students with purpose-setting scenarios applicable to real-world situations
- Require creation of a product, performance, or demonstration in response to those scenarios
- Promote critical thinking through highly interactive learning
- Encourage multiple approaches and solution methods
- Use task-specific scoring guide success criteria co-created by students and teachers
- Incorporate peer feedback and self-assessment using scoring guide success criteria
- Provide multiple opportunities to revise work based on educator and peer feedback
- Showcase work products and performances as credible evidence of degree to which learning intentions achieved
- Apply to all grades and all content areas including performance-based disciplines, such as visual and performing arts, physical education, career and technical education, world languages, and library-media technology

Readers interested in learning more about the design and effective use of classroom performance tasks will find Tracey Flach's book, *Engaging Students Through Performance Assessment: Creating Performance Tasks to Monitor Student Learning* (2011), very informative.

A PERFECT FIT WITH THE ALIGNED ASSESSMENT HIGHWAY

As represented in Figure 3.3, classroom performance tasks fit perfectly into the "highway of aligned assessments" model described in Chapter 1. As educators launch a new unit of study, they include performance tasks wherever appropriate in the instructional sequence. While students are working, teachers circulate throughout the classroom, monitoring and evaluating student progress to see what additional information or assistance is needed, either for individual students or for cooperative groups.

Figure 3.3 Authentic Learning: Classroom Performance Tasks

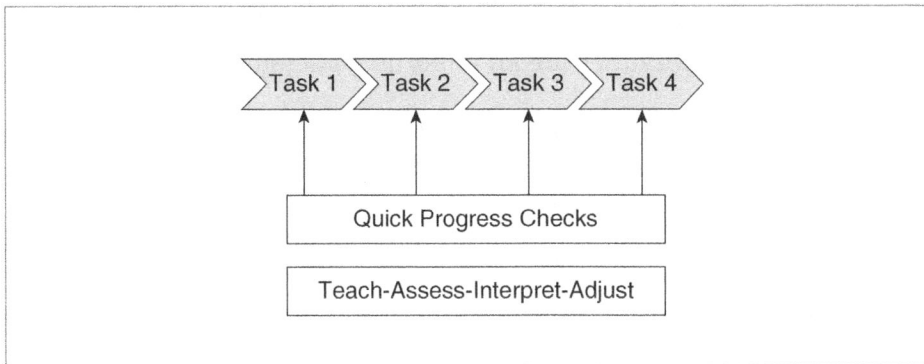

Task 1 〉 Task 2 〉 Task 3 〉 Task 4

Quick Progress Checks

Teach-Assess-Interpret-Adjust

Because students usually complete performance tasks collaboratively, educators often insert quick progress checks between the performance tasks. This enables them to determine specific learning needs of individual students and differentiate their instruction accordingly. Connecting classroom performance tasks and quick progress checks in this powerful way promotes the *group process, individual accountability* approach to teaching and learning.

PERFORMANCE TASKS ON LARGE-SCALE ASSESSMENTS

Even though classroom performance tasks are not part of the unit CFAs, they play an important role in preparing students for large-scale assessments that do include performance tasks. Students who regularly experience engaging and challenging classroom performance tasks combined with CFAs that require both short and extended responses will be familiar with and prepared for the multiple formats of large-scale assessments.

In creating national assessments aligned to the Common Core, both the Smarter Balanced Assessment Consortium (SBAC) and the Partnership for Assessment of Readiness for College and Careers (PARCC) included performance tasks in their overall assessment design. However, each consortium defines performance tasks somewhat differently. The SBAC performance tasks more closely resemble the characteristics of classroom performance tasks described in this chapter, whereas the PARCC tasks more closely resemble the formats of short and extended response questions used in the CFA 2.0 process. Teacher teams will benefit from reviewing sample items available online. At the time of the original publication of this book (2015), the following SBAC and PARCC links were active.

SBAC Performance Tasks

The Smarter Balanced Assessment Consortium (www.smarterbalanced.org) points out an important benefit of performance tasks and explains succinctly why they are an important assessment component:

> Performance tasks measure a student's ability to integrate knowledge and skills across multiple standards—a key component of college and career readiness. Performance tasks will be used to better measure capacities such as depth of understanding, research skills, and complex analysis, which cannot be adequately assessed with selected- or constructed-response items. (SBAC, n.d.)

On the SBAC home page, the drop-down menu under the navigation bar **Smarter Balanced Assessments** shows "Sample Items and Performance Tasks." Click on that link to see sample questions in both English language arts and math (http://www.smarterbalanced.org/sample-items-and-performance-tasks/). Scroll down to the specific links for English language arts/literacy and mathematics sample items and performance tasks. Clicking on the link for ELA and literacy samples, you will now be at http://sampleitems.smarterbalanced.org/itempreview/sbac/ELA.htm. Click on the navigation bar **View More English Language Arts/Literacy Sample Items** and then on any of the three performance tasks that appear there under the heading, "Grade Bands": Animal Defenses (3–5), Garden (6–8), and Nuclear Power (High School).

If you click on the link for the mathematics examples, you will now be at http://sampleitems.smarterbalanced.org/itempreview/sbac/index.htm. From here, click on the navigation bar **View More Mathematics Sample Items** and then on any of the three performance tasks for specific grade bands that appear there: Planting Tulips (3–5), Field Trip (6–8), and Crickets (High School).

PARCC Performance Tasks

The Partnership for Assessment of Readiness for College and Careers consortium (www.parcconline.org) provides information about the performance-based assessments that are part of their overall assessment components.

The summative assessment in the 3–8 grade band includes performance-based assessments (PBAs):

> Performance-Based Assessment (PBA) administered after approximately 75% of the school year. The English language arts/literacy

PBA will focus on writing effectively when analyzing text. The mathematics PBA will focus on applying skills, concepts, and understandings to solve multi-step problems requiring abstract reasoning, precision, perseverance, and strategic use of tools. (PARCC, 2014b)

The summative assessment in the high school grade band includes performance-based assessments (PBAs), identical in wording to the 3–8 grade band in ELA but different in math:

Performance-Based Assessment (PBA) administered after approximately 75% of the school year. The ELA/literacy PBA will focus on writing effectively when analyzing text. The mathematics PBA will focus on expressing mathematical reasoning and modeling real-world problems. (PARCC, 2014a)

To access content area sample questions, visit the PARCC Web site at www.parcconline.org. On their home page, click on the navigation bar **The PARCC Assessment** and then "Sample Questions" in the left column. There are two sections of samples, the first for ELA/Literacy and the second for Math. Once you have selected a subject area click on Sample Questions, in the center bar this time, and select the desired grade level in the left column.

NOTE: For readers in Canadian provinces and those in the United States not using the Common Core and the SBAC or PARCC assessments, access your state or provincial education Web site to look for sample performance-based items relevant to your location.

SUCCESS CRITERIA

At the beginning of this chapter, three learning intentions previewed the steps and content of the CFA 2.0 process. Those same learning intentions now reappear here as success criteria, written in the form of performance statements, for you to reflect upon and sum up what you have learned.

Success Criteria:

- Describe the sequential steps in designing a quality CFA.
- Summarize each of the CFA components represented in the ten design steps.
- Explain the role of performance tasks in assessing student understanding of the unit learning intentions.

Please take a few moments and write your responses to these success criteria, or simply evaluate your understanding of each performance statement on a scale of one (low) to five (high). Close any learning gaps you identify by rereading related sections or clarifying your understanding with a colleague. Again, if you are reading this book as part of a professional study group, share your thoughts and ideas with colleagues. When ready, begin Chapter 4 to learn about the critical role Priority Standards play in the CFA 2.0 design process.

4 Priority Standards and Learning Intentions

In This Chapter You Will Learn:

- The rationale for prioritizing standards.
- The pivotal role Priority Standards play in the CFA 2.0 design process.
- The relationship between Priority Standards, supporting standards, and unit learning intentions.

Now we are ready to look at the ten CFA 2.0 design steps individually and describe them in more detail. The first highlighted step in Figure 4.1 shows its foundational position in the linear sequence. CFAs are written to assess student understanding of the Priority Standards *only,* yet the supporting standards often provide the instructional scaffolds that students need to ultimately attain the priorities. Synopses of these two foundational steps will introduce the examples later in the chapter.

UNIT PREPLANNING

When educators are ready to create a unit of study, the first task is to decide what they want the unit to be about. They go about making this

Figure 4.1 CFA 2.0 Design Step 1

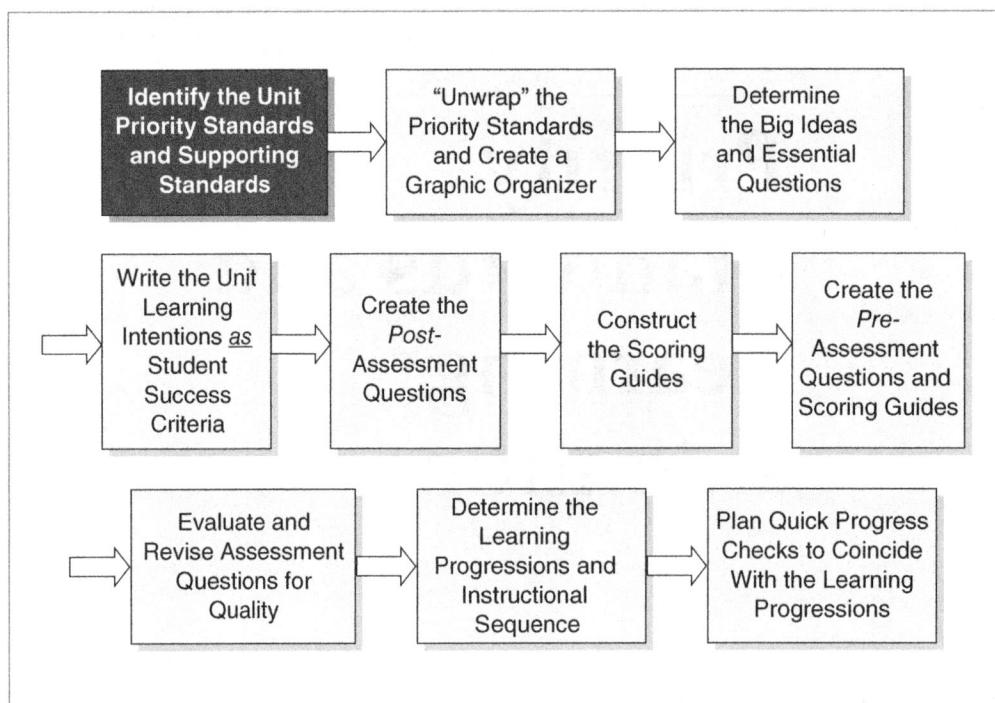

```
┌─────────────────┐     ┌─────────────────┐     ┌─────────────────┐
│ Identify the Unit│     │   "Unwrap" the  │     │   Determine     │
│ Priority Standards│ →  │ Priority Standards│ → │ the Big Ideas   │
│ and Supporting   │     │  and Create a   │     │ and Essential   │
│   Standards      │     │ Graphic Organizer│    │   Questions     │
└─────────────────┘     └─────────────────┘     └─────────────────┘

┌─────────────────┐     ┌─────────────────┐     ┌─────────────────┐     ┌─────────────────┐
│  Write the Unit │     │   Create the    │     │                 │     │   Create the    │
│    Learning     │     │      Post-      │     │    Construct    │     │      Pre-       │
│ Intentions as   │ →   │   Assessment    │ →   │  the Scoring    │ →   │   Assessment    │
│    Student      │     │   Questions     │     │     Guides      │     │  Questions and  │
│    Success      │     │                 │     │                 │     │  Scoring Guides │
│    Criteria     │     │                 │     │                 │     │                 │
└─────────────────┘     └─────────────────┘     └─────────────────┘     └─────────────────┘

┌─────────────────┐     ┌─────────────────┐     ┌─────────────────┐
│  Evaluate and   │     │  Determine the  │     │Plan Quick Progress│
│ Revise Assessment│ →  │    Learning     │ →  │ Checks to Coincide│
│  Questions for  │     │ Progressions and│     │  With the Learning│
│    Quality      │     │  Instructional  │     │   Progressions   │
│                 │     │    Sequence     │     │                 │
└─────────────────┘     └─────────────────┘     └─────────────────┘
```

decision in different ways. Either they have in mind an overall instructional focus that leads to their selection of the standards that match it, or they look over the standards in a particular content area and identify a few important standards to build a unit around. However, if their units of study are already organized and sequenced into a curriculum pacing calendar, most likely the standards have already been decided and included in those units. They simply select one of those predetermined units as their starting point. Whichever approach educators use, it results in a clear determination about what the unit focus will be.

Now the challenges begin to show up. All of the standards at every grade and in every content area need to be taught, and student understanding of those standards must be assessed. Yet educators know that certain standards are more important than others for students to learn, and those particular standards require more classroom instruction time to teach. Curriculum pacing guides lay out how long each unit of study is to last, but educators are often unable to keep pace due to their students' varying speeds of learning. Pressure to cover the entire curriculum to prepare students for spring standardized achievement tests too often leads to superficial instruction and shallow student understanding.

In the face of these challenges, educators are opting for the only logical solution. They are abandoning the ineffective practice of "inch deep, mile wide" instructional coverage of too many standards in favor of *prioritization.* They are sitting down together in separate K–12 grade-level teams to thoughtfully and systematically classify each grade-level standard as being either "priority" or "supporting." Then the large K–12 group comes together to vertically align all of the grade-level selections from kindergarten through Grade 12.

Here are the definitions of Priority Standards and supporting standards, key terms that are used throughout the CFA 2.0 design process.

> **Priority Standards** are "a carefully selected *subset* of the total list of the grade-specific and course-specific standards within each content area that students must know and be able to do by the end of each school year in order to be prepared for the standards at the next grade level or course. Priority standards represent the *assured student competencies* that each teacher needs to help every student learn, and demonstrate proficiency in, by the end of the current grade or course" (Ainsworth, 2013, p. xv).

> **Supporting standards** are "those standards that support, connect to, or enhance the Priority Standards. They are taught within the context of the Priority Standards, but do not receive the same degree of instruction and assessment emphasis as do the Priority Standards. The supporting standards often become the *instructional scaffolds* to help students understand and attain the more rigorous and comprehensive Priority Standards" (Ainsworth, 2013, p. xv).

THE RATIONALE FOR PRIORITY STANDARDS

The most compelling reason for prioritizing the standards or learning outcomes is the voluminous number of standards assigned to each grade level and course in nearly every content area, K–12. Ask classroom educators, and they will almost unanimously agree that it is an unrealistic expectation to thoroughly teach, assess, reteach, and reassess student understanding of all grade- or course-level standards in the limited amount of instructional time they have with their students. In addition, English language learners (ELLs) and students with any kind of special need generally require increased instruction and assessment time. And because the annual standardized achievement tests typically occur weeks before the end of school—educators have *less* than a full academic year to ensure that all students master all standards.

Obviously, educators would love it if every student in every grade and content area could learn every standard assigned at each grade level, but this is just not a realistic goal. For an educator to think it is more important to cover every standard than to focus on teaching high-leverage standards for depth of understanding is faulty reasoning. Students will not benefit from superficial coverage of the standards. They will not retain what they are superficially taught, and this will necessitate the reteaching of those standards in subsequent grade levels. This domino effect can continue for years, delaying educators in each succeeding grade level from teaching the standards they are supposed to be teaching.

Because a "spray and pray" approach to covering standards results in students falling further behind each year, educators are becoming increasingly aware of the vital need to prioritize K–12 standards in targeted content areas *prior to* any curriculum and assessment design or instructional planning. They can then emphasize grade-level Priority Standards repeatedly in different curricular units of study throughout the year. This is why CFAs assess student understanding of the Priority Standards *only*—to make sure that students have multiple opportunities to deepen their understanding of those standards that K–12 educators have determined to be the most critical for all students to learn.

Even though this makes sense intellectually, a simple count of the total number of grade-level standards in state and provincial documents tips the scales in favor of prioritizing standards and learning outcomes. It is the norm, not the exception, that the number of standards at each grade level in all content areas adds up to well over one hundred. In *Rigorous Curriculum Design* (2010), I showcased examples of such high numbers of standards from three randomly selected states and one Canadian province (see pp. 41–44).

STATISTICAL RATIONALE FOR IDENTIFYING PRIORITY STANDARDS

Not only does prioritizing seem the only logical solution to this dilemma from a practitioner's point of view, respected educational researchers and thought leaders agree.

W. James Popham (2003) has long supported this call for prioritization and an assessment focus on the priorities:

> Teachers need to prioritize a set of content standards so they can identify the content standards at which they will devote powerful,

thoroughgoing instruction, and then they need to *formally and systematically assess student mastery of only those high-priority content standards.* (p. 36; italics added)

Robert Marzano has also advocated a "less is more" approach to standards for well over a decade, and his statistical rationale for doing so is as relevant today as it was when first showcased in *Common Formative Assessments* (Ainsworth & Viegut, 2006):

The following calculations determine the time educators would need to effectively teach all the standards students are expected to learn by the end of high school.

- 5.6 instructional hours per day × 180 days in typical academic year = 1,008 hours per year × 13 years = *13,104* total hours of K–12 instruction.
- McREL (Mid-continent Research for Education and Learning) identified 200 standards and 3,093 benchmarks in national- and state-level documents across 14 different subject areas.
- Classroom teachers estimated a need for *15,465* hours to *adequately* teach them all. (pp. 32–33)

Furthermore, Marzano (2003) reveals a powerful "reality check" regarding how many of those instructional hours each school day are actually dedicated to instruction of students:

- Varies widely from a low of 21 percent to a high of 69 percent.
- Taking the highest estimate of 69 percent, only *9,042* hours are actually available for instruction out of the original math calculation of 13,104 hours total.
- 200 standards and 3,093 benchmarks needing *15,465* hours cannot be taught in only 9,042 hours of instructional time. (pp. 24–25)

Marzano concludes his statistics with an insightful quip: "To cover all this content, you would have to change schooling from K–12 to K–22" (interview by Scherer, 2001, p. 15). He recommends a fractional guideline for reducing the number of standards: "By my reckoning, we would have to cut* content by about *two-thirds,*" and ends with a dramatic assertion: "The sheer number of standards is the biggest impediment to implementing standards" (Scherer, p. 15).

Note the asterisk added after the verb "cut" in the quotation above. Marzano was not likely advocating the actual *elimination* of two thirds of the standards, but rather making the point that, in most standards, approximately one third of them are truly significant and worthy of in-depth instruction and assessment focus. The remaining two thirds can be taught within the context of the essentials but without the same degree of emphasis.

With more than a decade of experience guiding thousands of K–12 educators and leaders through the prioritization process, I have repeatedly found this "one third" fractional recommendation to be an accurate guide-line. In recent years, however, educators who prioritize the Common Core English language arts standards typically select as priorities between one third and one half of the total list of grade-specific standards due to the increased rigor of these standards in comparison to state standards. Let us look briefly at the internationally benchmarked Common Core standards to support my assertion that these too must be prioritized.

THE COMMON CORE STATE STANDARDS

The Common Core State Standards (CCSS) in English language arts actually include fewer standards at each grade level than most states and provinces do, yet they still are up there in number. Case in point: there are 73 grade-specific Common Core standards (inclusive of all ELA strands) in kindergarten, and the total number of standards equals or exceeds that number in all subsequent grades through high school (Ainsworth, 2013, p. 6).

The numbers of CCSS in mathematics are deceptively fewer than those in English language arts. Yet many grade-specific standards appear as full-paragraph descriptions with related subpoints beneath them rather than the single-sentence math standards typically found in state and provincial standards documents. Even though such "thick" and lengthy standards may really only be about "one connected mathematical idea . . . . the density of the content will prove formidable for educators to teach and for students to learn, both conceptually and procedurally" (Ainsworth, 2013, p. 13).

The Common Core State Standards have been intentionally designed to include *vertical learning progressions*, the grade-to-grade flow of stand-ards that progress in rigor from kindergarten through high school. Each standard is linked to a College and Career Readiness standard that stu-dents must master to be prepared for the standards at the next grade level. This fact—that the CCSS at each grade level are the prerequisites for the standards at the following grade level—underscores the need for prioriti-zation. Rather than attempting to hurriedly cover all of the standards each year, educators instead can strive to ensure that all students acquire the Priority Standards as *assured competencies.* This sensible approach is far more likely to prepare students for successful attainment of the standards at the next grade level.

When prioritizing the Common Core, educators must take great care not to "break" or interrupt these learning progressions because they all intentionally connect from one grade to the next. To prevent this from happening, after initially selecting the priorities at each grade level, teacher teams should track the progression of each Priority Standard *vertically* from K–12. Then the teams need to make whatever changes are necessary in the standards selected to ensure that the vertical learning progressions of these priorities remain intact.

THE NEED FOR OBJECTIVE SELECTION CRITERIA

Regardless of the standards to be prioritized (state, provincial, or Common Core), educators approach the prioritization process with questions: "Which standards do we choose as the priorities? How do we decide? What happens if and when we don't agree?" In response, here are a few important guidelines to keep in mind:

Teams of K–12 educators collaboratively determine those standards that are the most rigorous or comprehensive at each grade level, not those that are the most basic or foundational. Priority Standards should represent the "end game" of what students must know and be able to do by the end of each grade level.

To prevent differing professional opinions from getting in the way of reaching a consensus as to which standards to choose (state, provincial, or Common Core), K–12 teams use these objective selection criteria (Ainsworth, 2013):

- *Endurance* (lasting beyond one grade or course; concepts and skills needed in life)
- *Leverage* (crossover applications within the content area and to other content areas; i.e., interdisciplinary connections)
- *Readiness for next level of learning* (prerequisite concepts and skills students need to enter a new grade level or course of study)
- *External exam requirements* (national, state, provincial, college, and career) (pp. 25–27)

Standards that meet *all* of these established criteria qualify as Priority Standards. These preliminary selections are not set in stone, however. One of the great benefits of this process is how it depends upon professional discussion. The goal is for participating educators to reach an initial consensus regarding the Priority Standards selected. There will be opportunities to modify and change those preliminary selections along the way, particularly during the K–12 vertical alignment step when participants look to see how the selected priorities at one grade level mesh with the priorities selected at the grade level below and at the grade level above.

There is one additional criterion for educators to factor in when prioritizing the Common Core standards in math, and that is the *critical areas of focus*. Appearing in the preamble (introduction) of each grade level's math standards, the critical areas of focus specify where the greatest degree of instructional time should be spent. Standards that reflect these critical areas of focus should be strongly considered as priorities along with the four established criteria.

PRIORITIZATION, NOT ELIMINATION

Identifying Priority Standards is not an irresponsible recommendation to ignore any standards not designated as priorities. It is imperative to continually remind everyone in the school and district community, "The Priority Standards are *not* all we teach," even while allocating the greatest amount of instruction and assessment time to those standards determined to be absolutely essential for student success in current and succeeding grade levels.

Continually communicate to everyone this message: "Prioritization, not elimination," especially to those not involved in the selection process. *All standards must be taught.* The Priority Standards just receive *greater* instruction and assessment emphasis. The supporting standards play a key supporting role as instructional scaffolds, to help students understand the more rigorous Priority Standards.

SPECIAL EDUCATORS, SECOND LANGUAGE EDUCATORS, AND SPECIAL AREA EDUCATORS

Priority Standards can be of great benefit to special educators, to teachers of students whose primary language is other than English, and to educators of content areas not directly assessed on the annual standardized achievement tests.

Special educators who serve students in multiple grade levels and with diverse learning needs find that Priority Standards provide them with a sharp focus on those standards that have been determined as being the most essential. These specialists can write specific student learning goals required by Individual Education Plans that target the Priority Standards. Having this information enables classroom and special education teachers to plan needed modifications and alternative forms of assessment to help their students demonstrate progress toward learning the Priority Standards by the end of the full school year, even though the standardized achievement tests occur several weeks before.

Teachers of English language learners also find the Priority Standards extremely beneficial. In certain areas of the United States, for example, there may be one hundred or more different first languages represented in the student body. Rather than striving to assist students whose primary language is other than English to learn and demonstrate proficiency in *all* standards, educators can utilize their second-language acquisition skills to help ELLs attain the Priority Standards.

Educators in *all* content areas benefit from the identification of Priority Standards, not just those in the four "core" areas typically tested: English language arts, mathematics, science, and history/social science. Priority Standards have been successfully identified by educators in visual and performing arts, physical education, world languages, library media technology, career and technical education, junior ROTC, basic and advanced ceramics, early childhood education and development, computer applications, free enterprise and entrepreneurship, and in other content areas as well.

INTERDISCIPLINARY PRIORITY STANDARDS

After the Priority Standards are identified in the academic core, educators next identify those that have interdisciplinary applications. Since language arts is regarded as the "delivery system" for all the content areas, educators identify the particular reading, writing, and language Priority Standards that educators in all content areas can emphasize to improve student literacy. Such standards, representing the ability to read informational text, write in a variety of forms (narrative, explanatory, and persuasive), and so on, apply across the curricula.

In the Common Core, "K–5 literacy standards for history/social studies and science/technical subjects are embedded within the K–5 content strands. Secondary educators in these content areas need to determine how they will emphasize these literacy standards *in tandem with* their content-area standards" (Ainsworth, 2013, p. 45). Toward this end, secondary interdisciplinary teams do this by first prioritizing the Common Core 6–12 literacy standards for science and history/social studies and then integrating them with their prioritized content area standards in units of study.

Similarly, to improve student numeracy across the curricula, educators can assist students in learning many mathematics Priority Standards through other content areas, such as art, music, and physical education. Math Priority Standards typically include the ability to use

- all four basic number operations (+ – × ÷) with and without calculators;
- fractions, decimals, and percentages;
- two-dimensional scale models;
- graphs, charts, and tables;
- estimation; and
- [perform] tests of reasonability. (Ainsworth & Viegut, 2006, p. 36)

Such interdisciplinary English language arts and mathematics Priority Standards, as well as the Priority Standards identified in all other disciplines, are essential for students to understand and be able to apply, not only for success on high-stakes assessments but in daily life as well.

Readers interested in learning more about the step-by-step process for prioritizing the standards—applicable not only to the Common Core but also to all state standards and provincial learning outcomes—will find it fully explained and illustrated in *Prioritizing the Common Core* (Ainsworth, 2013). Profiled in the book are narratives contributed by leaders from six school systems across the United States, who personally directed the prioritization process. They describe in detail how they accomplished this important work with educators in their own districts.

LEARNING INTENTIONS AND SUCCESS CRITERIA

Even though the Priority Standards are the primary source for determining the unit learning intentions—the specifics of what students are to learn and be able to do—in the CFA 2.0 process they are not synonymous with those intentions. Otherwise, the standards statements verbatim could serve as the stand-alone learning intentions.

As introduced in previous chapters, the purpose of learning intentions for the educator is to sharply focus assessment design, curriculum choices, instructional delivery, and selection of learning activities for the entire unit. For students, learning intentions can be written *as* success criteria that state explicitly how they will be expected to demonstrate the learning intentions. Referencing these success criteria, students set personal learning goals for what they intend to achieve by the end of the unit of study.

John Hattie includes multiple references to the companion terms "learning intentions" and "success criteria" in *Visible Learning* (2009) and

Visible Learning for Teachers (2012), his two in-depth compilations of evidence-based research that have been derived from over a thousand educational studies in classrooms worldwide. Here are a few excerpts from these powerful volumes that convey the meaning and purpose of learning intentions and success criteria:

> **Learning intentions** describe what it is we want students to learn in terms of the skills, knowledge, attitudes, and values within any particular unit or lesson. Learning intentions should be clear, and provide guidance to the teacher about what to teach, help learners be aware of what they should learn from the lesson, and form the basis for assessing what the students have learnt and for assessing what the teachers have taught well to each student. (Hattie, 2009, pp. 162–163)

Success criteria describe for students how to be successful in attaining the unit learning intentions.

> The purpose of the success criteria, or "What are we looking for?" is to make students understand the criteria for judging their work and, of course, to ensure that the teacher is clear about the criteria that will determine if the learning intentions have been successfully achieved. . . . The success criteria, or "How will we know?" need to state as exactly as possible what the students and teacher will want to see. (Hattie, 2009, pp. 169–170)

> The more transparent the teacher makes the learning goals, the more likely the student is to engage in the work needed to meet the goal. Also, the more the student is aware of the criteria of success, the more the student can see and appreciate the specific actions that are needed to attain these criteria. (Hattie, 2012, p. 46)

Learning intentions let students know upfront, *before* any instruction and assessment take place, where they are headed in their learning journey. Some of those intentions will represent easier-to-grasp surface understandings, while others will signify deeper understanding to be acquired through exercise of higher-level thinking skills. Clearly understood learning intentions are indispensable to educators who are in charge of charting the course for that journey. They must first know exactly what students are to learn in order to decide how they will assess student understanding of that learning. It is the "where to?" step of knowing the destination prior to any actual trip planning.

Examples of ELA and math unit learning intentions and student success criteria are presented in Chapter 6.

ILLUSTRATING THE CFA 2.0 DESIGN PROCESS

The first step of the CFA 2.0 design process shown at the beginning of the chapter has two parts, summarized here.

> **CFA 2.0 Design Step 1: Identify the Priority Standards for the Unit.** From the complete list of grade- or course-level Priority Standards, select three to five standards maximum to be the learning focus of the unit. These specific Priority Standards should come from a *combination* of strands or domains within the content area, and not be limited to one strand or domain only. The Priority Standards assigned to the unit are the foundations from which the unit learning intentions will be decided.

> **CFA 2.0 Design Step 1: Identify the Supporting Standards.** The supporting standards are the standards that connect or relate to the Priority Standards but do not receive the same degree of instructional emphasis. The CFA assesses student understanding of the Priority Standards only, not the supporting standards. However, the supporting standards provide instructional supports, or scaffolds, to help students achieve understanding of those Priority Standards. Select a limited number of supporting standards that directly connect to the unit Priority Standards.

In the following two examples excerpted from two units of study, one in English language arts and the other in math, the Priority Standards and related supporting standards provide the foundations for determining the unit learning intentions. These same standards will be used to illustrate each of the nine remaining design steps in later chapters.

——————— ೞ ೞ ———————

CFA 2.0 DESIGN STEP 1

English Language Arts

Unit Focus: Reading Informational Text

Grade 5, Unit 5

Unit Name: Exploring the Role of Point-of-View in Argument

Unit Length: 30 days (25 instructional, 5 Bridge)

Informational Text

(Priority CCSS) RI.5.6 Analyze multiple accounts of the same event or topic, noting important similarities and differences in the point of view they represent.

> (Supporting Standard) RI.5.4 Determine the meaning of general academic and domain-specific words and phrases in a text relevant to a Grade 5 topic or subject area.

> (Supporting Standard) RI.5.8 Explain how an author uses reasons and evidence to support particular points in a text, identifying which reasons and evidence support which point(s).

Writing an Opinion

(Priority Standard) W.5.1 Write opinion pieces on topics or texts, supporting a point of view with reasons and information.

(Priority Standard) W.5.1a Introduce a topic or text clearly, state an opinion, and create an organizational structure in which ideas are logically grouped to support the writer's purpose.

(Priority Standard) W.5.1b Provide logically ordered reasons that are supported by facts and details.

(Priority Standard) W.5.1d Provide a concluding statement or section related to the opinion presented.

> (Supporting Standard) W.5.8 Recall relevant information from experiences or gather relevant information from print and digital sources; summarize or paraphrase information in notes and finished work, and provide a list of sources.

Note: Writing standard W.5.1c was not included as part of this particular unit of study.

Source: 5th Grade Curriculum Design Team, San Diego Unified School District, San Diego, CA.

ΟΒ ΚΟ

Note how **Priority Standard RI.5.6** is followed by its two supporting standards, *indented* to show their supporting role as instructional scaffolds necessary to help students achieve the more rigorous Priority Standard. In the same example, the **Priority Standard W.5.1** and its related subpoints, **Priority Standards W.5.1.a, b,** and **d** are followed by one supporting standard, also indented, to show its supporting role as an instructional scaffold. Positioning the supporting standards beneath the Priority Standards in this way underscores that relationship.

In the following math example, the two supporting standards listed at the end connect to and support *all five* of the unit Priority Standards.

———————— 03 80 ————————

CFA 2.0 DESIGN STEP 1

Mathematics

Standards Focus: Ratio and Proportion

Grade 6

Unit Name: Ratio and Proportional Relationships

Unit Length: 20 days (18 instructional, 2 Bridge)

Priority Standards (One Main Standard and Related Subpoints)

6.RP.A.3 Use ratio and rate reasoning to solve real-world and mathematical problems, e.g., by reasoning about tables of equivalent ratios, tape diagrams, double number line diagrams, or equations.

  a. Make tables of equivalent ratios relating quantities with whole number measurements, find missing values in the tables, and plot the pairs of values on the coordinate plane. Use tables to compare ratios.
  b. Solve unit rate problems including those involving unit pricing and constant speed. *For example, if it took 7 hours to mow 4 lawns, then at that rate, how many lawns could be mowed in 35 hours? At what rate were lawns being mowed?*
  c. Find a percent of a quantity as a rate per 100 (*e.g., 30% of a quantity means 30/100 times the quantity*); solve problems involving finding the whole, given a part and the percent.

d. **Use ratio reasoning to convert measurement units; manipulate and transform units appropriately when multiplying or dividing quantities.**

Supporting Standards

6.RP.A.1 Understand the concept of a ratio and use ratio language to describe a ratio relationship between two quantities. For example, "The ratio of wings to beaks in the bird house at the zoo was 2:1, because for every 2 wings there was 1 beak." "For every vote candidate A received, candidate C received nearly three votes."

6.RP.A.2 Understand the concept of a unit rate a/b associated with a ratio a:b with b ≠ 0, and use rate language in the context of a ratio relationship. For example, "This recipe has a ratio of 3 cups of flour to 4 cups of sugar, so there is 3/4 cup of flour for each cup of sugar." "We paid $75 for 15 hamburgers, which is a rate of $5 per hamburger."

Source: Jan Christinson, author-consultant.

———————— ☙ ❧ ————————

SURFACE AND DEEP LEARNING IN THE STANDARDS

The targeted Priority Standards and supporting standards in both of these units represent a blend of both deep and surface learning. Usually, the Priority Standard is more cognitively demanding than the less rigorous supporting standard.

For example, in the English language arts unit, the Priority Writing Standard W.5.1, "Write opinion pieces on topics or texts, supporting a point of view with reasons and information" will require more of students than the related, but less difficult-to-learn excerpt from the supporting standard W.5.8, "Recall relevant information from experiences or gather relevant information from print and digital sources."

In the math unit, the main Priority Standard, 6.RP.A.3, "Use ratio and rate reasoning to solve real-world and mathematical problems, e.g., by reasoning about tables of equivalent ratios, tape diagrams, double number line diagrams, or equations," requires a more comprehensive—deeper—understanding students need to attain through problem-based application. Yet part of 6.RP.A.3c, "Find a percent of a quantity as a rate per 100 (e.g., 30% of a quantity means 30/100 times the quantity)," represents a more straightforward—surface—learning outcome, even though it too is a Priority Standard.

EN ROUTE TO THE LEARNING INTENTIONS AND SUCCESS CRITERIA

After the Priority Standards are selected for the unit of study, they must be "unwrapped" to identify the concepts, skills, and levels of cognitive rigor they represent. The identification of these elements, along with Big Ideas and Essential Questions, will then enable educators to clearly pinpoint the unit learning intentions and student success criteria and then create the matching end-of-unit CFA questions.

Before reading on, please take a few moments and write your responses to the following success criteria for this chapter, or simply evaluate your understanding of each performance statement on a scale of one (low) to five (high). Identify and close any learning gaps you may have. Once again, if you are reading this book as part of a professional study group, share your thoughts and ideas with colleagues. When finished, you will be ready to start the "unwrapping" step in Chapter 5.

Success Criteria:

- Summarize the rationale for identifying Priority Standards.
- Explain the role of Priority Standards in the CFA 2.0 design model.
- Describe the relationship between Priority Standards, supporting standards, and learning intentions.

5 "Unwrapping," Big Ideas, and Essential Questions

In This Chapter You Will Learn:

- How to "unwrap" the unit Priority Standards.
- The function of the graphic organizer and its key role in assessment design.
- How to determine the unit Big Ideas and Essential Questions.

With the Priority Standards and supporting standards identified for the unit of study, the second step in the CFA 2.0 design process is to "unwrap" the Priority Standards, create a graphic organizer of the "unwrapped" concepts and skills, and determine the levels of cognitive rigor for each concept-skill pair. In the related third step, teacher teams derive Big Ideas and Essential Questions from the "unwrapped" Priority Standards.

Figure 5.1 CFA 2.0 Design Step 2

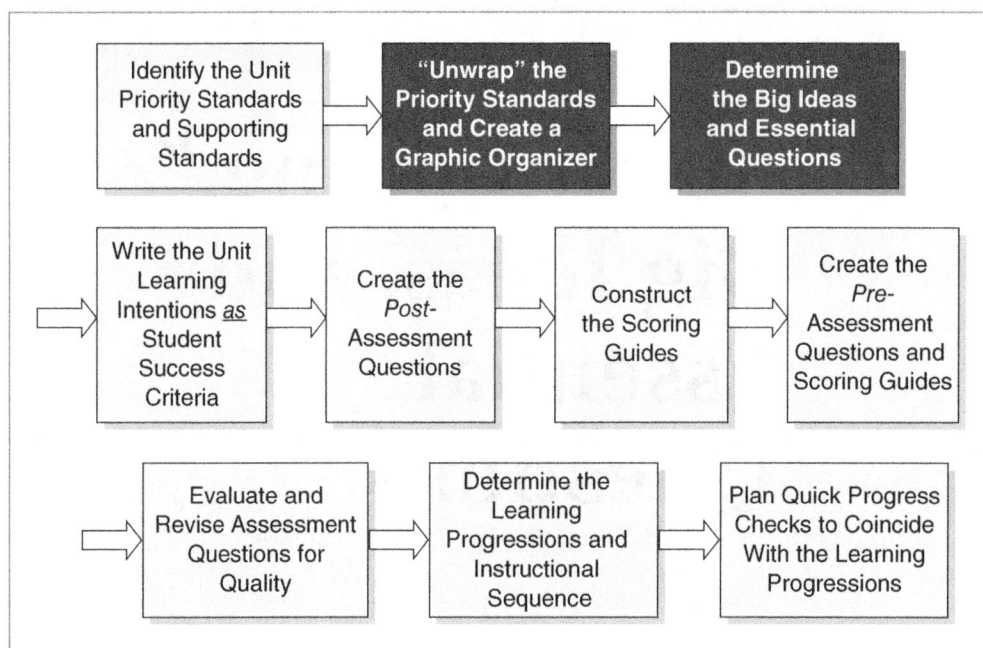

Identify the Unit Priority Standards and Supporting Standards	"Unwrap" the Priority Standards and Create a Graphic Organizer	Determine the Big Ideas and Essential Questions

Write the Unit Learning Intentions _as_ Student Success Criteria	Create the _Post-_ Assessment Questions	Construct the Scoring Guides	Create the _Pre-_ Assessment Questions and Scoring Guides

Evaluate and Revise Assessment Questions for Quality	Determine the Learning Progressions and Instructional Sequence	Plan Quick Progress Checks to Coincide With the Learning Progressions

CFA 2.0 Design Step 2: "Unwrap" the Priority Standards and Create a Graphic Organizer. Deconstruct the Priority Standards _only_ in order to identify the teachable concepts (what students need to know) and the assessible skills (what students need to be able to do). Create a graphic organizer representing all of the "unwrapped" concepts and skills. Assign to each concept-skill pair associated levels of cognitive rigor using the revised Bloom's Taxonomy and Webb's Depth of Knowledge matrices.

This second CFA 2.0 design step is critically important, because it guides all steps that follow it. Teacher teams review all of the "unwrapping" components, Big Ideas, and Essential Questions to formally decide their unit learning intentions and student success criteria. They then continually refer to the graphic organizer while creating CFA questions that directly match the "unwrapped" concepts, skills, and identified levels of cognitive rigor.

BACKGROUND OF "UNWRAPPING"

Donald Viegut introduced me to the idea of "unwrapping" standards in 2000, during my first professional development sessions with educators and leaders in Merrill, Wisconsin, where he served as the district supervisor for K–12 curriculum, instruction, and assessment.

In 2003, I wrote the book *"Unwrapping" the Standards: A Simple Process to Make Standards Manageable.* It contains more than 85 examples of "unwrapped" standards, with topical Big Ideas and Essential Questions specific to all four grade spans (primary, upper elementary, middle school, and high school) across numerous content areas. In 2014, I authored the second edition follow-up, *"Unwrapping" the Common Core: A Simple Process to Manage Rigorous Standards.* It includes 60 examples of "unwrapped" Common Core standards, graphic organizers, Big Ideas, and Essential Questions in English language arts and math distributed across the four grade spans.

"Unwrapping" the standards is a simple yet highly effective way to deconstruct any set of academic content standards. Across the United States and Canada, thousands of PreK–12 educators in all content areas who have applied the "unwrapping" process over the past decade and a half have enthusiastically endorsed it as a practical method to isolate and clarify the important concepts and skills within the wording of the Priority Standards or prioritized learning outcomes.

"Unwrapping" sharply focuses assessment design and curricular planning. It helps educators lift the level of their instruction to match the rigor of the "unwrapped" Priority Standards, which results in students exercising and developing their higher-order thinking skills.

HOW TO "UNWRAP" STANDARDS AND CREATE THE GRAPHIC ORGANIZER

In its simplest description, when educators "unwrap" standards, they underline the concepts (important nouns and noun phrases) and circle or CAPITALIZE the skills (verbs and verb phrases).

But don't let the seeming simplicity of the description minimize the importance of the practice. "Unwrapping" is much more than underlining and circling words. During the deconstruction of a standard, educators closely analyze its wording to identify exactly what students need to know (teachable ideas that are abstract or concrete) and be able to do (necessary skills students must demonstrate). Some of these concepts and skills represent surface learning (lower-level foundational knowledge and procedures) and others represent deeper learning (higher-level insights and applications). Collectively, these surface- and deep-learning targets, once identified, become key elements of the unit learning intentions and subsequent assessment questions.

After educators underline the teachable concepts and circle or CAPITALIZE the skills, they next create some type of graphic organizer (outline, bulleted list, concept map, or chart). By and large, educators prefer using a three-column chart in which they organize the concepts in the first column, the corresponding skills in the second column, and the levels of cognitive rigor in the third. And this is where the real fun begins!

ASSIGNING LEVELS OF COGNITIVE RIGOR

Assigning levels of rigor to each of the skills and its paired concept is both engaging and challenging. Design team members need to collectively agree on the assigned skill levels because the collaborative creation of the assessment questions must match those predetermined skill levels. While teams engage in this endeavor, productive discussions regularly take place about how to "teach up" to the identified levels of rigor so that students can successfully respond to the matching questions on the post-CFA.

To assign the levels of cognitive rigor to their "unwrapped" concepts and skills, educators typically use the revised Bloom's Taxonomy (Anderson & Krathwohl, 2001) and/or Webb's Depth of Knowledge levels (1997). In the CFA 2.0 process, teacher teams use *both* taxonomies to assign cognitive levels to each "unwrapped' concept-skill pair.

The revised Bloom's Taxonomy includes six cognitive process levels: remember, understand, apply, analyze, evaluate, and create. Each level is represented by a list of verbs that depict that particular level (Anderson & Krathwohl, 2001, pp. 67–68). The challenge in using this taxonomy to assign levels of cognitive rigor is that the verbs are listed in isolation (e.g., identify, make, observe) with no reference to any concepts that would help in determining the appropriate level. However, it is the taxonomy most educators are familiar with and use when making initial determinations of thinking-skill rigor.

Webb's Depth of Knowledge (DOK) taxonomy utilizes four cognitive process levels: recall and reproduction; skills and concepts; strategic thinking and reasoning; and extended thinking. In each of the four levels, verbs are paired with concepts (e.g., IDENTIFY main ideas or accurate generalizations of texts). These descriptive phrases greatly help in determining the DOK level of each concept-skill pair.

The DOK model is typically used to categorize the different levels of cognitive demand (or depth of knowledge) of assessment questions from external sources. But because teacher teams will be doing the actual writing of the assessment questions, they need to determine for themselves the level of rigor each targeted concept and skill represents *before* they can create assessment questions to match.

I recommend for use with the "unwrapping" process the DOK documents created by Karin Hess, specifically her updated publication for the Common Core Institute, *A Guide for Using Webb's Depth of Knowledge With Common Core State Standards* (2013). You can view this entire document online at http:// cliu21cng.wikispaces.com/file/view/WebsDepthofKnowledgeFlipChart. pdf/457670878/WebsDepthofKnowledgeFlipChart.pdf.

Hess first created three matrices to show the relationship between the six levels of the revised Bloom's Taxonomy and the four levels of Webb's Depth of Knowledge. One matrix is specific for close reading in English language arts and history/social studies, a second to math and science, and a third to written and oral communication across content areas. Since then, Dr. Hess has created additional matrices for multiple content areas. Readers may access these helpful matrices at: https://www.karin-hess.com/cognitive-rigor-and-dok. Permission is granted to use the matrices but only with a full citation (listed in the footer of each matrix).

For readers interested in learning more about how to effectively assign cognitive levels of rigor using the revised Bloom's Taxonomy and Hess' Cognitive Rigor Matrix, I have fully described and illustrated the process for doing so in *"Unwrapping" the Common Core* (2014).

"UNWRAPPED" EXAMPLES

The best way to realize the power of the "unwrapping" technique is to experience it firsthand. Yet for purposes here, illustrations will need to suffice. Continuing with the two examples of Priority Standards from the English language arts unit and the mathematics unit introduced in the previous chapter, here are the "unwrapped" versions of those Priority Standards. The concepts are underlined and the skills are CAPITALIZED. The two graphic organizers that follow show the organization of these concepts and skills in three columns, including the assigned levels of the revised Bloom's Taxonomy and DOK, respectively.

———————— ೮೩ ಜಿ ————————

CFA 2.0 DESIGN STEP 2

English Language Arts

Reading Informational Text

RI.5.6 ANALYZE <u>multiple accounts of the same event or topic</u>, NOTING important <u>similarities and differences</u> in the <u>point of view they represent</u>.

Writing (Opinion)

W.5.1 WRITE <u>opinion pieces</u> on topics or texts. SUPPORT <u>a point of view with reasons and information</u>.

W.5.1a INTRODUCE a <u>topic</u> or text clearly, STATE an <u>opinion</u>, and CREATE an <u>organizational structure in which ideas are logically grouped to support the writer's purpose</u>.

W.5.1b PROVIDE <u>logically ordered reasons</u> that are <u>supported by facts and details</u>.

W.5.1d PROVIDE a <u>concluding statement</u> or <u>section related to the opinion presented</u>.

Table 5.1 "Unwrapped" ELA Unit Graphic Organizer

"Unwrapped" Concepts	"Unwrapped" Skills	Levels of Rigor	
		Bloom's	DOK
• Same Events/Topic ○ multiple accounts	• ANALYZE (same events/ multiple accounts)	4	3
• Point of View ○ similarities ○ differences	• NOTE (similarities/differences in points of view	2	2
• Opinion Piece	• WRITE (opinion pieces)	6	4
• Point of View	• SUPPORT (point of view with reasons and information)	5	3
• Organizational Structure ○ with logical grouping of ideas	• INTRODUCE (topic or text)	2	1
• Reasons	• STATE (opinion)	5	2
○ supported by facts/ details	• CREATE (organizational structure with logical grouping of ideas to support writer's purpose)	2	4
• Concluding Statement ○ related to opinion	• PROVIDE (logically ordered reasons supported by facts/ details)	6	3
	• PROVIDE (concluding statement related to opinion)	5	3

Source: 5th Grade Curriculum Design Team, San Diego Unified School District, San Diego.

CFA 2.0 DESIGN STEP 2

Mathematics

Priority Standards (One Main Standard and Related Indicators)

6.RP.A.3 USE ratio and rate reasoning to SOLVE real-world and mathematical problems, e.g., by reasoning about tables of equivalent ratios, tape diagrams, double number line diagrams, or equations.

a. MAKE tables of equivalent ratios RELATING quantities with whole number measurements, FIND missing values in the tables, and PLOT the pairs of values on the coordinate plane. USE tables to COMPARE ratios.

b. SOLVE <u>unit rate problems</u>, including those involving <u>unit pricing</u> and <u>constant speed</u>. *For example, if it took 7 hours to mow 4 lawns, then at that rate, how many lawns could be mowed in 35 hours? At what rate were lawns being mowed?*

c. FIND a <u>percent of a quantity</u> as a <u>rate per 100</u> (*e.g., 30% of a quantity means 30/100 times the quantity*); SOLVE <u>problems</u> involving <u>finding the whole, given a part and the percent</u>.

d. USE <u>ratio reasoning</u> to CONVERT <u>measurement units</u>; MANIPULATE and TRANSFORM <u>units</u> appropriately <u>when multiplying or dividing quantities</u>.

Table 5.2 "Unwrapped" Math Unit Graphic Organizer

"Unwrapped" Concepts	"Unwrapped" Skills	Levels of Rigor Bloom's	DOK
Reasoning • ratio • rate Problems • real-world • mathematical *(e.g., by reasoning about tables of equivalent ratios, tape diagrams, double number line diagrams, or equations)*	USE to SOLVE	3	3
Tables • equivalent ratios Quantities • whole number measurements	MAKE RELATING	6	2
Missing Values • in the tables	FIND	4	2
Pairs • on the coordinate plane	PLOT		
Tables	USE	3	2
Ratios	to COMPARE	3	3

(Continued)

(Continued)

"Unwrapped" Concepts	"Unwrapped" Skills	Levels of Rigor	
		Bloom's	DOK
Unit Rate Problems • unit pricing • constant speed *(For example, if it took 7 hours to mow 4 lawns, then at that rate, how many lawns could be mowed in 35 hours? At what rate were lawns being mowed?)*	SOLVE	4	3
Percent of a Quantity • as a rate per 100 *(e.g., 30% of a quantity means 30/100 times the quantity)*	FIND	3	2
Problems • finding the whole • given a part and the percent	SOLVE	3	3
Ratio Reasoning Measurement Units • measurement units	USE to CONVERT	3	2
Units • multiplying quantities • dividing quantities	MANIPULATE (appropriately)	3	2
Units • multiplying quantities • dividing quantities	TRANSFORM	3	2

Source: Jan Christinson, author-consultant.

_____ ☙ ❧ _____

Even though the transfer of "unwrapped" concepts and skills from within the Priority Standards to the graphic organizer may look a bit like "word shuffling," educators have repeatedly affirmed the value of doing so. Reorganizing the Priority Standards elements in this way greatly helps them understand each standard's exact meaning. Organizing all of the concepts together in one column makes it easier to determine the Big Ideas in the next step of the process. Also, listing the concepts in this way helps educators determine their unit vocabulary terms—a key part of the unit learning intentions.

By itself, the skills column shows at a glance everything that students must be able to do by the end of the unit. Educators reference this column in particular to write their post- and pre-CFA questions. They then use it to plan their learning progressions and decide where to insert their quick progress checks (described in Chapter 10).

As educators analyze and deconstruct the standards, they really get to know exactly what they need to teach and what students need to learn. The standards become less daunting. Preparing the graphic organizer enables the "unwrappers" to organize all the concepts and skills in a way that makes the most sense to them. It helps them consider how best to teach those elements because they are now crystal clear.

The graphic organizer of "unwrapped" concepts, skills, and assigned levels of cognitive rigor represents the *what* and the *how* of the unit Priority Standards. The *why*—the reasons these concepts and skills are important for students to understand and be able to do—are known as the Big Ideas.

CFA 2.0 Design Step 3: Determine the Big Ideas and Essential Questions. The Big Ideas represent the three or four foundational understandings specific to the unit that are important for students to discover on their own as they learn and apply the "unwrapped" concepts and skills. To introduce the unit of study to students, educators present three or four corresponding Essential Questions derived from the "unwrapped" concepts and skills that will guide all instruction and learning activities throughout the unit. The expectation is that students will respond to the Essential Questions with their own corresponding Big Ideas on the post-CFA at the end of the unit.

DETERMINE THE BIG IDEAS

The third step of the CFA 2.0 process is to identify the **Big Ideas,** or key understandings, that students are to discover for themselves during the course of the unit. Big Ideas are generalizations that make explicit the connections between related "unwrapped" concepts. For example, these "unwrapped" concepts—same event/topic, firsthand (primary source), secondhand (secondary source)—can be connected to show the benefit for learning them, as expressed in this one Big Idea: "Reading about something from first- and second-hand accounts influences our understanding about an event or a topic" (4th Grade Curriculum Design Team San Diego Unified School District, San Diego, CA, 2012–2013 school year).

Written as full sentences to express a complete thought, Big Ideas communicate to students the benefit or value of learning the standards in focus. These Big Ideas often occur to students during the "Ah-ha!" moments of the learning process, particularly when teachers guide their students to make connections and draw conclusions about what they have been studying. Such insights, when personally discovered, endure long after instruction ends.

In *Understanding by Design,* Grant Wiggins and Jay McTighe (1998) describe Big Ideas as enduring understandings, "the important understandings that we want students to 'get inside of' and retain after they've forgotten many of the details" (p. 10).

H. Lynn Erickson (2002), long a champion of promoting students' conceptual understanding, states that teachers need to know how to

think beyond the facts, to understand the conceptual structure of the disciplines, and to have the ability to clearly identify key ideas that illustrate deep knowledge. Deep knowledge transfers across time and cultures and provides a conceptual structure for thinking about related new ideas. (p. 7)

In *Visible Learning* (2009), John Hattie writes,

Teachers are successful to the degree that they can move students from single to multiple ideas, and then relate and extend these ideas [so that] learners construct and reconstruct knowledge and ideas. It is not the knowledge or ideas, but rather the learner's construction of the knowledge and ideas that is critical. (p. 37)

BIG IDEAS BENEFIT STUDENTS *AND* TEACHERS

Mere recall of newly learned information (knowledge) is not sufficient in and of itself. Being able to make connections between new information and prior learning utilizes a higher-level thinking skill that leads to enhanced understanding. Teaching students how to connect new and different concepts and skills to prior learning prepares them to use that ability throughout their lives. Learning how to articulate Big Ideas *in their own words* paves the way for students to make these kinds of important connections on their own.

From my own 24 years of classroom teaching experience, I know how challenging it can be at times to convey to students a purpose for learning—especially when they are not interested. In my ongoing efforts to motivate students, I eventually came to this realization about the power of Big Ideas (Ainsworth, 2014): "Big Ideas bring relevancy to students by answering their often unspoken mental question: 'Why do I have to learn this anyway?' or 'When will I ever use this in real life?'" (p. 55).

Collaboratively determining the Big Ideas benefits educators as well. It helps them to "think bigger" when setting out to plan their units of study. When educators understand the value of helping students make greater meaning from what they are learning, their instruction changes and deepens. They become more focused on helping students understand the *why* of learning, and not just the *what* and *how*.

To determine the Big Ideas, teacher teams look at the "unwrapped" concepts on their graphic organizer and discuss what might be the three or four key ideas they would want their students to take away from the unit. When drafting their Big Ideas, they will often cluster together related concepts to generate a Big Idea statement for each cluster. It is often helpful to think of each Big Idea as an "umbrella statement" under which the clustered concepts gather.

BIG IDEA EXAMPLES

Here again are the graphic organizers for the English language arts and mathematics "unwrapped" Priority Standards. Following each graphic organizer are the Big Ideas derived from the "unwrapped" concepts. Note the *specificity* of these Big Ideas to the concepts in focus. These are not broad generalizations, but rather essential understandings specific to the unit standards that the educators want the students to realize and be able to articulate in their own words.

In Big Ideas, the benefit for learning is often represented by the word *helps*. Here are two examples:

- Identifying the main idea and details in nonfiction texts *helps* me understand the topic.
- Visual representations *help* me understand math rules and patterns.

Inclusion of the word *helps* indicates a direct benefit to the students, one that provides them with meaning and relevancy. Another example of this appears in the first Big Idea statement within the English language arts example.

Table 5.1 "Unwrapped" ELA Unit Graphic Organizer

"Unwrapped" Concepts	"Unwrapped" Skills	Levels of Rigor	
		Bloom's	DOK
• Same Events/Topic o multiple accounts	• ANALYZE (same events/multiple accounts)	4	3

• Point of View
  o similarities
  o differences
	• NOTE (similarities/differences in points of view	2	2

• Opinion Piece	• WRITE (opinion pieces)	6	4
• Point of View	• SUPPORT (point of view with reasons and information)	5	3
• Organizational Structure o with logical grouping of ideas	• INTRODUCE (topic or text)	2	1
• Reasons o supported by facts/details	• STATE (opinion)	5	2
	• CREATE (organizational structure with logical grouping of ideas to support writer's purpose)	2	4
• Concluding Statement o related to opinion	• PROVIDE (logically ordered reasons supported by facts/details)	6	3
	• PROVIDE (concluding statement related to opinion)	5	3

Source: 5th Grade Curriculum Design Team, San Diego Unified School District, San Diego, CA; Tracey Shiel.

CFA 2.0 DESIGN STEP 3

English Language Arts Unit Big Ideas

1. Analyzing varying points of view from multiple accounts of an event/topic helps me form my own opinion.

2. When writing my opinion, it will be stronger with supported reasons and relevant information.

3. Writing requires an organizational structure so that the author's ideas are presented, supported, and summarized effectively.

Source: 5th Grade Curriculum Design Team, San Diego Unified School District, San Diego, CA.

Commentary: Notice how the first Big Idea is a summary statement for several clustered concepts (point of view, similarities, differences, multiple accounts of same event/topic). The second Big Idea also incorporates several concepts (opinion reasons, supported by facts/details). The third Big Idea clusters the remaining concepts (organizational structure, logical grouping of ideas, concluding statement). The first and second Big Ideas are written in the first person to show their direct benefits to the students. The third Big Idea is broader and expresses the value of organizational structures to all writers.

Now let's look at how math concepts on the graphic organizer can be clustered together as Big Ideas.

Table 5.2 "Unwrapped" Math Unit Graphic Organizer

"Unwrapped" Concepts	"Unwrapped" Skills	Levels of Rigor	
		Bloom's	DOK
Reasoning • ratio • rate Problems • real-world • mathematical *(e.g., by reasoning about tables of equivalent ratios, tape diagrams, double number line diagrams, or equations)*	USE to SOLVE	3	3
Tables • equivalent ratios Quantities • whole number measurements	MAKE RELATING	6	2
Missing Values • in the tables	FIND	4	2
Pairs • on the coordinate plane	PLOT		
Tables	USE	3	2
Ratios	to COMPARE	3	3

(Continued)

"Unwrapped" Concepts	"Unwrapped" Skills	Levels of Rigor	
		Bloom's	DOK
Unit Rate Problems • unit pricing • constant speed *(For example, if it took 7 hours to mow 4 lawns, then at that rate, how many lawns could be mowed in 35 hours? At what rate were lawns being mowed?)*	SOLVE	4	3
Percent of a Quantity • as a rate per 100 *(e.g., 30% of a quantity means 30/100 times the quantity)*	FIND	3	2
Problems • finding the whole • given a part and the percent	SOLVE	3	3
Ratio Reasoning Measurement Units • measurement units	USE to CONVERT	3	2
Units • multiplying quantities • dividing quantities	MANIPULATE (appropriately)	3	2
Units • multiplying quantities • dividing quantities	TRANSFORM	3	2

Source: Jan Christinson, author-consultant.

CFA 2.0 DESIGN STEP 3

Math Unit Big Ideas

1. Reasoning with ratios involves coordinating two quantities. Tables of equivalent ratios, tape diagrams, and double line diagrams are mathematical tools used to solve real-world ratio problems.

2. A unit rate is a rate that is expressed as a quantity of one. A unit rate describes how many units of the first type of quantity correspond to one unit of the second type of quantity.

3. A percent is a ratio that compares a quantity to 100. A percent can be used to find the whole or a given part in a problem situation.

Commentary: As in the English language arts examples, the math unit's Big Ideas are summary statements representing the clustering of several concepts. In this example, there are two statements for each of the three Big Ideas. The first statement represents *surface* knowledge, a foundational math definition that is necessary for all students to grasp. The second statement represents a *deeper* understanding that is more representative of a true mathematical Big Idea. Together, they articulate three essential learning intentions for this unit on mathematical ratios and rates.

WRITE THE ESSENTIAL QUESTIONS

The final part of the "unwrapping" process is to formulate **Essential Questions** matched to the Big Ideas. Essential Questions serve three important functions. They (1) center instruction on the "unwrapped" Priority Standards, (2) align instruction with preplanned assessments, and (3) lead students to the discovery of the Big Ideas on their own by the end of the unit of study. These multiple purposes of Essential Questions are conveyed in this broader description (Ainsworth, 2014):

> Essential Questions are engaging, open-ended questions that educators use to spark student interest in learning the content of the unit about to commence. Even though plainly worded, they carry with them an underlying rigor. Responding to them in a way that demonstrates genuine understanding requires more than superficial thought. Along with the "unwrapped" concepts and skills from the Priority Standards, educators use the Essential Questions *throughout the unit* to sharply focus curriculum, instruction, and assessment. (p. 78)

Educators present these open-ended questions to students at the beginning of a unit as part of the learning intentions and student success criteria. They then engage their students in a challenge—to discover the answers to these important questions during the unit and be able to write them in their own words on the post-CFA.

The Essential Questions, the "unwrapped" Priority Standards concepts and skills, and the unit vocabulary terms are then posted in the classroom for the duration of the unit. Together they serve as constant reminders—to students and educators alike—of the learning focus of the unit.

As instruction progresses, educators use the Essential Questions to filter and select particular textbook pages and instructional materials that will advance student understanding of the "unwrapped" Priority Standards. They continually refer to the Essential Questions to connect each day's lessons and activities to them and to informally check the progress of student understanding in order to plan instructional next steps. Students periodically reflect on their own progress in terms of being able to respond to the Essential Questions and use that feedback to adjust their learning strategies.

ATTRIBUTES OF EFFECTIVE QUESTIONS

Here are a few attributes or characteristics of effective questions to keep in mind when teacher teams are drafting and refining their Essential Questions (Ainsworth, 2014):

- Cannot be answered with a *yes* or *no*
- Have no single obvious right answer
- Cannot be answered from rote memory (simple recall of facts)
- Reflect the rigor of the "unwrapped" Priority Standards
- Go beyond who, what, when, and where to how and why (p. 83)

"ONE-TWO PUNCH" ESSENTIAL QUESTIONS

Educators know that students need to acquire surface learning *and* deep learning. Effective Essential Questions meet both of these needs. They ask students to respond to both lower- and higher-level questions. I call these types of combination inquiries *one-two punch* or two-part questions (Ainsworth, 2014):

> The first part asks students to demonstrate their *recall* of information. It validates the need to acquire a knowledge base about the question at hand. But the second part asks students to *apply* that information. It communicates the message that facts alone are not enough; they must be utilized if they are to be of real value. (pp. 83–84)

Here are a few examples of one-two punch Essential Questions in ELA and math, respectively (Ainsworth, 2014). They initially ask students for surface knowledge and then challenge them to go deeper.

- What is the writing process? Why do accomplished writers use it?
- What is point of view? How does it affect the story?
- What are the differences between fact and opinion? When is it appropriate to use fact or opinion?

- How do people use data? Why are certain representations of data more useful than others?
- Which strategy works best for me to add and subtract big numbers? Why?
- What are linear equations? How can we use them in real life? (p. 84)

TIPS FOR WRITING ESSENTIAL QUESTIONS

Essential Questions and Big Ideas share a "question-answer" relationship. One effective way educators write an Essential Question is to look at a particular Big Idea statement and think, "If that's the answer or desired student response, what's the question?"

Be careful not to give the Big Idea away in the Essential Question by including too much of it in the wording of the question. For example, if an elementary science Big Idea is, "Animals have developed certain adaptations that help them survive," the Essential Question should not be, "What adaptations do animals have that help them survive?" The two are almost identical, asking only for a recall of information with nothing for the student to discover. A better Essential Question might be a one-two punch worded like this: "What are adaptations? Why are adaptations important to animals?" The Big Idea answers the second of these two questions.

Some educators find the writing of Essential Questions easier to do than the identification of Big Ideas, and vice versa. Just experiment with the process, draft your initial Essential Questions, and then revise as needed. The only critical guideline to remember is that the Big Idea is the student's answer or response to the teacher's Essential Question and provides the evidence of learning.

EXAMPLES OF ESSENTIAL QUESTIONS AND CORRESPONDING BIG IDEAS

Here are the two sets of Essential Questions and Big Ideas from the same English language arts and mathematics units shown earlier in the chapter. The Big Ideas in the second column are the intended student responses to the educators' Essential Questions. Notice in the mathematics example, the repeated use of one-two punch Essential Questions that represent both surface and deep learning.

CFA 2.0 DESIGN STEP 3

English Language Arts

Essential Questions	Corresponding Big Ideas
Why is it important to understand different points of view?	Analyzing points of view from multiple accounts of an event/topic helps form your own opinion.
How can you write a strong opinion piece that communicates your point of view?	When writing my opinion, it will be stronger with supported reasons and relevant information.
Why is an organizational structure necessary to a writer?	Writing requires an organizational structure so that the author's ideas are presented, supported, and summarized effectively.

Source: 5th Grade Curriculum Design Team, San Diego Unified School District, San Diego, CA.

Mathematics

Essential Questions	Corresponding Big Ideas
What does it mean to reason with ratios? *What mathematical tools are used to solve real-world ratio problems?*	Reasoning with ratios involves coordinating two quantities. Tables of equivalent ratios, tape diagrams, and double line diagrams are mathematical tools used to solve real-world ratio problems.
What is a unit rate? *What information does it provide?*	A unit rate is a rate that is expressed as a quantity of one. A unit rate describes how many units of the first type of quantity correspond to one unit of the second type of quantity.
What is a percent? *How can it be used to solve problems?*	A percent is a ratio that compares a quantity to 100. A percent can be used to find the whole or given part in a problem situation.

Source: Jan Christinson, author-consultant.

Readers interested in more in-depth information on how to write Big Ideas and Essential Questions that engage students, along with 60 ELA and math examples across the four grade spans, will find *"Unwrapping" the Common Core: A Simple Process to Manage Rigorous Standards* (Ainsworth, 2014) to be a useful resource. Although focused on the Common Core State Standards, the information is directly relevant and applicable to all state standards as well as all grades and all content areas.

FROM "UNWRAPPED" PRIORITY STANDARDS TO UNIT LEARNING INTENTIONS

After teacher teams complete the four parts of the "unwrapping" process, there is only one more step to take before they are ready to collaboratively design the common formative post-assessment. They need to revisit all of the "unwrapped" elements and finalize the unit learning intentions in the form of student success criteria. How teams do this is described and illustrated in the next chapter.

But first, on your own or with colleagues please again take a few moments to write your responses to these success criteria, or simply evaluate your understanding of each performance statement on a scale of one (low) to five (high). Be sure to close any learning gaps you may have.

Success Criteria:

- Explain how to "unwrap" the Priority Standards.
- Summarize the function of the graphic organizer.
- Describe how to write Big Ideas and Essential Questions and how these benefit instruction and student learning.

6 Unit Learning Intentions and Student Success Criteria

In This Chapter You Will Learn:

- How to finalize the unit learning intentions.
- How to develop the success criteria for students that parallel the unit learning intentions.
- How to introduce the success criteria to students.

In this fourth step of the CFA 2.0 design process, teacher teams review all of the standards elements created in the previous three steps and finalize the specific *learning intentions* for the unit. They then write these learning intentions in the form of *student success criteria.* Introduced in Chapter 4, learning intentions and success criteria represent the specific knowledge and skills students are to acquire and be able to demonstrate by the end of the unit. Representing a combination of surface knowledge and deeper understanding, these elements will "drive" the creation of the unit assessments (pre-, post-, and quick progress checks) and inform the identification of learning progressions and related instruction.

Figure 6.1 CFA 2.0 Design Step 4

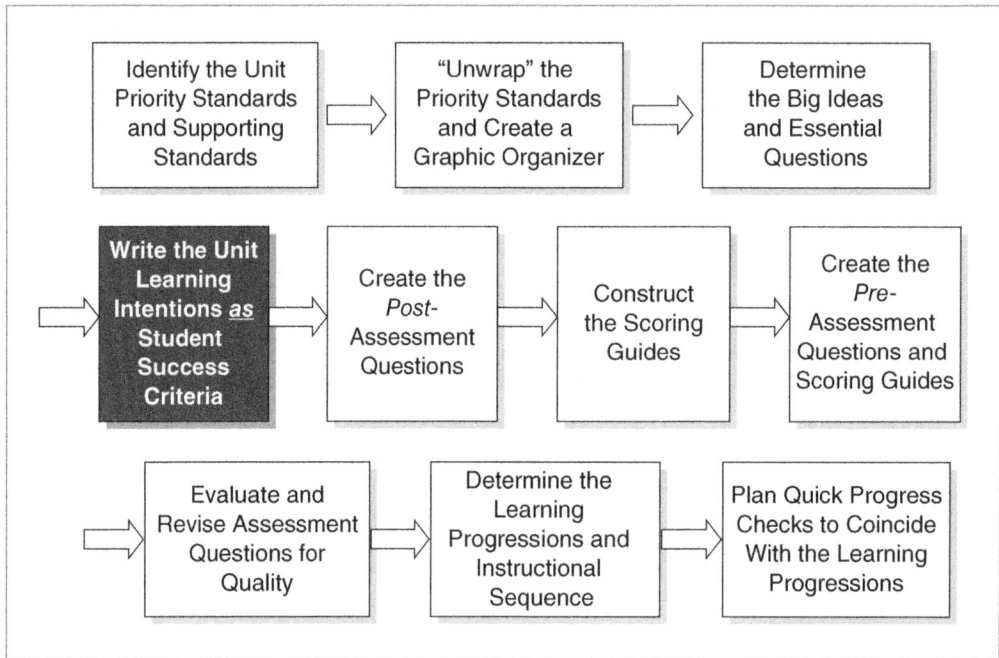

```
┌─────────────────┐     ┌─────────────────┐     ┌─────────────────┐
│ Identify the Unit│     │  "Unwrap" the   │     │   Determine     │
│ Priority Standards│ ──> │ Priority Standards│ ──> │  the Big Ideas  │
│ and Supporting   │     │  and Create a   │     │  and Essential  │
│   Standards      │     │ Graphic Organizer│     │   Questions     │
└─────────────────┘     └─────────────────┘     └─────────────────┘

┌─────────────────┐     ┌─────────────────┐     ┌─────────────────┐     ┌─────────────────┐
│ Write the Unit  │     │  Create the     │     │                 │     │  Create the     │
│   Learning      │     │    Post-        │     │   Construct     │     │     Pre-        │
│ Intentions as   │ ──> │  Assessment     │ ──> │  the Scoring    │ ──> │  Assessment     │
│   Student       │     │  Questions      │     │    Guides       │     │  Questions and  │
│   Success       │     │                 │     │                 │     │  Scoring Guides │
│   Criteria      │     │                 │     │                 │     │                 │
└─────────────────┘     └─────────────────┘     └─────────────────┘     └─────────────────┘

┌─────────────────┐     ┌─────────────────┐     ┌─────────────────┐
│  Evaluate and   │     │  Determine the  │     │ Plan Quick Progress│
│ Revise Assessment│     │    Learning     │     │ Checks to Coincide │
│  Questions for  │ ──> │  Progressions and│ ──> │ With the Learning  │
│    Quality      │     │  Instructional  │     │   Progressions     │
│                 │     │    Sequence     │     │                 │
└─────────────────┘     └─────────────────┘     └─────────────────┘
```

LEARNING INTENTIONS AND FORMATIVE ASSESSMENT

For educators, the learning intentions directly inform *all* of their decisions about the entire unit, from assessment design and curriculum selections to daily instructional planning and delivery. For students, the unit learning intentions—written as student success criteria—let them know exactly where they are headed in their learning journey. It answers their often-unspoken question, "Where are we going?" before setting out on the trip.

Describing learning intentions and their critical connection to assessment, John Hattie (2012) writes,

> Good learning intentions are those that make clear to the students the type of mastery they need to attain, so that they understand where and when to invest energies, strategies, and thinking, and where they are positioned along the trajectory towards successful learning . . .
>
> Learning intentions describe what it is that we want students to learn, and their clarity is at the heart of formative assessment. Unless teachers are clear about what they want students to learn (and what

the outcome of this learning looks like, i.e. success criteria), they are hardly likely to develop good assessment of that learning. (p. 47)

STUDENT SUCCESS CRITERIA

Student success criteria are similar in appearance to performance statements, in that they typically begin with a verb and describe what students must *do* with regard to the learning intentions. The learning intentions and success criteria include nearly identical wording, much like the stated learning intentions and success criteria that bookend the beginning and end of each chapter in this book.

For example, one of the learning intentions for readers of this chapter is, "Learn how to introduce the success criteria to students." The matching success criterion is "*Describe* how to introduce the success criteria to students." Both of these nearly verbatim statements begin with a verb *(learn* and *describe),* but only the verb *describe* calls for an observable outer demonstration of performance on the part of the reader. In the process of describing how to share the success criteria with students, the reader's response will certainly include details and additional information—all of which can be assessed.

In *Visible Learning* (2009), Hattie gives this example of a learning intention: "To learn to use effective adjectives." Such a nebulous phrase, he says, "does not give the students the success criteria or how they will be judged. . . . . For too many students, this is what learning feels like" (pp. 50–51). Hattie then suggests two specific success criteria for that vague learning intention: "use at least five effective adjectives; . . . . use an adjective before a noun on at least four occasions that will help to paint a detailed picture" (p. 51).

Success criteria must specify for students the necessary evidence they will need to produce to show whether or not they have achieved the related learning intentions. Accompanying scoring guides (described in Chapter 8) provide the *details* of the success criteria.

> **CFA 2.0 Design Step 4: Write the Unit Learning Intentions *as* Student Success Criteria.** The "unwrapped" concepts and skills, the levels of cognitive rigor, the Big Ideas and Essential Questions, and the unit vocabulary terms derived from both the Priority Standards and the supporting standards collectively represent the unit learning intentions that students are to achieve by the end of the unit. In this step, teacher teams write these unit learning intentions in the form of student success criteria—performance statements that describe how students will show they have achieved the learning intentions.

COMPREHENSIVE SET OF ELA LEARNING ELEMENTS

To illustrate, here are all of the learning elements for the ELA unit on informational text and opinion writing, reprinted from earlier chapters.

———————— ℭ ℬ ————————

COMPREHENSIVE SET OF LEARNING INTENTIONS ELEMENTS

English Language Arts Unit

"Unwrapped" Priority Standards and Indented Supporting Standards

Reading Informational Text

RI.5.6 ANALYZE <u>multiple accounts of the same event or topic</u>, NOTING important <u>similarities and differences</u> in the <u>point of view they represent</u>.

> RI.5.4 Determine the meaning of general academic and domain-specific words and phrases in a text relevant to a Grade 5 topic or subject area.

> RI.5.8 Explain how an author uses reasons and evidence to support particular points in a text, identifying which reasons and evidence support which point(s).

Writing (Opinion)

W.5.1 WRITE <u>opinion pieces</u> on topics or texts. SUPPORT a <u>point of view</u> <u>with reasons and information</u>.

W.5.1a INTRODUCE a <u>topic</u> or text clearly, STATE an <u>opinion</u>, and CREATE an <u>organizational structure</u> in which <u>ideas are logically grouped to support the writer's purpose</u>.

W.5.1b PROVIDE <u>logically ordered reasons</u> that are <u>supported by facts and details</u>.

W.5.1d PROVIDE a <u>concluding statement</u> or <u>section related to the opinion presented</u>.

W.5.8 Recall relevant information from experiences or gather relevant information from print and digital sources; summarize or paraphrase information in notes and finished work, and provide a list of sources.

ELA Unit Graphic Organizer of "Unwrapped" Priority Standards Concepts, Skills, and Levels of Rigor

"Unwrapped" Concepts	"Unwrapped" Skills	Levels of Rigor	
		Bloom's	DOK
• Same Events/Topic 　o multiple accounts	• ANALYZE (same events/ multiple accounts)	4	3
• Point of View 　o Similarities 　o differences	• NOTE (similarities/ differences in points of view)	2	2
• Opinion Piece	• WRITE (opinion pieces)	6	4
• Point of View	• SUPPORT (point of view with reasons and information)	5	3
• Organizational Structure 　o with logical grouping of ideas	• INTRODUCE (topic or text)	2	1
• Reasons 　o supported by facts/details	• STATE (opinion)	2	2
• Concluding Statement 　o related to opinion	• CREATE (organizational structure with logical grouping of ideas to support writer's purpose)	6	4
	• PROVIDE (logically ordered reasons supported by facts/details)	5	3
	• PROVIDE (concluding statement related to opinion)	5	3

Source: 5th Grade Curriculum Design Team, San Diego Unified School District, San Diego, CA.

──────── Cʒ ঙ⃝ ────────

ESSENTIAL QUESTIONS AND CORRESPONDING BIG IDEAS

1. *Why is it important to understand different points of view?*

Analyzing points of view from multiple accounts of an event/topic helps me form my own opinion.

2. *How can you write a strong opinion piece that communicates your point of view?*

When writing my opinion, it will be stronger with supported reasons and relevant information.

3. *Why is an organizational structure necessary to a writer?*

Writing requires an organizational structure so that the author's ideas are presented, supported, and summarized effectively.

In Box 6.1, all of these learning elements now appear together as the comprehensive set of unit learning intentions—with the exception of the supporting standards. However, as indicated in Number 4 in the box, unit vocabulary terms will be drawn from certain concepts in the supporting standards. Learning these terms, plus the vocabulary words derived from the "unwrapped" Priority Standards concepts in Number 3, will be a key part of the student success criteria.

Important: Teacher teams need to retain the completed graphic organizer as a separate document for reference when designing all of the unit assessment questions (pre-, post-, quick progress checks). These questions must all be directly aligned to the revised Bloom's Taxonomy and DOK levels of cognitive rigor, which appear only on the graphic organizer.

CHARTING THE LEARNING INTENTIONS _AS_ SUCCESS CRITERIA

Given the close relationship between the unit learning intentions and the student success criteria, it will be less complicated for students to understand the unit learning intentions if they are written *as* success criteria. The success criteria include everything that the students need to know and be able to do in the unit—plus the action verbs (e.g., analyze, write, introduce, and so on) specify how students will be expected to demonstrate their learning.

Box 6.1 Comprehensive Set of ELA Unit Learning Intentions

1. <u>Priority Standard</u>: Analyze multiple accounts of the same event or topic, noting important similarities and differences in the point of view they represent.

2. <u>Priority Standards</u>: Write opinion pieces on topics or texts, supporting a point of view with reasons and information.

   a. Introduce a topic or text clearly, state an opinion, and create an organizational structure in which ideas are logically grouped to support the writer's purpose.
   b. Provide logically ordered reasons that are supported by facts and details.
   c. Provide a concluding statement or section related to the opinion presented.

3. "Unwrapped" *Priority Standards* concepts from which to develop unit vocabulary terms:

   - Multiple accounts of a topic or event
   - Point of view, including similarities and differences
   - Opinion piece
   - Organizational structure with logical grouping of ideas
   - Reasons supported by facts and details
   - Concluding statement related to opinion

4. Concepts from *supporting standards* to include in unit vocabulary terms:

   - Academic and domain-specific words
   - Supporting reasons and evidence
   - Relevant information from variety of sources
   - Summary
   - Paraphrase

5. Essential Questions and Big Ideas for the unit:

   - *Why is it important to understand different points of view?*

   Analyzing points of view from multiple accounts of an event/topic helps me form my own opinion.

   - *How can you write a strong opinion piece that communicates your point of view?*

   When writing my opinion, it will be stronger with supported reasons and relevant information.

   - *Why is an organizational structure necessary to a writer?*

   Writing requires an organizational structure so that the author's ideas are presented, supported, and summarized effectively.

To create the student success criteria, teacher teams transfer the comprehensive set of unit learning intentions into a three-column chart. The Essential Questions appear in the first column, the "unwrapped" Priority Standards appear in the second column, and the vocabulary terms for the unit (derived from the Priority Standards *and* the supporting standards) in the third. The contents of each column are prefaced with bolded performance descriptors that state what students will be expected to demonstrate.

Note: The Big Ideas are included in the educators' set of unit learning intentions, but they are obviously not shared with students since the goal is for them to discover the Big Ideas on their own.

Table 6.1 Learning Intentions *as* Student Success Criteria for the ELA Unit

Essential Questions	Priority Standards	Vocabulary

Respond correctly with your Big Ideas to the unit's three Essential Questions:
 	
1. *Why is it important to understand different points of view?*
 	
2. *How can you write a strong opinion piece that communicates your point of view?*
 	
3. *Why is an organizational structure necessary to a writer?*
	Demonstrate your ability to do each of the following:
	
	1. ANALYZE <u>multiple accounts</u> of the <u>same event or topic</u>.
	  • NOTE important <u>similarities</u> and <u>differences</u> in the <u>point of view</u> they represent.
	
	2. WRITE <u>opinion pieces</u> on topics or texts.
	  • SUPPORT a <u>point of view</u> with <u>reasons</u> and <u>information</u>.
	
	3. INCLUDE:
	  • An <u>introduction</u>
	  • A stated <u>opinion</u>
	  • An <u>organizational structure</u>
	  • Logically grouped <u>ideas</u> to <u>support writer's purpose</u>
	  • Logically ordered <u>reasons</u> <u>supported by facts/details</u>
	  • <u>Concluding statement</u> related to opinion
		Define and use the unit vocabulary terms appropriately:
		
		• Multiple accounts
		• Point of view
		• Similarities
		• Differences
		• Opinion piece
		• Organizational structure
		• Reasons
		• Facts
		• Details
		• Concluding statement
		• Academic words
		• Domain-specific words
		• Supporting reasons
		• Evidence
		• Relevant information
		• Summary
		• Paraphrase

In the second column of Table 6.1, the Priority Standards appear in their "unwrapped" form to focus students' attention on the key aspects of the standards they will be learning and applying throughout the unit. The underlined concepts and CAPITALIZED skills also help students see the direct connections between what students are expected to know and be able to do and the vocabulary terms they need to learn, which are listed in the third column.

Often this begs the question: "Why not translate some of the formal academic language in the standards into more student friendly terms?" Students need to know the specific language of the standards, not only to add to their knowledge base but also to become familiar with these same terms before they encounter them on standardized achievement tests.

Now, refer again to Box 6.1. Note the italicized verbs in the three writing Priority Standards listed under Number 2:

a. *Introduce* a topic or text clearly, *state* an opinion, and *create* an organizational structure in which ideas are logically grouped to support the writer's purpose.

b. *Provide* logically ordered reasons that are supported by facts and details.

d. *Provide* a concluding statement or section related to the opinion presented.

See how these standards have been paraphrased at the bottom of the second column of Table 6.1. The underlined concepts now appear under one main verb, "INCLUDE." INCLUDE collectively stands for the italicized skills: *introduce, state, create*, and *provide*. As students write their opinion piece and INCLUDE the underlined concepts, they will be demonstrating all of the italicized skills. This reduces the amount of text on the student success criteria chart and makes these particular standards more "student friendly" without losing any of their full meaning

COMPREHENSIVE SET OF MATH LEARNING ELEMENTS

Let's now look at how the comprehensive set of learning elements for the math unit can be written in the form of student success criteria.

The main Priority Standard is detailed by the four related subpoints, also identified as priorities for this unit. Even though they have not been indented, as are the supporting standards in the ELA example, the two supporting math standards placed at the end will serve as instructional scaffolds to help students attain the Priority Standards.

The remainder of the math learning elements includes the "unwrapped" Priority Standards concepts and skills, the levels of cognitive rigor, the Big Ideas, and the Essential Questions.

——————— ❧ ❧ ———————

COMPREHENSIVE SET OF LEARNING INTENTIONS ELEMENTS

Mathematics Unit

Priority Standards (One Main Standard and Related Subpoints)

6.RP.A.3 USE ratio and rate reasoning to SOLVE real-world and mathematical problems, e.g., by reasoning about tables of equivalent ratios, tape diagrams, double number line diagrams, or equations.

    a. MAKE tables of equivalent ratios RELATING quantities with whole number measurements, FIND missing values in the tables, and PLOT the pairs of values on the coordinate plane. USE tables to COMPARE ratios.

    b. SOLVE unit rate problems including those involving unit pricing and constant speed. *For example, if it took 7 hours to mow 4 lawns, then at that rate, how many lawns could be mowed in 35 hours? At what rate were lawns being mowed?*

    c. FIND a percent of a quantity as a rate per 100 (*e.g., 30% of a quantity means 30/100 times the quantity*); SOLVE problems involving finding the whole, given a part and the percent.

    d. USE ratio reasoning to CONVERT measurement units; MANIPULATE and TRANSFORM units appropriately when multiplying or dividing quantities.

SUPPORTING STANDARDS

6.RP.A.1 Understand the concept of a ratio and use ratio language to describe a ratio relationship between two quantities. For example, "The ratio of wings to beaks in the bird house at the zoo was 2:1, because for every 2 wings there was 1 beak." "For every vote candidate A received, candidate C received nearly three votes."

6.RP.A.2 Understand the concept of a unit rate a/b associated with a ratio a:b with b ≠ 0, and use rate language in the context of a ratio relationship. For example, "This recipe has a ratio of 3 cups of flour to

4 cups of sugar, so there is 3/4 cup of flour for each cup of sugar." "We paid $75 for 15 hamburgers, which is a rate of $5 per hamburger."

Completed Graphic Organizer of "Unwrapped" Priority Standards Concepts, Skills, and Levels of Rigor

"Unwrapped" Concepts	"Unwrapped" Skills	Levels of Rigor	
		Bloom's	DOK
Reasoning • ratio • rate Problems • real-world • mathematical *(e.g., by reasoning about tables of equivalent ratios, tape diagrams, double number line diagrams, or equations)*	USE to SOLVE	3	3
Tables • equivalent ratios Quantities • whole number measurements	MAKE RELATING	6	2
Missing Values • in the tables	FIND	4	2
Pairs • on the coordinate plane	PLOT	3	2
Tables Ratios	USE to COMPARE	3	3
Unit Rate Problems • unit pricing • constant speed *(For example, if it took 7 hours to mow 4 lawns, then at that rate, how many lawns could be mowed in 35 hours? At what rate were lawns being mowed?)*	SOLVE	4	3
Percent of a Quantity • as a rate per 100 *(e.g., 30% of a quantity means 30/100 times the quantity);*	FIND	3	2

(Continued)

(Continued)

"Unwrapped" Concepts	"Unwrapped" Skills	Levels of Rigor	
		Bloom's	DOK
Problems • finding the whole • given a part and the percent	SOLVE	3	3
Ratio Reasoning Measurement Units • measurement units	USE to CONVERT	3	2
Units • multiplying quantities • dividing quantities	MANIPULATE (appropriately)	3	2
Units • multiplying quantities • dividing quantities	TRANSFORM	3	2

Source: Jan Christinson, author-consultant.

Essential Questions	Big Ideas
What does it mean to reason with ratios?	Reasoning with ratios involves coordinating two quantities.
What mathematical tools are used to solve real-world ratio problems?	Tables of equivalent ratios, tape diagrams, and double line diagrams are mathematical tools used to solve real-world ratio problems.
What is a unit rate?	A unit rate is a rate that is expressed as a quantity of one.
What information does it provide?	A unit rate describes how many units of the first type of quantity correspond to one unit of the second type of quantity.
What is a percent?	A percent is a ratio that compares a quantity to 100.
How can it be used to solve problems?	A percent can be used to find the whole or given part in a problem situation.

Source: Jan Christinson, author-consultant.

———————— 03 80 ————————

Following the same procedure described in the ELA example, all of these learning elements will now appear together in a boxed set of comprehensive unit learning intentions—with the exception of the supporting standards. However, as indicated in Number 4, key concepts from the supporting standards will be used to identify unit vocabulary terms. These terms, plus those derived from the "unwrapped" Priority Standards concepts in Number 3, will be a key part of the student success criteria.

Remember that teacher teams need to retain their completed graphic organizer as a separate document for reference when designing all of the unit assessment questions (pre-, post-, quick progress checks). These questions must all be directly aligned to the revised Bloom's Taxonomy and DOK levels of cognitive rigor that appear only on the graphic organizer.

Box 6.2 Comprehensive Set of Math Unit Learning Intentions

Priority Standards:

1. Use ratio and rate reasoning to solve real-world and mathematical problems, e.g., by reasoning about tables of equivalent ratios, tape diagrams, double number line diagrams, or equations.

   a. Make tables of equivalent ratios relating quantities with whole number measurements, find missing values in the tables, and plot the pairs of values on the coordinate plane. Use tables to compare ratios.
   b. Solve unit rate problems, including those involving unit pricing and constant speed.
   c. Find a percent of a quantity as a rate per 100 (e.g., 30% of a quantity means 30/100 times the quantity); solve problems involving finding the whole, given a part and the percent.
   d. Use ratio reasoning to convert measurement units; manipulate and transform units appropriately when multiplying or dividing quantities.

2. Define and use the following *Priority Standards* vocabulary terms and phrases appropriately:

   - Reasoning (ratio and rate)
   - Equivalent ratios
   - Tape diagrams
   - Double number line diagrams
   - Equations
   - Missing values

- Pairs on coordinate plane
- Unit rate
- Unit pricing
- Constant speed
- Percent of quantity

3. Define and use the following *supporting standards* vocabulary terms and phrases appropriately:

- Ratio relationship
- Rate language

4. Respond correctly with Big Ideas for the unit's three Essential Questions:

- *What does it mean to reason with ratios? What mathematical tools are used to solve real-world ratio problems?*

Reasoning with ratios involves coordinating two quantities. Tables of equivalent ratios, tape diagrams, and double line diagrams are mathematical tools used to solve real-world ratio problems.

- *What is a unit rate? What information does it provide?*

A unit rate is a rate that is expressed as a quantity of one. A unit rate describes how many units of the first type of quantity correspond to one unit of the second type of quantity.

- *What is a percent? How can it be used to solve problems?*

A percent is a ratio that compares a quantity to 100. A percent can be used to find the whole or given part in a problem situation.

To create the student success criteria, teacher teams now transfer the comprehensive set of unit learning intentions into a three-column chart. As previously described in the ELA section, the Essential Questions appear in the first column, the "unwrapped" Priority Standards appear in the second column, and the vocabulary terms for the unit (derived from the Priority Standards *and* the supporting standards) in the third. The contents of each column are prefaced with performance descriptors in bold type that state what students will be expected to demonstrate.

The Priority Standards, appearing in their "unwrapped" form, will focus students' attention on the key aspects of the standards they will be learning and applying throughout the unit. The underlined concepts and CAPITALIZED skills will also help students see the direct connections between what they are expected to know and be able to do and the unit vocabulary terms they need to learn.

Table 6.2 Learning Intentions as Student Success Criteria for the Math Unit

Essential Questions	Priority Standards	Vocabulary
Respond correctly with your Big Ideas to the unit's three Essential Questions: 1. *What does it mean to reason with ratios? What mathematical tools are used to solve real-world ratio problems?* 2. *What is a unit rate? What information does it provide?* 3. *What is a percent? How can it be used to solve problems?*	**Demonstrate your ability to do each of the following:** 6.RP.A.3 USE ratio and rate reasoning to SOLVE real-world and mathematical problems—by reasoning about tables of equivalent ratios, tape diagrams, double number line diagrams, or equations. a. MAKE tables of equivalent ratios RELATING quantities with whole number measurements, FIND missing values in the tables, and PLOT the pairs of values on the coordinate plane. USE tables to COMPARE ratios. b. SOLVE unit rate problems including those involving unit pricing and constant speed. c. FIND a percent of a quantity as a rate per 100. SOLVE problems involving finding the whole, given a part and the percent. d. USE ratio reasoning to CONVERT measurement units; MANIPULATE and TRANSFORM units appropriately when multiplying or dividing quantities.	**Define and use the unit vocabulary terms appropriately:** • Ratio reasoning • Rate reasoning • Equivalent ratios • Tape diagrams • Double number line diagrams • Equations • Missing values • Pairs on coordinate plane • Unit rate • Unit pricing • Constant speed • Percent of quantity • Ratio relationship • Rate language

PRESENTING THE STUDENT SUCCESS CRITERIA

How do educators present the success criteria to students at the beginning of a new unit of study? Certainly this is up to each teacher to decide, but here are my recommendations for doing so:

1. First set the stage for what students are about to see. Explain to them that the student success criteria represent their learning goals for the new unit that will take place over *several weeks,* not during one week or one class period only!

2. Present one section of the success criteria at a time. First, show students the Essential Questions on one large chart, explaining to the class that by the end of the unit each student will be able to provide a Big Idea response in his or her own words to each of these questions.

3. Next, show students the "unwrapped" Priority Standards concepts and skills on a second chart, explaining that the underlined and capitalized words are what students are going to learn and be able to do throughout the unit.

4. Then, introduce the new unit vocabulary terms on a third chart, explaining to students that they will be learning what each of these terms means and using the terms in their unit lessons and learning activities. Point out that the vocabulary words come directly from the "unwrapped" concepts on the second chart and show them how they correlate.

5. Finally, post the charts in a prominent location in the classroom so that students can daily make connections between what they are learning and the success criteria they are expected to achieve by the end of the unit.

6. Distribute a one-page chart that includes all three columns of the success criteria. Students can keep this chart in their binders to refer to as needed throughout the unit and/or take it home to share with their parents.

After educators complete this "student orientation" to the unit success criteria, it's time to administer the unit pre-CFA (described in Chapter 8). Explain the purpose of the pre-assessment and ask students to complete it to the best of their ability. Reassure students that they are not expected to already know what they are about to learn and that their responses will only be used to help plan instruction.

CHAPTER SUCCESS CRITERIA

Now, please take a few moments and write your responses to the success criteria for this chapter, or simply evaluate your understanding of each mastery statement on a scale of one (low) to five (high). Clarify your understanding of any particular information as needed. Once again, if you are reading this book as part of a professional study group, share your thoughts and ideas with colleagues.

Success Criteria:

- Explain how the unit learning intentions are finalized.
- Summarize how to develop the success criteria for students that parallel the unit learning intentions.
- Describe how to introduce the success criteria to students.

After writing the unit learning intentions as student success criteria, teacher teams are now ready to create their post-CFA questions in multiple formats directly aligned to the "unwrapped" Priority Standards concepts, skills, and levels of cognitive rigor. This is the learning focus of Chapter 7.

7 Writing Assessment Questions in Multiple Formats

In This Chapter You Will Learn:

- Why educators create a multiple-format CFA.
- How to directly align each assessment question to the rigor of the "unwrapped" concepts and skills.
- Helpful guidelines to keep in mind when creating the post-CFA.

In the highlighted fifth step of the CFA 2.0 design process, grade- and course-level teams collaboratively design a post-CFA that includes a blend of questions in the selected-response and constructed-response formats. Specifically, these questions will be in the form of multiple-choice, short-response, *and* extended-response questions. The last section of the CFA will ask students to provide their Big Idea responses to the Essential Questions—another form of short-response question. Every assessment question will *directly align* to one or more of the "unwrapped" Priority Standards concepts, skills, and levels of cognitive rigor. In total, the assessment will address all unit learning intentions and student success criteria.

Figure 7.1 CFA 2.0 Design Step 5

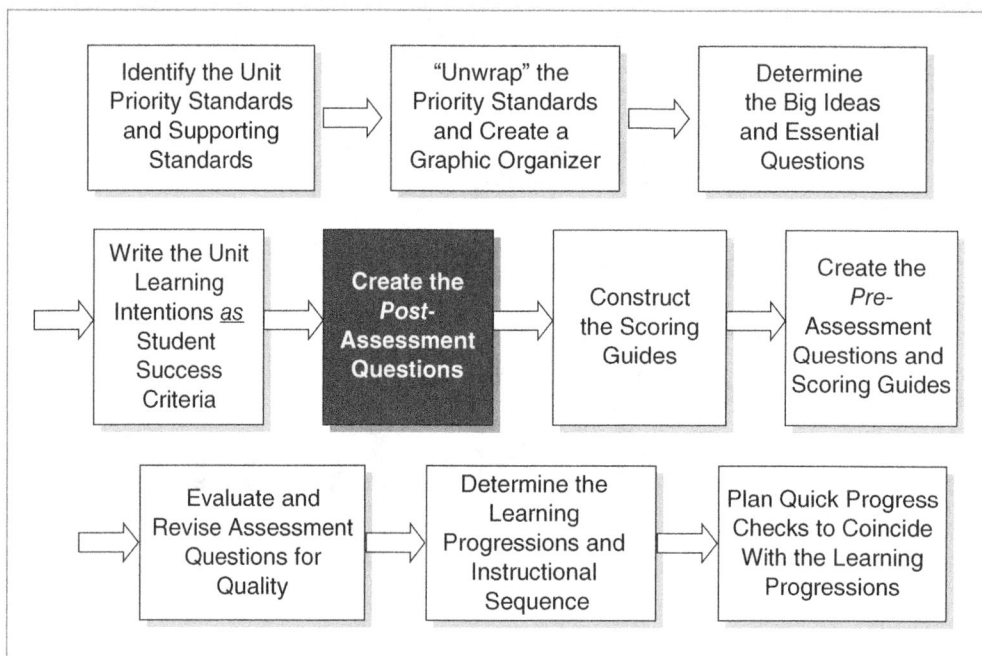

CFA **Design Step 5: Create the** *Post*-**Assessment Questions.** The CFA is a multiple-format assessment that includes a blend of selected-response and constructed-response questions directly aligned to the unit learning intentions ("unwrapped" concepts, skills, corresponding levels of cognitive rigor, targeted vocabulary, Essential Questions, and Big Ideas). When combined together effectively, these assessment formats help educators determine students' overall understanding of the learning intentions in focus during the unit. Beginning with the end in mind, educators create the post-CFA *before they plan instruction* so they have a clear picture of what they want their students to show they have learned by the end of the unit.

BEGIN WITH THE END

Up to this point in the CFA 2.0 design process, we have focused solely on the standards as the foundation for the unit. Now it's time to shift attention to the assessments that will be used to determine student attainment of those standards. We begin with the end—the unit *post*-assessment that the teacher team creates together. By starting with the post-CFA, the educators can then work backwards to write their pre-assessment, determine the instructional sequence of learning progressions, and plan out their quick progress checks. After that, they will be ready to prepare unit instruction, select appropriate curriculum materials, begin teaching the unit, and differentiate ongoing instruction to meet the specific learning needs of all students.

Many educators admit to having had little or no prior training in assessment design. So even if this is also true for you, "No worries!" Constructing the post-CFA is a very linear procedure, and the instructions for doing so are specific and straightforward.

This doesn't mean, however, that it's an easy thing to do. It requires a great deal of thought and collaborative effort to produce a quality assessment, but that's what makes the CFA 2.0 design process a perfect task for teacher teams—everyone has a share in the work. The good news is, like most things in life, the more you do it the easier it gets. However, if this is your first experience designing a CFA, remind yourself as often as needed that you are moving steadily through a new learning curve.

CHARACTERISTICS OF EFFECTIVE CFAS

Quick to Administer, Easy to Process: Because CFAs are *formative,* they need to be fairly quick to administer and easy to process so they can produce timely feedback. Educators need the assessment results immediately to inform next steps in their instructional planning. Students need to know as soon as possible how they are doing so they can decide what adjustments they need to make in their learning strategies.

Clearly Worded Questions: The CFA questions need to be clear and easily understood by students, with no trick questions allowed! The goal is to "test mastery of material, not students' ability to figure out what you're asking" (Stiggins, 1997, p. 134).

Apply Knowledge, Not Just Recall It: Students should not be able to answer from memory; they must be able to *apply* their knowledge, not just recall it. And the questions should be based, in part, on *new* material (i.e., be able to read or interpret a passage of text or a graph they have never seen before) to determine if students can apply or transfer their knowledge and skills to different contexts.

Academic Vocabulary and External Assessment Formats: Effective CFA questions include proper academic vocabulary from the standards—not simplified terms—that students need to learn and are likely to encounter on large-scale assessments. The assessment questions should be written in formats similar to those used on external exams so that students become familiar with the *ways* in which their understanding of the standards will be assessed.

How Many Questions? Educators often want a recommendation of how many questions to include on the post-CFA. There is no hard-and-fast rule in this regard. The number of questions depends on several factors:

- Grade level of the students (lower grades, fewer questions; higher grades, more questions);
- How many standards and learning intentions the unit addresses; and
- Amount of instructional time allocated to each standard or learning intention: "A good guideline is that the percentage of instructional time and the percentage of (related) assessment items should be roughly equal" (Stiggins, Arter, Chappuis, & Chappuis, 2004, p. 114).

Limit the total number of CFA questions to no more than needed. Why give students a 25-question assessment when you can find out what you need to know about student understanding in 5, 10, or 15 questions? A simple guideline to keep in mind is this: "How many questions do we need to be able to make an *accurate inference* or correct interpretation about what students know now and need next in their learning?"

Fair and Bias Free: Lastly, strive to design fair and bias-free questions (no bias based on gender, ethnicity, language, religion, sexual orientation, socioeconomic status, and so on). Make assessment items *valid* (measure what they are supposed to measure) and *reliable* (consistent each time used to assess student understanding of the same learning intentions in the same way). Additional information regarding validity and reliability is presented in Chapter 9.

ROADBLOCKS TO EFFECTIVE ITEM WRITING

W. James Popham (2003) cautions educators to be aware of five roadblocks to effective item writing:

* *Unclear Directions*—Read the test directions from a student's perspective to see if they make sense.

- *Ambiguous Statements*—Replace words having double meanings with single meanings and faulty-reference pronouns with the specific words to which they refer.
- *Unintentional Clues*—Keep answer choices of equal length (not unintentionally making the correct answer the longest) and avoid grammatical tip-offs: a *pachyderm* is <u>an</u> (a) elephant (b) turtle (c) lion (d) pigeon.
- *Complex Phrasing*—Avoid lengthy sentences and strive for simplicity in sentence structure.
- *Difficult Vocabulary*—Use everyday language wherever possible so students can understand the question and concentrate on answering it correctly. (p. 64)

One qualification to make regarding the roadblock of difficult vocabulary: the more difficult standards-derived unit vocabulary terms are an important part of the unit learning intentions and student success criteria. As stated in previous chapters, students should be expected to learn and use these terms appropriately throughout the unit and therefore they should be included on the post-CFA.

THE SELECTED-RESPONSE FORMAT

Many educators rely primarily on **selected-response questions,** which include multiple-choice, matching, true/false, and fill-in items with a provided answer bank. As its name signifies, students are *selecting* their answer from a set of answer choices. This format continues to be favored by many educators for legitimate reasons:

1. *The Time Factor:* Student responses can be scored quickly using an answer key.

2. *Larger Sampling of Standards:* Educators can often assess student understanding of a greater number of standards.

3. *Continuation of Past Practice.* Educators may depend primarily on the selected-response format because it is the format they are most accustomed to using.

THE CONSTRUCTED-RESPONSE FORMAT

Because a student really needs to understand something in order to construct a response based on that understanding, students' responses to these sorts of items will better contribute to *valid inferences* (about their actual levels of mastery) than will students' answers to selected-response items. (Popham, 2003, p. 87)

Whenever a student must produce an answer from his or her own mind, that student is *constructing* a response. **Constructed-response questions** are an essential part of the post-CFA and include both types: short and extended. **Short** constructed responses include individual words, phrases, single sentences, short paragraphs, and computational work. **Extended** constructed responses include multiple sentences or paragraphs, essays, and problem solving with an explanation of steps and/or verification of answer.

Only when students are asked to "show what they know" can educators correctly interpret the depth of their knowledge because what they do or don't know is on full display. Even though it requires additional time to thoughtfully score written responses, that investment of time will always yield valuable insights into student understanding.

REMEMBER YOUR PURPOSE—CHOOSE FORMAT ACCORDINGLY

This is where educators need to be clear about their *purpose* for assessing students. If it is to measure students' concrete, defined knowledge and mental skills, selected-response questions can prove quite effective for doing so. However, accurate inferences are harder to make from students' bubbled-in responses. Students can simply get lucky by selecting correct answers without knowing the content whatsoever. For educators to then conclude that the students "got it" is faulty reasoning.

On the other hand, students live in an education world that continues to rely heavily on the selected-response testing format. Doing away with multiple-choice questions altogether because they do not provide sufficient insights into student understanding would be a great disservice to students who must continue taking multiple-choice standardized achievement tests each year. CFAs provide students with regular opportunities throughout the school year to practice answering questions in that format.

If the purpose of assessment is to gain qualitative feedback (credible and convincing evidence) about students' ability to, for example, write a paragraph or explain a problem-solving process—both complex abilities—then a constructed-response question is the only appropriate format to use.

The bottom line is this: no single assessment format is appropriate for evaluating every type of student learning to be measured. Each assessment format has its own benefits and drawbacks. Both formats are necessary.

Know your purpose and choose your assessment format accordingly. Here are a few pros and cons to keep in mind when doing so.

SELECTED-RESPONSE FORMAT: PROS AND CONS

In his book *Writing Test Items to Evaluate Higher-Order Thinking* (1997), Thomas Haladyna points out a few of the benefits and drawbacks—pros and cons—to using the selected-response format:

Pros

- *Broader Sampling of the Content Area*—Students can answer more multiple-choice items covering more content in the same amount of time it would take them to complete one or two constructed-response questions.
- *Higher Reliability*—Multiple-choice questions tend to produce greater consistency and dependability of student responses over time than constructed-response questions addressing the same content.
- *Greater Efficiency*—"The effort you put into writing test items as well as the time spent administering and scoring the test is part of its efficiency. [When comparing both formats in this regard,] multiple-choice is probably more efficient" (pp. 65–66).
- *Objectivity*—Multiple-choice questions will be scored the same by different people whereas scoring students' constructed-response questions will be more subjective. "Objectivity/subjectivity relates to reliability. The more subjective the scoring process [even with the use of a rubric], the larger the error component in test scores is likely to be" (p. 66).
- *Measurability for Higher-Level Thinking*—Constructed-response questions to measure higher-level thinking may be easier to write, but selected-response questions can and should be written to assess students' higher-level thinking. They are not limited to assessing recall of information or memorization only.
- *Mechanical Scoring*—Student responses can be rapidly and accurately scored to provide teachers and students quick feedback from the results.

Cons

- *Emphasis on Learning Isolated Facts*—If educators write selected-response questions to assess lower-level recall only, "Multiple-choice testing can lead to multiple-choice teaching," according to Lori Shepard (cited in Haladyna, 1997).

- *Inappropriate for Some Purposes*—specifically, writing and creative thinking.
- *Lack of Student Writing*—unless intentionally part of assessment design.

CONSTRUCTED-RESPONSE FORMAT: PROS AND CONS

Benefits and drawbacks to using the constructed-response format (applicable to both short- and extended-response questions) include the following:

Pros

- Typically more cognitively challenging than selected-response questions;
- Students *generate* a response of their own, not simply select one;
- More effective for revealing student thinking; provides authentic evidence of learning; makes possible deeper insights into student understanding than may be incorrectly inferred from selected-response items;
- More likely used to inform instructional next steps;
- Usually easier to write than higher-level selected-response questions;
- Good source of common student errors and misconceptions to use as distracters in multiple-choice questions;
- Several "unwrapped" concepts and skills from the unit Priority Standards/learning intentions can often be measured with one or two constructed-response questions.

Cons

- Greater expenditure of time required to score student responses;
- More difficult to accurately score—even with scoring guide—due to personal interpretation of the response by the evaluator;
- Highly subjective wording in scoring guides caused by overuse of adverbs and adjectives (e.g., *clearly/generally/partially* describes the main idea of the passage; *limited* or *little* understanding of the problem);
- Lack of student writing ability may mask what students actually understand but cannot effectively communicate.

START WITH SELECTED-RESPONSE FORMAT

When teacher teams are ready to create their end-of-unit CFA, they start with the selected-response format. Even though the other types of selected-response questions (matching, true/false, choosing answer from provided word bank) have their own inherent value, the focus in the CFA 2.0 process is on the effective design of multiple-choice questions.

Multiple-choice questions are fairly easy to write if they target *lower-level* thinking skills (i.e., recall of information, memorized knowledge). More challenging to write are multiple-choice questions that assess students' higher-level thinking skills (i.e., analysis, synthesis, and evaluation of content).

It bears frequent repeating that the rigor of each question must match the rigor of the targeted skill. If, for example, the skill requires students to "analyze" or "evaluate," the assessment question must reflect that same higher level of cognition, not one that asks students merely to "recall" or "compare." The majority of "unwrapped" concepts and skills in the Priority Standards, especially those from the Common Core, are rigorous and representative of deep versus surface learning. For this reason teacher teams will need to devote sufficient thought and energy to the writing of higher-level questions in the multiple-choice format.

Each multiple-choice question includes the question stem with four answer choices—one correct response and three distracters. Distracters are incorrect answer choices. They should all be plausible so that students cannot easily eliminate any of them. A key recommendation is to include distracters that represent common student errors or misconceptions. When students incorrectly select an answer choice that is a common error, educators can use that feedback diagnostically to determine what misconceptions the students are having and then adjust instruction to correct them.

WRITE THE QUESTION STEM

When your team is ready to create a multiple-choice question, look at your graphic organizer and choose one "unwrapped" concept and matching skill. Note the pre-assigned levels of the revised Bloom's Taxonomy and Webb's Depth of Knowledge. Think about the meaning of the *skill*, and practice writing a multiple-choice question stem.

For example, if the reading skill is "DETERMINE" and the related concept is "<u>author's point of view</u>," the question stem could simply combine the two in reference to a reading passage and be worded like this: "In the article/story you just read, which of the following *best* represents the author's point of view?"

To determine the author's point of view is a Bloom's level 4 and DOK level 2 thinking skill. It requires the student to *analyze* and *infer*. The sample question above reflects this—particularly because of the words "best represents." The student must first understand what the author's point of view is (understanding) and then determine which of the four answer choices best expresses that point of view (analysis, inference).

WRITE THE ANSWER CHOICES

Next write the correct answer and three distracters (incorrect but plausible choices). Normally, this is the process to follow when writing each of the possible answer choices. When using the word *best* in the question stem, however, *all* of the answer choices must be correct, but only one of them is the best choice. Writing a question stem this way bumps up the rigor because students will need to think about each answer choice and determine which answer is the best of the four.

For example, here is a question directly aligned to the Priority Standard above it that asks students to best support their answer to a *previous* question (not shown here):

RI.4.1 REFER to <u>details and examples in a text</u> when explaining what the text says explicitly and when DRAWING <u>inferences</u> from the text.

1. Which of the following statements *best supports* your answer to the previous question?

   a. A study found that most of the foods advertised on these shows are very unhealthy.
   b. Some people think kids would be healthier if they saw fewer junk-food ads.
   c. Consumers should study both sides of the debate and decide.
   d. Many teens love chips, candy, and soda.

Source: 5th Grade Curriculum Design Team, San Diego Unified School District, San Diego, CA.

All four answer choices can be considered correct statements, but which choice best supports the student's answer to the question before it? To answer, the student must reread that previous question, the related reading passage, and his or her answer choice to decide which answer option best supports that choice.

Compared to the ordinary kind of multiple-choice questions of the past where there was one correct answer, one *nearly* correct answer (often referred to as the "attractive distracter"), and two easy-to-eliminate answer choices, this is a more rigorous question that will require deeper thought on the part of the student—and it will reflect the rigor of the targeted standard.

This is not to say that every multiple-choice CFA question your team writes must include the word *best* in the stem or must refer to a previous question. Yet large-scale assessments—particularly those developed by the Smarter Balanced Assessment Consortium (SBAC) and the Partnership for Assessment of Readiness for College and Careers (PARCC)—are including this more challenging type of multiple-choice question.

MULTIPLE-CHOICE EXAMPLES FROM ELA AND MATH UNIT LEARNING INTENTIONS

Shown here are four multiple-choice questions aligned to the English language arts and math learning intentions that were presented in the previous chapter. Note the direct alignment between each question and the "unwrapped" concept(s), skills, and levels of the revised Bloom's Taxonomy and Webb's DOK. The entire Priority Standard appears in bold type and is the assessment focus of each question.

Every CFA question does not need to assess student understanding of the entire standard, however. Some questions may only apply to certain underlined phrases and capitalized verbs. Other questions may address a few concepts and skills in the related supporting standard even though the primary focus remains on the "unwrapped" Priority Standard.

Accompanying each question is a "distracter analysis" that explains *why* the distracters are incorrect. This is very helpful for educators to think through while they are creating their assessment questions and answer choices. It will help them more quickly interpret the errors students make on the post-CFA and adjust follow-up instruction accordingly while students are "on the Bridge" at the end of the unit.

English Language Arts Multiple-Choice Examples With Distracter Analyses

Students will read two informational text passages (not included here due to their length) about Rosa Parks and then answer the related questions. Here are the online links to those passages and closely approximated lexile levels:

Rosa Parks

http://www.ncsu.edu/project/lancet/fifth.htm

Lexile Level 940L

Rosa Parks: The Story Behind the Bus

http://www.thehenryford.org/exhibits/rosaparks/story.asp

Lexile Level 1000L

Reading Question #1

(Priority Standard) RI.5.6 ANALYZE <u>multiple accounts of the same event or topic</u>, NOTING important <u>similarities and differences</u> in the <u>point of view they represent</u>.

(Supporting Standard) RI.5.8 Explain how an author uses reasons and evidence to support particular points in a text, **<u>identifying which reasons and evidence support which point(s)</u>**.

What evidence <u>best</u> supports Rosa Parks being called the "mother of the civil rights movement"?

   a. Rosa Parks rode a segregated bus and was arrested.
   b. Her arrest started nonviolent protests to support civil rights in the United States.
   c. Rosa Parks was awarded the Congressional Gold Medal.
   d. Rosa Parks refused to give up her bus seat to a white man.

Distracter Analysis:

   a. This is an accurate detail from the two texts but not enough to support the claim.
   b. <u>This is the best response as it is a main point of both passages.</u>
   c. This is an accurate detail from the first reading passage but not enough to support the claim.
   d. Her action was a catalyst for the boycott moving the Civil Rights Movement forward, but this is not the *best* response.

Reading Question #2

(Priority Standard) RI.5.6 ANALYZE <u>multiple accounts of the same event or topic</u>, NOTING important <u>similarities and differences</u> in the <u>point of view they represent</u>.

(Supporting Standard) RI.5.8 Explain how an author uses reasons and evidence to support particular points in a text, **identifying which reasons and evidence support which point(s).**

Which point-of-view statement can be supported in BOTH reading passages?

    a. Rosa Parks purposefully did not to give up her seat on the bus to support the boycott.

    b. Rosa Parks and her actions played an important role in the civil rights movement.

    c. Rosa Parks encouraged Martin Luther King, Jr., to organize the Montgomery Bus Boycott.

    d. Transportation was the most challenging place to enforce segregation of blacks and whites.

Distracter Analysis:

    a. Rosa Parks did not do what she did because the boycott was taking place. Her actions *initiated* the boycott.

    b. Correct: Authors of both texts demonstrate her pivotal role in the civil rights movement.

    c. Martin Luther King was selected by other ministers and activists to lead the boycott, not Rosa Parks.

    d. This statement is clearly indicated in the second passage, but would need to be deduced from a close reading of the first.

Source: Tracey Shiel, author-consultant.

Math Multiple-Choice Examples With Distracter Analyses

In the following two math examples, the format differs slightly from the ELA examples. The term *distracter analysis* is replaced by the statement, "Incorrect answers may indicate the following about student understanding." This statement underscores the purpose of assessment, which is to correctly interpret student understanding.

Math Question #4

(Priority Standard) 6.RP.3b SOLVE unit rate problems including those involving unit pricing and constant speed ("constant speed" not the assessment focus in this question).

A 24-pound bag of dog food sells for $10.56. What is the unit price per pound?

    a. $.44/pound
    b. $.53/pound
    c. $13.44/pound
    d. $34.56/pound

Correct answer: a

Incorrect answers may indicate the following about student understanding:

Answer b shows calculation error and incorrect division.

Answers c and d indicate the student has not reasoned that the answer needs to be less than $1.00. Student selection of either of these two answer choices shows a lack of number sense and/or the ability to determine a reasonable answer. Student does not understand the concept of unit rate.

Math Question #6

(Priority) 6.RP.3c FIND <u>a percent of a quantity as a rate per 100;</u> SOLVE problems involving finding the whole, given a part and the percent.

At a local zoo, 12 iguanas represent 30% of the total iguana population. What is the total iguana population at the local zoo?

    a. 12
    b. 30
    c. 40
    d. 360

Correct answer: c

Incorrect answers may indicate the following about student understanding:

Answers a and b might indicate that the student is just using answers listed in the problem. It is likely student does not understand the problem.

Answer d is the most common mistake and indicates that the student is multiplying the numbers listed in the problem. This choice demonstrates a lack of number sense or a sense of what quantity would be reasonable as an answer.

Source: Jan Christinson, author-consultant.

SHORT CONSTRUCTED-RESPONSE QUESTIONS

After writing the first-draft multiple-choice questions, the teacher team shifts its focus to creating the **short** constructed-response questions. One benefit of this format is that a single constructed-response question can often be used to assess student understanding of several skill-concept pairs, as shown in bold print just before each question in the two examples below. Again, these questions are aligned to the same ELA and math learn-ing intentions and associated levels of cognitive rigor presented in the previous chapter.

The commentary that follows each of the two questions below should be developed by the teacher team in conjunction with the writing of the questions, just as the distracter analyses are developed in conjunction with the creation of the multiple-choice questions. After scoring the assessments, team members will reference these commentaries that include the elements of a correct response to help correctly interpret student learning needs and then adjust follow-up instruction accordingly.

English Language Arts Example

(Priority Standard) RI.5.6 ANALYZE <u>multiple accounts of the same event or topic</u>, NOTING important <u>similarities and differences</u> in the <u>point of view they represent</u>.

(Supporting Standard) RI.5.8 Explain how an author uses reasons and evidence to support particular points in a text, **<u>identifying which reasons and evidence support which point(s)</u>.**

How does the portrayal of Rosa Parks by the author of the first passage differ from the author of the second passage? Use evidence from the two passages to support your response.

> **Commentary (In paragraph form here; a <u>bulleted</u> format of same content could be easier to refer to when processing student responses):**

In the first passage, Rosa Parks is portrayed as a simple working-woman. The author shares limited background information— only that she grew up in Tuskegee, Alabama, and that she worked as a seamstress in Montgomery when she got older. The second pas-sage portrays her as a black woman actively engaged in the Civil Rights Movement who worked as a seamstress and who appealed her conviction leading to the U.S. Supreme Court decision to rule segregation as being unconstitutional.

Another difference could be that the first article focuses on Rosa Parks's recognitions earned from her actions in the Civil Rights Movement. These recognitions include being awarded the Presidential Medal of Freedom and the Congressional Gold Medal. The second passage focuses on Rosa Parks's specific action of refusing to give up her seat on the bus and how she became the woman that lawyers chose to support in order to challenge the segregation laws.

Short Constructed-Response Math Example

6.RP.3a MAKE tables of equivalent ratios RELATING quantities with whole number measurements, FIND missing values in the tables, and plot the pairs of values on the coordinate plane. Use tables to compare ratios.

The table below shows equivalent ratios to 7:5.

Fill in the missing values.

7	5
21	
	20
35	
	30

Explain how you determined the missing values: _____

_____

_____

_____

_____

Correct answer: Student completes the table by adding the following numbers in **bold** type.

7	5
21	**15**
28	20
35	**25**
42	30

Commentary (Again, a bulleted format with the same elements of a correct response could be easier to refer to when processing student responses):

Students must explain how they used the relationship between the numbers at the top of each column and the numbers below to determine the missing values. For example, 21 is 3 × 7, so the number below 5 would be 3 × 5, which equals 15.

Note the part of the same standard that was *not* underlined and assessed in the above question: "Plot the pairs of values on the coordinate plane." A second short-response question would be added to ask students to "show each ordered pair from the table correctly plotted on the coordinate grid."

A third question would target the last sentence of the standard, "Use tables to compare ratios," by asking students to create a second table of equivalent ratios and then compare it to the first one shown above.

In this way, three short constructed-response questions would effectively assess student understanding of the entire Priority Standard in focus.

FLEXIBILITY IN FORMATTING

Even though educators often separate the multiple-choice section from the short constructed-response section, formatting of the CFA should be flexible and dependent on what makes the most sense. Often teams position their short constructed-response questions right after the related selected-response questions. For example, a math multiple-choice question stem and answer choices can be immediately followed by a short constructed-response prompt that states, "Show your work" or "Verify your answer mathematically." Doing so will reveal students' actual understanding of the concepts and skills in focus far better than an isolated multiple-choice question that the student may simply have guessed at. Discuss as a team whether to separate the multiple-choice questions from the short constructed-response items or to blend them together.

THE EXTENDED-RESPONSE QUESTION

The great benefit to creating one comprehensive **extended**-response question is that it can effectively assess student comprehension of most, if not *all*, of the unit's "unwrapped" concepts, skills, and levels of rigor. Presenting students with a rich, multifaceted question can lead to a huge payoff in revealing the depth and breadth of student understanding. It's a powerful way for educators to see their full impact on student learning and for students to see how much they have learned during the course of the unit.

English Language Arts Extended-Response Question

The English language arts learning intentions used throughout this book to illustrate the CFA 2.0 design process are based on a combination of one Priority Standard in reading and four Priority Standards in writing. The extended-response question from this CFA is a writing prompt that directly aligns to *all* four of the "unwrapped" writing Priority Standards. And because students must reference *both* reading passages in their responses, the extended-response question also targets the full reading standard. Note the specific success criteria in the bulleted directions.

W.5.1 WRITE <u>opinion pieces</u> on topics or texts. SUPPORT a <u>point of view with reasons and information</u>.

W.5.1a INTRODUCE a <u>topic</u> or text clearly, STATE an <u>opinion</u>, and CREATE an <u>organizational structure</u> in which <u>ideas are logically grouped to support the writer's purpose</u>.

W.5.1b PROVIDE <u>logically ordered reasons</u> that are <u>supported by facts and details</u>.

W.5.1d PROVIDE a <u>concluding statement</u> or <u>section related to the opinion presented</u>.

RI.5.6 ANALYZE <u>multiple accounts of the same event or topic</u>, NOTE important <u>similarities and differences</u> in the <u>point of view they represent</u>.

Using information from both reading passages, write a three- to five-paragraph opinion piece that explains whether or not you agree that Rosa Parks should be considered the "mother of the Civil Rights Movement." In your response, be sure to

- *State your point of view*
- *Support your point of view with reasons and information from reading passages 1 and 2*
- *Include a clear introduction*
- *Organize your ideas logically to support your opinion*
- *Use unit vocabulary terms in your writing*
- *Include a concluding statement related to your opinion*

Math Extended-Response Question

The learning intentions and student success criteria for the math unit state that students need to demonstrate understanding and application of the mathematical concepts, skills, and the correct use of vocabulary related to rates and ratios. The following extended-response problem-solving question for this unit includes multiple parts. Taken as a whole, it effectively "nails" nearly all of the underlined concepts and CAPITALIZED skills. Any concepts not addressed in this one extended-response question are assessed in either the multiple-choice and/or the short constructed-response sections of the post-CFA.

Question 10 Extended-Response Problem Solving

6.RP.3 USE ratio and rate reasoning to SOLVE real-world mathematical problems, e.g., by REASONING about tables of equivalent ratios, tape diagrams, double number line diagrams, or equations.

6.RP.3a MAKE tables of equivalent ratios relating quantities with whole number measurements, FIND missing values in the tables, and PLOT the pairs of values on the coordinate plane. Use tables to compare ratios.

6.RP.3b SOLVE unit rate problems including those involving unit pricing and constant speed.

6.RP.3c FIND a percent of a quantity as a rate per 100; SOLVE problems involving finding the whole, given a part and the percent.

6.RP.3d USE ratio reasoning to CONVERT measurement units; MANIPULATE and TRANSFORM units appropriately when MULTIPLYING or DIVIDING quantities.

Thunder and Lightning

Thunder and lightning have a relationship that can be used to determine your distance from a lightning strike.

When you see the flash of a lightning bolt you can start counting by seconds until you hear thunder. If it takes 10 seconds to hear the thunder, the lightning struck 2 miles away.

1. *John is standing in the middle of a field and sees the flash of a lightning bolt. He counts to 15 seconds. How far away from John is the lightning strike? Show your work.*

2. *Identify the unit rate for thunder and lightning strikes. What does the unit rate mean?*

3. *Create a table that shows equivalent ratios for the relationship between thunder and lightning strikes from 0 seconds to 25 seconds.*

4. *Use the values in the table in Number 3 to graph the relationship between thunder and lightning on the coordinate plane.*

5. *Determine the number of seconds that John counted before he heard the thunder if he was 10 miles away from the lightning strike. Explain your answer using ratio ideas.*

6. *Sound travels at the speed of 1,087 feet per second.*

   How far would a sound travel in 5 seconds?

   Write a ratio for the speed of sound.

   Use the ratio to answer the question.

7. *If the lightning strike was 3 miles from John, how many feet away was John?*

   How many yards away was John?

   Use ratio ideas to find your answers. Show your work.

8. *John lives in Oklahoma where there are numerous lightning strikes in a month. One day there were 84 lightning strikes where John lived. If the 84 lightning strikes represented 12% of the total lightning strikes for the month, how many lightning strikes were there for the month?*

   Show that your answer is correct. Show all of your work.

This one extended-response question with multiple parts is purposely designed to simulate a real-life math problem-solving situation. It may appear too ambitious or challenging for sixth-grade students to tackle in an on-demand assessment situation. But it is not. Students *can* solve this kind of rigorous multistep math question when educators give them the math tools for doing so, along with multiple opportunities to succeed through trial and error. The message to students must be: "If you follow these steps, you *can* do this."

Keep in mind that students will be acquiring the ability to answer this kind of multiple-part problem in increments throughout the unit. By working backwards from the unit learning intentions, the team will lay out the sequence of learning progressions (building blocks of instruction), plan the related classroom learning activities, and create the quick progress checks.

Several of these quick progress checks will be individual parts of this kind of multistep problem. As teachers scaffold instruction throughout the duration of the unit and regularly check on student progress, students will be generating several pieces of concrete evidence that they are achieving the unit's success criteria. In this way, by the end of the unit they will be prepared to show all they have learned to do incrementally by applying their learning in an integrated way to this one extended-response question.

BIG IDEA RESPONSES TO ESSENTIAL QUESTIONS

The last section of the post-CFA is the easiest for educators to write. All they need to do is copy the Essential Questions from the unit learning intentions and student success criteria and paste them into the last section of the post-CFA document, leaving space between each question for students to provide their Big Idea responses. By responding to the unit's Essential Questions with their own Big Ideas—gradually acquired as the unit begins, continues, and concludes—students will produce the final piece of evidence that they have achieved or exceeded all of the success criteria for the unit.

DOUBLE CHECK

When teams are finished drafting all of their post-CFA questions, they need to make sure that all of the "unwrapped" concepts and skills and unit learning intentions are sufficiently represented in the collection of questions. Again, some of these elements will be assessed with multiple-choice questions, some with short-response questions, and many included in the one extended-response question. But this intentional match-up between all of the learning intentions and all of the assessment questions must be confirmed to ensure full alignment. In this way, the post-CFA serves as a *quality* assessment that is sure to provide credible evidence of student learning.

IMPLICATIONS FOR ENGLISH LANGUAGE LEARNERS

In her excellent book, *Common Formative Assessments for English Language Learners* (2012), Rachel Syrja offers guidance for teacher teams to keep in mind when using common formative assessments with ELLs:

When differentiating common formative assessments, teachers of English learners must be sure to simplify the language of the assessment enough so that the students can comprehend the task or assignment. When scoring the assessment, teachers also need to be sure to score English learners on the content of their responses and not on their use of the English language. . . . Students learning a second language need a variety of ways to demonstrate their understanding of concepts that are not wholly reliant on advanced language skills. This allows the English learners, particularly at the earliest levels of language acquisition, to demonstrate what they know about the topic. It allows teachers to provide feedback to English learners that helps them close the gap between where they are in the learning continuum and where they need to be. (p. 52)

MAKING CONNECTIONS TO LARGE-SCALE ASSESSMENTS

As pointed out in Chapter 2, teacher teams can benefit from a careful analysis of their state or provincial large-scale assessment questions. By studying how the external tests are formatted, the kind of vocabulary they use, and the levels of rigor they represent, teams can reflect that design in their own assessment questions.

Regarding the U.S. assessments created by the two assessment consortia, Smarter Balanced (SBAC) and PARCC, those test developers have posted sample multiple-choice, constructed-response, and performance-task questions at benchmark grades to familiarize teams in Common Core states with the types of questions their students will encounter. Educators who seek to incorporate or reflect these formats in their formative assessment design are using this information to their students' advantage. To access these sample questions, please refer again to the online links presented at the end of Chapter 3.

WHY ALIGN TO EXTERNAL ASSESSMENT FORMATS?

This idea of deliberately designing CFA questions to align with large-scale assessment formats may initially offend educators' professional sensibilities, and even add fuel to the already smoldering fire of their feeling at times like a "test-prep factory." Yet to be clear: this is not an endorsement for *teaching to the test* (providing students with leading hints to help them select or provide correct answers). Rather it is a recommendation to become aware of how those standardized achievement-test questions are written, so as to prepare students for how they will be expected to show what they have learned on those external exams.

Why do this? Ask teachers how often they have seen students successfully show their understanding of a concept in the classroom but then be unable to *transfer* their understanding of that concept to a new and unfamiliar format—particularly the annual, high-stakes assessment.

Students need to know the specific "rules of the game" and then practice those rules all "season" long. This logic applies to many testing situations in life (e.g., taking a practice driver's license written test as preparation for the similar licensing exam). Why shouldn't it also apply to assessment design in education? "Students, here is what you need to know and be able to do, and this is how you will be expected to show what you have learned during the 'big game' at the end of the year." Such fair disclosure promotes equity for all students, levels the "playing field," and gives everyone a better chance to "win."

ANSWER KEY AND SCORING GUIDES

To complete the post-CFA, the teacher team now needs to prepare an answer key for the multiple-choice questions and write the scoring guides (rubrics) for the constructed-response questions.

Preparing the answer key is something educators are quite adept at doing. Yet creating the scoring guides to quickly and accurately assess students' written responses has proven to be problematic. Often educators use rubrics from outside sources (textbooks, curricular programs, online tools) that are filled with vague and imprecise terminology. In the next chapter, you will learn how teacher teams create objectively worded scoring guides directly matched to the specific constructed-response questions. These scoring guides will provide students with the *details* of the success criteria and help them know up front how their responses will be evaluated.

CHAPTER SUCCESS CRITERIA

Before beginning Chapter 8, please take a few moments and write your responses to the success criteria for this chapter, or simply evaluate your understanding of each performance statement on a scale of one (low) to five (high). Close any learning gaps you may have by rereading or talking with a colleague. As suggested at the conclusion of prior chapters, if you are reading this book as part of a professional study group, share your thoughts and ideas with colleagues.

Success Criteria:

- Explain the rationale for creating a multiple-format CFA.
- Describe how to directly align each assessment question to the rigor of the "unwrapped" concepts and skills.
- Summarize one or two guidelines you found especially helpful to keep in mind when creating the post-CFA.

8 Scoring Guides: *Detailed* Success Criteria

In This Chapter You Will Learn:

- The rationale and key points to consider when creating scoring guides.
- How to write scoring guides as *detailed* success criteria specific to the constructed-response questions on the post-CFA.
- What to consider when designing the *pre*-CFA.

In the highlighted sixth step of the CFA 2.0 design process, grade- and course-level teams collaboratively create scoring guides—*detailed* success criteria specific to the constructed-response questions. In the seventh step, they design the pre-CFA directly matched to the post-CFA so that improvement in student learning from the beginning to the end of the unit can be reliably determined. Students receive the scoring guides *before* beginning the pre- or post-CFAs, so they are able to refer to the criteria while responding to the constructed-response assessment questions.

WHY SCORING GUIDES?

Detailed **scoring guides** make the performance expectations of success criteria explicit. They communicate in specific, objective terms exactly what students need to include in their constructed responses on the CFA

132

Figure 8.1 CFA 2.0 Design Steps 6 and 7

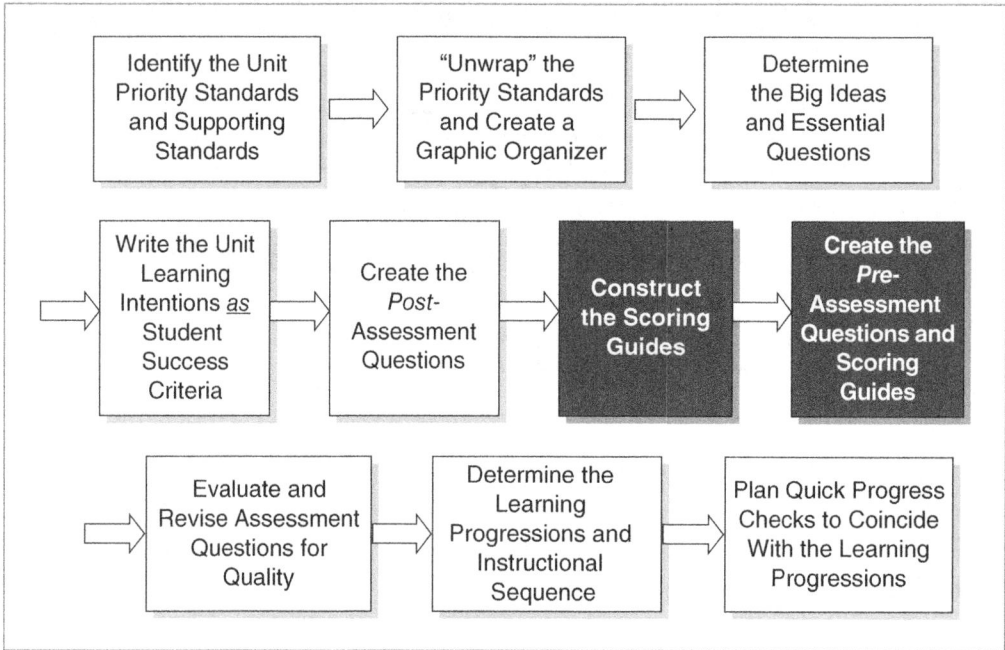

Identify the Unit Priority Standards and Supporting Standards	"Unwrap" the Priority Standards and Create a Graphic Organizer	Determine the Big Ideas and Essential Questions

Write the Unit Learning Intentions *as* Student Success Criteria	Create the *Post*-Assessment Questions	Construct the Scoring Guides	Create the *Pre*-Assessment Questions and Scoring Guides

Evaluate and Revise Assessment Questions for Quality	Determine the Learning Progressions and Instructional Sequence	Plan Quick Progress Checks to Coincide With the Learning Progressions

to show they have achieved the learning intentions upon which the assessment questions are based.

For example, one of the success criteria for this chapter is, "Explain how to write the scoring guides as *detailed* success criteria specific to constructed-response questions." By itself, this one performance statement is insufficient for communicating exactly what the reader's response should include. Details are needed. The response must include how to

- Match the criteria in the scoring guide to the directions of the task.
- Make certain all of the criteria are objectively worded.
- Provide explanations to clarify key points.
- Describe the differences between scoring guides for short- and extended-response questions.
- Specify how to go "above and beyond" the task directions to produce an advanced response.

Scoring guides show students how to succeed by explaining in plain language what is expected. Shared with students up front, the scoring criteria serve as reference points to help students make sure they have carried out all the directions stated in the task.

Well-crafted scoring guides greatly expedite the fair and accurate scoring of students' constructed responses that typically take much longer to score than multiple-choice items do. This is a great benefit to busy teachers who need immediate feedback for informing next-day instructional planning and to students who can reflect on their performance while it's still fresh in their minds and make immediate adjustments in their learning tactics.

AVOID SUBJECTIVE LANGUAGE

Scoring guides, when written effectively, demystify for students and teachers alike the often murky expectations for "a job well done." The problem with most scoring guides (rubrics) is their subjectivity. The language descriptors are so vague and general that educators and students cannot help but interpret them differently. Therefore, the most important direction to keep in mind when writing scoring guides is to *avoid subjective language.*

For example, here is a four-level rubric that is permeated with subjectivity, as shown by the underlined terms (in the performance level headings and double bullets):

4. *Demonstrates Complete Understanding*

   •• Demonstrates internalized understanding of major content and concepts
   •• Communicates clearly and with originality

3. *Demonstrates Adequate Understanding*

   •• Demonstrates general understanding of most major content and concepts
   •• Communicates successfully

2. *Demonstrates Limited Understanding*

   •• Demonstrates partial understanding of major content and concepts
   •• Communicates on a limited basis

1. *Demonstrates Little or No Understanding*

   •• Shows little, if any, understanding of major content and concepts
   •• Attempts to communicate

When creating scoring guides, educators are cautioned against using words such as "some, few, good, many, most, little, creative," and any of the other underlined terms in the above example (Ainsworth, 2008, p. 89).

Such descriptors convey ambiguity rather than clarity. Instead, strive to use language that is observable by and understandable to everyone—students, teachers, parents, and administrators. Write the scoring guide criteria so that each phrase directly links to the constructed-response directions. In this way, everyone can share a common understanding: "This is what the students need to include in their response, and this is how it will be scored."

If a subjective term is to be included in a scoring guide, make sure there is consistent understanding between and among the educators and students about what that term means, providing an example that represents it. The potential of scoring guides to help students understand and achieve performance expectations lies in direct proportion to the objectivity of the language descriptors used.

A FEW DECISIONS FIRST

Before creating the scoring guides, the grade- or course-level teams of educators need to make a few decisions. They can decide these matters on their own as an individual team or, as is the case in most schools, decide them with the entire faculty. Doing so promotes greater consistency and familiarity with the scoring guide formats, language, and performance levels—not only among the educators but particularly among the students as they advance from grade to grade and course to course.

Here are six key issues to discuss and agree upon prior to designing the scoring guides for the CFA 2.0 constructed-response questions.

1. Definition of Proficiency. The term *proficiency* has been in widespread use for a number of years. Yet it is a problematic choice of label for the desired level of student performance because it means different things to different people. Ask any group of educators to generate a list of synonyms for the word *proficient* and the results will look something like this: competent, adequate, meets expectations, minimal, satisfactory, good, basic, mastery.

What level of achievement should students aim for? Educators need to decide where to set the bar for a desired student performance. One effective way to resolve this is to look at examples of student responses to constructed-response questions that fulfill the task requirements. Ask, "If students correctly include in their responses everything the question requires, like we see in these papers, what should we call that? Proficient? Meets Expectations? Mastery?" Discuss different terms and strive to reach an initial consensus on the term everyone agrees to use. Then "table the conversation" until the other performance levels are discussed and tentatively titled.

2. Number of Performance Levels. How many performance levels will you include on your scoring guides? For short constructed-response scoring guides, educators tend to favor three levels that categorize answers as being correct, partially correct, or incorrect. Because the student responses are short, the use of three levels makes scoring them a fairly quick process.

The usual number of performance levels for extended-response questions is four, which spans the range of student responses from minimum to maximum in terms of quality and quantity. Rather than requiring four performance levels, however, consider starting with only two—one for the "achieves goal" level and the other for the "above and beyond" level. This keeps students' focus fixed on the desired result. Then decide what to do about the performance levels for student responses that do not achieve the goal criteria.

3. Names of Performance Levels. What performance level names will you and your colleagues choose? Because of the variance in agreement as to the meaning of the word *proficiency*, consider a level name that more effectively communicates what the desired level of performance is. *Goal*, for example, is a good choice because most adults and children share a common understanding of what that word means. Many educators prefer numerical names for the levels, such as "3-2-1" for short constructed-response questions or "4-3-2-1" for extended-response questions. Perhaps you want to use a phrase such as "Achieves Success Criteria," followed by a colon. Then list the specific performance expectations below it, each preceded by an open box symbol that can be checked when included in the response. It's also important to show students on the scoring guide how they can excel. The phrase "Exceeds Success Criteria" represents this level and provides the specific criteria of how to do so. The choice is yours! Just remember to keep the focus on where you want students to perform: "at the goal" and "beyond the goal" levels.

4. Holistic or Analytic Format. The scoring guide for the extended-response question can be written in either a *holistic* format (all criteria listed beneath each level) or in an *analytic* format (chart with specific criteria for several different categories, like those used for the traits of writing: ideas, organization, voice, conventions, and so on). The majority of educators and students prefer the holistic format; it's efficient, and less wordy than the analytic format while still including all needed criteria.

5. Blend of Quantitative and Qualitative Criteria. Scoring guides include a blend of *quantitative* criteria ("Includes <u>3</u> supporting details" or "Provides <u>2</u> examples from the text") and *qualitative* criteria ("Solves the equation with graphic representation" or "Compares main character to supporting character, noting similarities and differences"). A student who can achieve either of these criteria is demonstrating quality that is both objective and observable.

It's much easier to write quantitative criteria because this only requires the insertion of a specific number or quantity into the criteria ("includes at least <u>2</u> mathematical operations"). Qualitative criteria, however, must describe quality without resorting to subjective terms ("includes <u>elaborative</u> use of literary devices" or "provides <u>effective</u> and <u>comprehensive</u> explanation of the story's theme"). It's more challenging to describe quality objectively so students can produce it. The most effective way to do this is by referring to examples of student work. Identify the desired quality elements in student work products and then strive to describe those elements in specific words that students would use and understand. (How educators involve students in scoring guide design is presented later in the chapter.)

6. Task Specific or Generic. A scoring guide is either *task specific* (written for the specific requirements of a particular constructed-response question), or *generic* (written for frequent or multiple uses, such as a generic writing scoring guide or generic math problem-solving scoring guide). For example, a generic writing scoring guide includes criteria applicable to any piece of student writing: writes to topic and specific audience, supports ideas with details, uses appropriate vocabulary, and so on. A generic math problem-solving scoring guide includes criteria applicable to any math process writing that students do: solves the problem correctly, uses graphic representation (words, pictures, numbers), writes the steps used to solve the problem, verifies the answer mathematically, and so on.

In the CFA 2.0 process, the scoring guides for the short- and extended-response questions are task specific. The last section of the CFA requires students to respond to the unit's Essential Questions with their own Big Ideas. For this particular section only, the scoring guide is *generic* because the criteria for responding to the Essential Questions will be the same on every unit's post-CFA throughout the school year. Examples of task-specific and generic scoring guides that are part of the ELA and math CFAs appear later in this chapter.

When you and your colleagues have discussed the six issues presented in this section and made decisions accordingly, you are ready to create the scoring guides for your constructed-response questions.

CFA 2.0 Design Step 6: Construct the Scoring Guides. First prepare an answer key to score the selected-response questions on the CFA, if your team has not already done so. Next write a task-specific, three-level scoring guide for each short constructed-response question. Then create a task-specific, four-level scoring guide for the extended-response question. Finally, create a generic scoring guide to evaluate students' Big Idea responses to the unit's Essential Questions.

SCORING GUIDES FOR SHORT CONSTRUCTED-RESPONSE QUESTIONS

A good place to begin creating scoring guides is with the short constructed-response questions. To create a three-level scoring guide, start with the top level. Read the first question and underline or highlight the specific elements that students need to include in their response. Write that first element as a phrase beginning with a verb, such as "Summarizes the central idea of passage" or "Shows steps used to solve problem." Then repeat the same process with the next underlined or highlighted element, and so on. Because this is a short constructed-response question, there will usually be only two or three criteria in all. These detailed success criteria represent a complete student response.

Next, write the specific criteria for the middle level of the scoring guide to reflect a partially correct response, such as "Identifies the central idea but does not summarize it" or "Shows two correct steps to solving the problem, but not all steps."

Finally, write the criteria for the bottom level of the scoring guide to indicate an incorrect response, such as "Does not summarize the central idea of the passage" or "Does not show any correct steps used to solve the problem."

KEEP IT POSITIVE, KEEP IT SIMPLE

See any drawbacks to this approach? The wording of the criteria becomes increasingly negative (and discouraging to students) as the levels descend. Also, it becomes difficult for educators to anticipate how to describe the ways students *might* respond if their answer is only partially correct. What if a student correctly summarizes the central idea or shows the math steps correctly but does not meet the other criteria listed on the scoring guide for that level? How do you score that response?

A much simpler and more effective way to resolve these challenges is to only detail the criteria for the *top* level. Student responses are then scored as having met all of those criteria, one or two of those criteria, or none of the criteria. Scores of 3–2-1 are easily determined by educators and understood by students.

Another reason for writing specific criteria for the top level of the scoring guide only is that there are likely to be three or more short constructed-response questions on the post-CFA. Writing three descriptive levels for three or more scoring guides will be time-consuming, not only to create the criteria but also to score the student responses. Writing one level of criteria representing a complete and correct response to each question is much more efficient. Student responses can then be scored correct, partially correct, or incorrect.

SCORING GUIDE FOR THE EXTENDED-RESPONSE QUESTION

The process of writing the scoring guide for the extended-response question is the same as for the short constructed-response questions, with one exception: it includes the addition of a fourth performance level to represent the student response that *exceeds* the success criteria.

To create a four-level scoring guide, write the *goal-level* criteria first. Read the directions of the extended-response question, one sentence at a time, and underline or highlight the specific elements students need to include in their response. On the scoring guide, write the first underlined or highlighted element as a phrase beginning with a verb. Then repeat the same process with each of the other elements. Collectively, these detailed success criteria represent a complete student response. Now, discuss with your colleagues how students can go "above and beyond" a complete response to produce one that exceeds the success criteria. Write those criteria using both quantitative and qualitative descriptors.

Creating the criteria for a student response that exceeds the success criteria is usually the most challenging part of designing a scoring guide. It's easy to include quantitative descriptors to boost the "goal-level" response ("Includes 3 supporting facts") to an "exceeds" response ("Includes 4 or more supporting facts"). It is more difficult to come up with objectively worded *qualitative* descriptors.

THE CHALLENGE OF WRITING QUALITATIVE CRITERIA

The way educators write qualitative criteria for the top performance level is to look at each of the goal-level criteria and decide which ones can be "bumped up" in quality. Then they brainstorm how to describe that in specific language.

For example, a goal-level descriptor in math might be, "Correctly identifies the mathematical pattern." A related advanced-level descriptor would be, "Correctly extends the mathematical pattern." The qualitative enhancement is expressed in the verb, *extends.* Students would need to show they knew how to extend the pattern, not just identify it. In doing so, they would exceed the related expectation of the goal-level response.

Many math educators are now using the phrase *statement of proficiency* to represent the goal-level criteria. To help students exceed the statement of proficiency, educators are showing them how to verify or justify their answers by proving them correct mathematically. Being able to do so is representative of an advanced-level response.

As an example in English language arts, a goal-level descriptor for writing a persuasive essay would be, "Supports position with facts." A related advanced-level descriptor might be, "Provides anecdotal evidence or personal experience in support of position." The qualitative enhancement is expressed by asking students to include these specific explanations in their response. Students who can do so would exceed the goal-level success criteria.

In an extended-response scoring guide, the goal-level success criteria are the most numerous because this level reflects *all* of the directions included in the question. Achieving the advanced-level success criteria presupposes that students have already met all of the goal-level criteria. They now must provide x number of additional quantitative and qualitative enhancements. The specific number of those criteria is up to the design team to determine.

My recommendation is to detail the success criteria for only the top two performance levels—"goal" and "exceeds." For the two levels below those—"progressing" and "beginning"—evaluate student responses according to how many of the goal-level criteria were met since that level represents a complete and correct response and serves as the target. Student responses achieving that target to a lesser degree can be indicated with a descriptor that uses a numerical range, such as "Meets 3–4 of the goal-level criteria" for a progressing-level response and "Meets fewer than 3 of the criteria" for a beginning-level response.

Again, regardless of the specific level names your team decides to use, the scoring guide needs to keep students' focus *fixed* on the goal-level success criteria and how to achieve the advanced-level success criteria.

GENERIC SCORING GUIDE FOR ESSENTIAL QUESTIONS

The last section of the post-CFA asks students to respond to the unit's Essential Questions with their own Big Ideas, a key component of the unit learning intentions and student success criteria. The scoring guide for this purpose is generically worded because it can be used repeatedly with subsequent post-CFAs, all of which include the same requirement that students provide their Big Idea responses to the Essential Questions.

Because student responses in this section of the post-CFA are typically brief, this generic scoring guide focuses on the one performance level, "Goal" or "Achieves success criteria." Certainly an "Exceeds success criteria" level can be added for all students willing and able to explain in greater detail all they have learned with regard to the Big Ideas for the unit.

Here is an example of the generic scoring guide teams can use to evaluate students' understanding of the Big Ideas. Again, two lower-performance levels with related descriptors can be added if design teams prefer.

Achieves Success Criteria:

- ☐ Correctly states Big Idea for *each* Essential Question
- ☐ Provides supporting explanations
- ☐ Uses unit vocabulary terms

FORMAT SCORING GUIDES WITH CHECK BOXES

Often educators want to know if a scoring guide isn't really just a checklist of requirements students need to include in their responses. The scoring guide is not a simple laundry list of items to include, mainly because it represents *different levels* of student performance. Yet it does resemble the appearance of a checklist because of the check boxes that precede the criteria within each performance level.

The purpose of the check boxes is twofold. While answering the constructed-response questions, students reference the accompanying scoring guide and check off each of the criteria as they include them in their response. When educators score the student responses, they check the boxes corresponding to the criteria that students met and highlight with a marker the criteria they did not.

When the scored papers are returned to the students, the unchecked, highlighted criteria draw attention to their learning gaps. This gives students a chance to stop, understand their errors, receive instructional help, readjust their learning approach, and be reassessed. As soon as they can produce evidence that they have met the highlighted criteria, the corresponding boxes are checked. In this way, the scoring guide serves students as a road map to their success.

ADD A SPACE FOR COMMENTS

At the end of the extended-response *task-specific* scoring guide and the Essential Questions-Big Ideas *generic* scoring guide, consider adding a few lines for written feedback to accompany the checked boxes and highlighted criteria. This feedback will be useful for students to receive kudos and/or next-steps instructional suggestions. When educators meet with students to review the feedback together, the comments will serve as helpful reminders to focus the discussion on what students need next instructionally and what adjustments, if any, students need to make in their learning strategies.

EXAMPLES OF SHORT CONSTRUCTED-RESPONSE SCORING GUIDES

Here again is one of the ELA short constructed-response questions and related commentary from Chapter 7, now with the task-specific scoring guide added. The commentary provides information referred to in the scoring guide criteria.

ELA Short Constructed-Response Question With Scoring Guide

How does the portrayal of Rosa Parks by the author of the first passage differ from the author of the second passage? Use evidence from the two passages to support your response.

Commentary (Reminder: The commentary can be in a <u>bulleted</u> format)

In the first passage, Rosa Parks is portrayed as a simple working-woman. The author shares limited background information—only that she grew up in Tuskegee, Alabama, and that she worked as a seamstress in Montgomery when she got older. The second passage portrays her as a black woman actively engaged in the Civil Rights Movement who worked as a seamstress and who appealed her conviction leading to the U.S. Supreme Court decision to rule segregation as being unconstitutional.

Another difference could be that the first article focuses on Rosa Parks's recognitions earned from her actions in the Civil Rights Movement. These recognitions include being awarded the Presidential Medal of Freedom and the Congressional Gold Medal. The second

142

passage focuses on Rosa Parks's specific action of refusing to give up her seat on the bus and how she became the woman that lawyers chose to support in order to challenge the segregation laws.

The following success criteria are met:

❐ Correctly states one of the above differences
❐ Correctly provides evidence from the <u>first</u> reading passage to support the difference
❐ Correctly provides evidence from the <u>second</u> reading passage to support the difference

In the math example, reprinted from Chapter 7, the three scoring guide criteria directly match the requirements of the question. To produce a correct response, students must demonstrate all three success criteria.

Math Short Constructed-Response Question With Scoring Guide

The chart below shows equivalent ratios to 7:5.

Fill in the missing values. (Correct values appear in bold type.)

7	5
21	**15**
28	20
35	**25**
42	30

*Explain how you determined the missing values:*_____
_____
_____
_____
_____

The following success criteria are met:

❐ Correctly includes missing values
❐ Correctly explains how relationship between numbers at top and bottom of each column are used to determine missing values
❐ Correctly explains how values were added to table

(For educators use in evaluating students' explanations: 21 = 3 × 7, so number below 5 would be 3 × 5, or 15; 28 = 4 x 7, so number below 15 would be 4 x 5 = 20, and so on.)

EXAMPLES OF EXTENDED-RESPONSE SCORING GUIDES

Here is the extended-response question and top two levels of the related scoring guide on the ELA common formative post-assessment. Note: The "Achieves success criteria" performance level appears *before* the "Exceeds success criteria," to emphasize to students that this is their initial target or goal.

ELA Extended-Response Question

Using information from both reading passages, write a three- to five-paragraph opinion piece that explains whether or not you agree that Rosa Parks should be considered the "mother of the Civil Rights Movement." In your response, be sure to

- *State your point of view*
- *Support your point of view with reasons and information from reading pas-sages 1 and 2*
- *Include a clear introduction*
- *Organize your ideas logically to support your opinion*
- *Use unit vocabulary terms in your writing*
- *Include a concluding statement related to your opinion*

Achieves Success Criteria:

- ❐ States point of view
- ❐ Includes at least 2 pieces of evidence (reasons and information), one from each passage, that supports point of view
- ❐ Organizes writing to include
  - * Introduction
  - • Body
  - • Specific concluding statement related to your point of view
  - • 3–5 unit vocabulary terms

Exceeds Success Criteria:

- ❐ Includes more than 2 pieces of evidence, from both passages, to support point of view

❏ Introduces opinion with attention-grabbing "hook"
❏ Includes challenging language
❏ Uses varied sentence structures
❏ Uses more than 5 unit vocabulary terms

In the third check box in this example, "Includes challenging language," the descriptor *challenging* must be explained to students with examples so they understand what the term means in the context of this writing prompt; otherwise it is a subjective descriptor.

Math Extended-Response Problem-Solving Question

For brevity, here is the final part only of the multiple-part math question presented in Chapter 7. The accompanying success criteria describe a correct student response.

John lives in Oklahoma where there are numerous lightning strikes in a month. One day there were 84 lightning strikes where John lived. If the 84 lightning strikes represented 12% of the total lightning strikes for the month, how many lightning strikes were there for the month? Show that your answer is correct. Show all your work.

Achieves Success Criteria:

❏ Supports calculations with correct mathematical reasoning
❏ Includes correct solution to problem
❏ Supports solution with appropriate justification
❏ Correctly expresses equivalent ratios as percentages
❏ Correctly uses math unit vocabulary

When scoring students' responses, math educators can refer to a "statement of proficiency" that they created along with the extended-response scoring guide. This will greatly assist them in scoring students' responses quickly and accurately. Here is the accompanying statement of proficiency that includes the key information specific to this math problem:

Correct student work should include the following:

❏ $12/100 = 84/x$
❏ Possible reasoning: 12 multiplied by 7 equals 84. To make an equivalent ratio you would multiply 100 by 7, which equals 700.
❏ Correct answer: There were 700 lightning strikes for the month where John lives in Oklahoma.

❏ Possible justification of solution: expand the ratio 12 to 100 (12%).

12	24	36	48	60	72	84
100	200	300	400	500	600	700

❏ The table shows that 12/100 and 84/700 are equivalent ratios.
❏ 12% of 700 = 84

Students who meet all of the "Achieves Success Criteria" requirements can then challenge themselves to include in their response one or more of the "Exceeds Success Criteria" requirements:

Exceeds Success Criteria:

❏ Supports correct answer with mathematical concepts
❏ Includes equivalent ratios that show the same relationship using different values

STUDENT INVOLVEMENT IN SCORING GUIDE DESIGN

Educators who involve students in the design of scoring guides know the tremendous value of doing so. However, scoring guides to evaluate student responses to the constructed-response questions on CFAs are typically created by the teacher team *only*. Here's one reason why.

Involving students in creating the post-CFA scoring guides would likely "skew" or invalidate the student results. Students might gain too much "insider information" during the construction of the scoring guides that could then too-favorably influence how they responded on the assessment. Certainly we want students to succeed, but we also must keep in mind the purpose of the post-CFA—to determine what they have learned and can demonstrate *on their own* by the end of the unit.

But here's the good news! Students are much more likely to understand the post-CFA scoring guide success criteria created by the teacher team and be able to use it independently to guide the completion of their responses *if* they've already learned how to coauthor scoring guides with their teachers during the unit. Classroom performance tasks (described in Chapter 3) provide the perfect opportunity to show students how to do this. While engaged in completing their performance tasks, students refer continually to the scoring guide criteria they helped create to make sure they are including the required elements in their work products.

After completing their performance tasks, they again refer to the scoring guide criteria during a peer review and self-assessment of their finished results.

TAKING STUDENT INVOLVEMENT FURTHER

Teacher teams may decide that they *want* to go further than this in involving their students. CFAs are formative assessments after all, and the goal is for students to achieve the learning intentions and success criteria for the unit. If educators see greater benefits to be had by creating the constructed-response scoring guides with their students before the students sit to take the post-CFA, certainly that should be considered. Just be sure that doing so will not invalidate the purpose of that end-of-unit assessment—to accurately infer from the assessment evidence you collect exactly what students have learned and can show on their own.

However your team decides this matter, it is important to understand how educators can eventually involve their students to a greater degree in the scoring guide design process. Reprinted here from the original edition of *Common Formative Assessments* (Ainsworth & Viegut, 2006) are the still-relevant guidelines for not only involving students in scoring guide design but also for teaching them how to peer- and self-assess their finished work products.

> With the scoring guide [they created] now complete, the teachers returned to their classes and distributed the rubric [extended-response scoring guide] to the students. Because these teachers were truly interested in demystifying the assessment process for their students, they wanted to share their expectations and criteria for [quality] work with students *before* asking them to produce it. However, in reviewing the scoring guide with students, an interesting thing occurred. The students in several classes expressed confusion over the rubric criteria and began asking their teachers for detailed clarification.

TEACHER-DESIGNED, STUDENT-*REVISED* SCORING GUIDES

> The teachers met together during their common planning period to share this unexpected development and decided to take the process one step further. The next day, they asked their students to

suggest changes to the scoring guide that might make it more student friendly. The students suggested replacing vague and subjective criteria with more objective criteria. Each individual teacher of the collaborative team recorded his or her students' suggestions and then met again to incorporate that feedback into the final draft of the rubric they would all use. The result—shared the following day with all the students in each participating class—was a teacher-designed, student-*revised* scoring guide that everyone understood.

Because the students helped refine the rubric, they understood the criteria more thoroughly than they did before. They were noticeably more motivated than usual, and they were better prepared to actually produce the corresponding quality work because they understood what was expected. Lastly, they anticipated receiving the type of specific feedback on their performance that would show them *how* to improve in the future.

PEER- AND SELF-ASSESSMENT BY STUDENTS

There is one further practice for the participating educators to consider: teaching their students how to peer- and self-assess their own performance on the common formative assessment—using the scoring guide they helped create—prior to having that assessment formally scored by the teacher team. "For formative assessment to be productive, pupils should be trained in self-assessment so that they can understand the main purposes of their learning and thereby grasp what they need to do to achieve" (Black & Wiliam, 1998[a], p. 10).

Students can learn how to self-assess their work against a set of established scoring guide criteria. Such self-assessment enables students to identify where their strengths lie and where they need to improve. "Engaging in self-assessment prior to receiving feedback . . . shifts the primary responsibility for improving the work to the student, where it belongs" (Stiggins et al., 2004, p. 195).

Teachers who do involve their students in the evaluation of assessments using the scoring guide the students help create will enjoy several benefits for their efforts:

• The assessments will already be pre-scored by students (peer-, self-, or both), which will expedite the time it takes the teachers to evaluate each paper.

* Students will take an active, rather than passive, role in the assessment of their own work.

- Student analysis skills will increase as students consider whether or not the work they evaluate meets the performance criteria they helped design.
- In reviewing the work of their peers, students reinforce their own understanding of the "unwrapped" concepts and skills they were taught and expected to learn.
- Students will be better able to set their own goals for future improvement by knowing where they are already capable and where they need to improve.
- Students will have an even greater ownership in the entire process—a truly "student-centered" assessment experience. (Ainsworth & Viegut, 2006, pp. 84–86)

As soon as teacher teams finish creating the scoring guides for their short- and extended-response questions on the post-CFA, they are ready to move to Step 7 in the CFA design process: creating their *pre*-CFA.

CFA 2.0 Design Step 7: Create the Pre-Assessment Questions and Scoring Guides. The CFA process is based on a pre- to post-assessment comparison of student growth in understanding. After designing the post-CFA, educators create a pre-CFA to align with the post-assessment and the related answer key and scoring guides.

ABOUT THE CFA PRE-ASSESSMENT

The CFA model is based on a pre-/post-assessment design whereby the pre-assessment is directly aligned to the post-assessment so that educators and students can see an apples-to-apples comparison of growth in student understanding from the beginning to the end of the unit.

The first important reason to pre-assess students before beginning instruction is to find out what they already understand about the standards and content soon to be taught. Because educators design the unit post-assessment *first*, they have already decided what students must know and be able to demonstrate by the end of the unit. An effective pre-assessment reveals the learning gaps between where students currently are in their understanding of the unit learning intentions and where they need to be. Educators use the pre-assessment results to inform ongoing unit instruction and help students close those gaps. "The improvement between the pre-test and post-test constitutes credible evidence of the teacher's instructional success" (Popham, 2003, p. 51).

A key message for educators to consider when developing their pre- and post-assessments is this:

> If you are using teacher-made pre- and post-tests to calculate an effect size, it is important that the students complete the same test at or near the start of the learning period as they do at the end—not an easy test at the start and then a comparatively difficult test later on. (Masters, 2014, p. 12)

This underscores the need for teacher teams to discuss two different approaches to the design of their pre-assessment. They can create a *mirrored* pre-assessment, an exact replica of the post-assessment, or they can prepare an *aligned* pre-assessment, which samples a few of the post-assessment questions only. There are benefits and drawbacks to both approaches (Ainsworth, 2010, pp. 152–153).

The Mirrored Pre-Assessment

The mirrored pre-assessment will likely provide greater statistical reliability of student growth in understanding between the pre- and post-assessment because the two assessments are essentially the same. However, it is difficult for educators to create a matched pair of assessments that are *equal* measures of student understanding. For students, the downside is they may greatly struggle to complete a longer, multi-format assessment of unfamiliar concepts and rigorous skills they have not yet learned. They may see the assessment as being too difficult, not do their best, and/or quit entirely, thus invalidating the assessment results and yielding no helpful information to inform instructional planning.

Whereas math educators can use the same questions from the post-CFA and simply change the numbers in the math problems to have a different yet almost identical pre-assessment, English language arts educators face a more time-consuming challenge. To create a mirrored pre-CFA, ELA educators may decide they need to find a *second* reading passage to use with their pre-CFA so as not to familiarize students with the passage content and possibly skew the results on the post-CFA. If so, that second reading passage needs to closely match the lexile level of the first reading passage used with the post-CFA, and it needs to include similar literary elements or informational text concepts.

The Aligned Pre-Assessment

The aligned pre-CFA is a shorter assessment since it includes only a few representative sample questions from the post-CFA. Educators often choose this kind of pre-CFA because it takes less classroom time to administer while still providing a good starting point for determining what students currently know and don't know about the targeted learning intentions. Because the purpose of assessment is to inform instruction, the aligned pre-CFA can effectively meet this purpose.

The downside here is that the post-CFA questions selected for inclusion on the pre-CFA may not be the best ones for revealing students' entry-level understanding of the new unit learning intentions. Why? If the pre-CFA is mainly selected-response questions, with only one or two short-response questions and no extended-response question, then the inferences the educators make from the student results may be limited and/or inaccurate. The learning needs of students may not be as evident on an aligned assessment as they would be on a mirrored assessment.

Ultimately, the pre-assessment format decision is one that educators need to make, either as a grade- or course-level team, or as an entire school faculty. When discussing this issue, keep this question uppermost in mind: "Which type of pre-CFA—mirrored or aligned—will best inform our instructional planning regarding what students currently know and what they need next in order to attain the unit learning intentions?"

As part of your discussion, see Popham's inventive plan in *Test Better, Teach Better* (2003) for creating a matched pair of pre- and post-assessments, which he calls the "Split-and-Switch Data-Gathering Design" (pp. 151–155). In brief, this rather ingenious plan involves creating only *one* complete set of assessment questions to use with the pre- *and* the post-assessment. When ready to administer the pre-assessment, educators divide the class of students into two groups, A and B. They administer half of the assessment questions to group A and the other half to group B. On the post-assessment, they switch the questions so that each group answers the *other* half of assessment questions that did not appear on their pre-assessment. This approach will save educators time and, as Popham says, "skirt the difficulties associated with the standard pretest/post-test design" (p. 152).

PRE-ASSESSING STUDENTS IN SOCIAL SCIENCES

Educators in history/social studies, science, and other content areas face a different challenge than their colleagues in English language arts and mathematics when designing a pre-CFA for their unit of study. Because students have yet to learn the specific content of the upcoming unit, it is unlikely that the majority of them will be able to answer *any* of the planned assessment questions appearing on the post-CFA. What purpose then is there in designing and administering a pre-CFA?

Pre-CFAs administered in any subject matter area where students know little of the new content to be learned should assess students' *prerequisite skills.* This will give educators insights into students' current level of background knowledge and readiness for the new content. Pre-assessments that help reveal to what extent students have the necessary foundations for the new learning will prove useful instructionally. They can also be helpful in determining any prior misconceptions students have so as to more appropriately plan entry-level instruction. This kind of pre-CFA will not allow for as much pre/post comparison of student results, but it will better help teachers know where to begin instruction. Remember the purpose of the pre-CFA—to find out where students currently are with regard to the more distant learning intentions for the new unit.

QUALITY CONTROL CHECKS

Collectively, the student responses to *all* of the CFA questions (extended response, short constructed response, multiple-choice, unit vocabulary, and Big Ideas) will provide the evidence of student attainment of the unit learning intentions and student success criteria. So it is critical that the assessment questions are well written and of quality.

When the first draft of the post-CFA is completed, educators often say, "We've written it, but now we're not sure how good it is." In Chapter 9, you will learn how to apply established guidelines from assessment experts to evaluate the *quality* of your first-draft assessment questions. These guidelines will assist your team in making any needed revisions to those questions.

CHAPTER SUCCESS CRITERIA

Now that you have learned how you and your colleagues can create better scoring guides for constructed-response questions (short, extended, and Big Idea-Essential Questions), please again take a few moments and write your responses to the success criteria for this chapter, or simply evaluate your understanding of each mastery statement on a scale of one (low) to five (high). Close any learning gaps you may have. As suggested at the conclusion of prior chapters, if you are reading this book as part of a professional study group, share your thoughts and ideas with colleagues.

Success Criteria:

- Point out the rationale and key points to consider when creating scoring guides.
- Explain how to write the scoring guides as *detailed* success criteria specific to constructed-response questions.
- Summarize the key points regarding the design of the unit *pre*-CFA.

9 Evaluating Quality of CFA 2.0 Questions

In This Chapter You Will Learn:

- Established guidelines for ensuring that assessment questions are of high quality:

    o Fairness
    o Validity
    o Reliability
    o Alignment
    o Multiple-choice questions
    o Short constructed-response questions
    o Extended-response questions

- How to use assessment quality criteria to refine or revise CFA questions after they are initially written.

Inferences that educators make about student understanding can only be as good as the assessment evidence they collect, and the evidence can only be as good as the source from which it comes. Credible student feedback is essential if educators are to infer and interpret student understanding accurately and correctly plan instructional next steps. In the highlighted eighth step of the CFA design process, grade- and course-level teams collaboratively critique all of their first-draft CFA questions for quality, using established criteria for doing so. These quality control checks and subsequent revisions to questions are critical for teams to carry out. Only then can they be confident that their CFA questions will produce sound student results.

Figure 9.1 CFA 2.0 Design Step 8

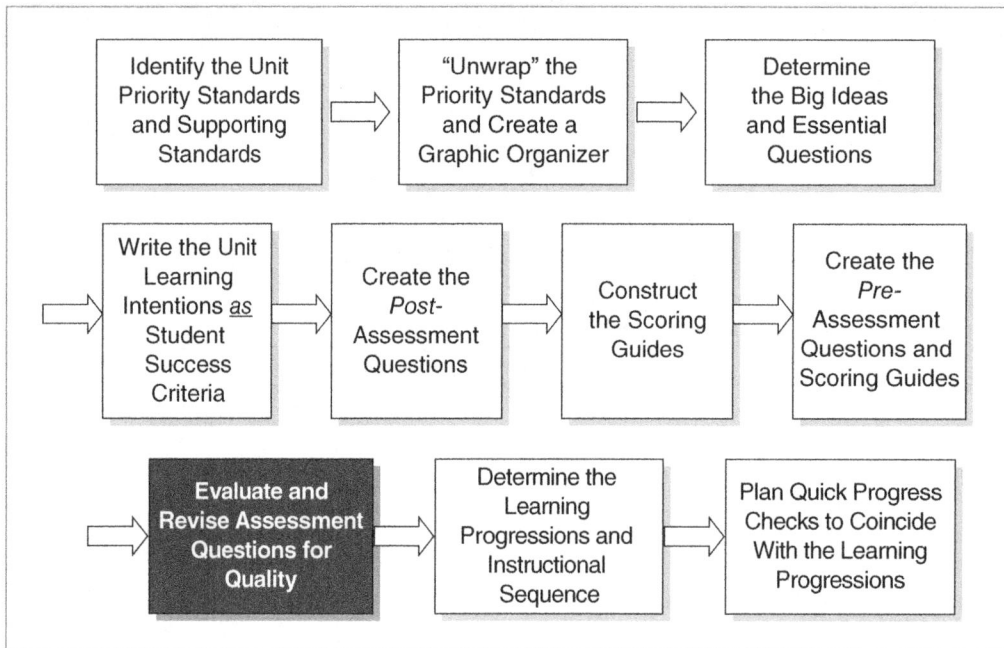

Identify the Unit Priority Standards and Supporting Standards	"Unwrap" the Priority Standards and Create a Graphic Organizer	Determine the Big Ideas and Essential Questions

Write the Unit Learning Intentions _as_ Student Success Criteria	Create the _Post-_Assessment Questions	Construct the Scoring Guides	Create the _Pre-_Assessment Questions and Scoring Guides

Evaluate and Revise Assessment Questions for Quality	Determine the Learning Progressions and Instructional Sequence	Plan Quick Progress Checks to Coincide With the Learning Progressions

CFA 2.0 Design Step 8: Evaluate and Revise Assessment Questions for Quality. After creating the post- and pre-CFA questions and related scoring guides, the grade- or course-level team now uses established guidelines associated with quality assessment questions to evaluate and revise as needed each of their post- and pre-CFA questions, in that order.

"WORKS IN PROGRESS"

Each grade- and course-level team will design, administer, score, and analyze the student results of as many as twenty pre- and post-CFAs (two per month) during the academic school year. For this reason, teacher teams need to commit a part of their collaborative work sessions to learning and applying the tools for improving the quality of their CFA questions.

Educators are usually well aware of the need to revise and refine their first-draft assessments. Typically, these first-draft efforts do not meet many of the guidelines for well-written assessment items—understandably due to the fact that most educators have not been formally trained in assessment design. When common formative assessments are rightly regarded as "works in progress," educators will not feel the pressure to produce outstanding questions during their early attempts. Improving assessment design skills is an ongoing endeavor.

Strive to keep the team's focus on *process*, not on results. Since all great visions require a great deal of work to bring them into being, a "write first, refine later" approach to authoring CFAs will do much in helping educators willingly do the work needed to produce high-quality assessments.

WRITE FIRST, REFINE LATER

Learning the attributes of well-written assessment questions *after* writing first drafts of CFAs makes that information highly relevant and pertinent. If that same information is presented prematurely, teams often feel constraint in writing their initial assessment items, being overly concerned that each item passes muster according to the assessment experts.

This is not to say that it would never be appropriate to provide teams with such criteria before they begin the actual design work for the first time. This is, in effect, comparable to telling students that they can see the scoring guide that will be used to evaluate their work *after* they finish it rather than before they begin. It only makes sense that educators would rather see these guidelines before they invest their time, thought, and energy into creating questions.

While I understand and respect that position, my recommendation is that teacher teams should wait to reference these established guidelines until *after* they have created their first-draft questions. The guidelines presented in this chapter contain many detailed points to think about, and simultaneously attempting to learn and apply them all while creating the assessment questions can become a bit overwhelming. It would be like pushing the revision phase onto writers before they have even begun formulating their initial drafts. However, the good news is that once teams are familiar with these guidelines, these guidelines will automatically influence the teams' design of *future* CFAs.

FAIRNESS, VALIDITY, AND RELIABILITY

The first three quality checks teacher teams conduct are to verify that their CFA questions pass the tests of fairness, validity, and reliability.

- **Fairness** means that the assessment items are not biased by factors (including race, gender, religion, ethnicity, socioeconomic status) that have nothing to do with student understanding of the stand-ards being assessed. Popham (2003) advises educators to write bias-free questions:

"Assessment bias occurs whenever test items *offend* or *unfairly penalize* students for reasons related to students' personal characteristics" (p. 55).

- **Validity** means that the inferences educators are able to draw from student responses are correct. The assessment questions need to measure what they are intended to measure (in the CFA context, student understanding of the predetermined unit learning intentions and student success criteria), so that educators can infer accurately.
- **Reliability** means consistency of what the assessment measures over time. If an assessment is reliable, students provide similar responses to the particular assessment questions at different times and/or under different circumstances.

The Visible Learning Plus Inside Series seminar *Using Data to Evaluate Your Impact* (Masters, 2014, p. 12) presents key attributes of validity and reliability (see box).

Validity of Assessments

- The validity of an assessment tool is the extent to which it measures what it was designed to measure, without contamination from other characteristics.
- "Validity is the most important single attribute of a good test. The emphasis is on the interpretation (of student understanding by the educators)."
- There are several types of validity:

  - Face validity—do the assessment questions appear to be appropriate?
  - Content validity—does the assessment content cover what we want to assess?
  - Criterion-related validity—how well does the test measure what we want it to?
  - Construct validity—are you measuring what you think you are measuring?

Reliability of Assessments

- "When the results of an assessment are reliable, we can be confident that repeated or equivalent assessments will provide consistent results."
- Factors affecting reliability are the length of the test, the suitability of the questions or tasks for the students being assessed, the phrasing and terminology of questions, the consistency in administration, and the design of marking and moderation.

A common misunderstanding about validity and reliability is that these two terms pertain only to the assessment itself. For example, educators will usually say that a valid assessment is one that measures what it sets out to measure and a reliable assessment is one that produces consistent results each time it is administered. When an *assessment* is determined to be both valid and reliable, the assumption is that these traits remain with that assessment indefinitely. W. James Popham (2003) corrects these misconceptions:

> It's not the test itself that can be valid or invalid, but, rather, the *inference* that's based on a student's test performance. . . . All validity analysis should center on the test-based inference, rather than on the test itself. If the interpretation is accurate, we say that the teacher has arrived at a valid test-based inference. If the interpretation is inaccurate, then the teachers' test-based inference is invalid. (p. 43)

> *An unreliable test will rarely yield scores from which valid inferences can be drawn.* . . . If a test is unreliable—inconsistent—how can it contribute to accurate score-based inferences and sound instructional decisions? Answer: It can't. (p. 54)

THE QUALITY CONTROL CHECKS

Not only is it important for educators to ensure that they have written fair, bias-free questions that make valid and reliable inferences possible, teams must also check their questions for *proper alignment* to the unit learning intentions and corresponding levels of cognitive rigor. Last, they need to reference established guidelines for well-written assessment questions from notable assessment experts to critique their CFA questions and then revise them as needed.

The following quality control checks and follow-up revision plan will assist teacher teams in completing this important CFA design step.

- Check for Alignment
- Use Established Criteria to Evaluate CFA Questions:
  - Selected Response (Multiple Choice)
  - Short Constructed Response
  - Extended Constructed Response
- Plan for Revision of Assessment Questions

Each of these helpful tools is described in the sections that follow.

CHECK FOR ALIGNMENT

For each CFA question, conduct an item-by-item match to the targeted Priority Standards upon which they should be based, noting which questions directly align and which do not. Conducting this kind of "gap analysis" enables you to determine if your assessment questions have achieved the purpose for which they were intended—accurate measures of the unit's learning intentions. While evaluating each question, note where changes need to occur in a subsequent revision of those questions.

Here are seven alignment questions to guide your team's discussions when reviewing each CFA question:

Alignment Guidelines

1. Does this assessment question directly align to our "unwrapped" Priority Standards included on the graphic organizer?

2. Does this assessment question match the level of cognitive rigor of the "unwrapped" concepts and skills?

3. Does this assessment question include correct standards vocabulary, as opposed to more student-friendly wording (i.e., "identify" rather than "label"; "hypothesis" rather than "educated guess")?

4. Will this question enable us to make reliable and valid inferences about student understanding?

5. Is this question free of bias (in its various forms)?

6. Do we need to revise this question to make certain there is a closer, more intentional alignment?

The following two multiple-choice questions meet these six quality criteria for proper alignment. The first is from a kindergarten math CFA and the second from a ninth- and tenth-grade reading CFA that is a combination multiple-choice and short constructed-response question. Note the bolded elements in each standard. The assessment questions directly align *only* to those bolded elements. Other CFA questions address the remaining elements.

ALIGNMENT TO EXTERNAL TESTS

Two additional questions address the alignment of CFA questions to large-scale assessments, the first to state and provincial exams, and the second

Figure 9.2 Standards-Aligned Assessment Questions

K.CC.6 **IDENTIFY** whether the number of objects in one group is greater than, less than, or **equal to** the number of objects in another group (Bloom 4, DOK3).

Kindergarten Unit 5 Post Test – Selected Response Questions

Name _____

6. Choose the picture that represents <u>an equal</u> amount as the stars.

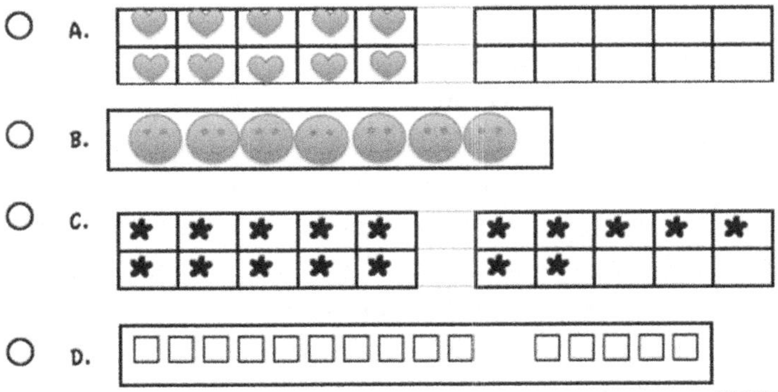

○ A.

○ B.

○ C.

○ D.

5   5Post TestSR

Source: Karen Gomez, San Diego Unified School District, San Diego, CA.

SL. 9-10.3 **EVALUATE a speaker's point of view**, reasoning, and **use of evidence** and **rhetoric**, identifying any fallacious reasoning or exaggerated or distorted evidence (Bloom 5, DOK 4).

In the excerpt from Hillary Rodham Clinton's speech, she primarily uses which of the following rhetorical appeals?

a. Ethos

b. Logos

c. <u>Pathos</u>

d. Fallacies

In your opinion, is that rhetorical device effective in conveying her point of view? Cite evidence from the speech to support your response.

Source: High School ELA Curriculum Design Team, San Diego Unified School District, San Diego, CA.

to Common Core assessments designed by the Smarter Balanced and PARCC assessment consortia:

- Does this assessment question align with the formats of our state or provincial exams so that students will be familiar with those formats? _or_
- Does this assessment question align with the formats of Common Core assessments (SBAC or PARCC) so that students will be familiar with those formats?

USE ESTABLISHED GUIDELINES TO EVALUATE CFA QUESTIONS

Numerous textbooks used in educational measurement and evaluation courses at the college and university level, and assessment books written for the education profession, all share the same important purpose: to inform educators about the attributes of effective assessments. Teachers who want to write better assessments need to know the research- and evidence-based criteria that assessment experts use and look for when writing and evaluating assessment questions for quality.

For this expanded new edition, I have synthesized in particular the item-writing guidelines for selected-response and constructed-response questions from the following publications:

- Thomas M. Haladyna, _Developing and Validating Multiple-Choice Test Items_ (3rd ed., 2012)
- Thomas M. Haladyna, _Writing Test Items to Evaluate Higher-Order Thinking_ (1997)
- W. James Popham, _Test Better, Teach Better: The Instructional Role of Assessment_ (2003)

Also included here are other excellent sources for designing assessment questions and evaluating the quality and rigor of those items:

- Anthony J. Nitko and Susan M. Brookhart, _Educational Assessment of Students_ (6th ed., 2010)
- Albert Oosterhof, _Classroom Applications of Educational Measurement_ (3rd ed., 2001)
- Richard J. Stiggins et al., _Classroom Assessment for Student Learning: Doing It Right—Using It Well_ (2004)

Selected-Response (Multiple-Choice) Guidelines for Quality

The following 12 guidelines derived from Haladyna and Popham (noted parenthetically in the list below as H and P) will assist teacher teams in evaluating the quality of their multiple-choice questions.

1. Is the <u>stem</u> written as a direct question? (H, P)

2. Is the <u>stem</u> written as an incomplete statement? (H, P)

3. Is the <u>stem</u> self-contained, containing all necessary information *only?* (H, P)

4. Is the <u>stem</u> worded positively, avoiding negatives such as *not, never, except?* (H, P)

5. Does this <u>stem</u> require a correct answer or a best answer? (P)

6. Is there only <u>one</u> clearly correct or best answer to this question? (H, P)

7. Are all distracters (incorrect answer choices) credible or plausible, with no easy eliminations? (H, P)

8. Do the distracters in this question include common student errors or misconceptions? (H, P)

9. Does this question avoid use of "all of the above" as an answer choice? (H, P)

10. Are all of the answer choices in this question approximately the same length? (H)

11. Is this question free of any leading clues to the right answer (e.g., inconsistent grammar)? (H, P)

12. Does this question target a specific concept and skill that will yield a valid inference of student understanding? (P)

In reviewing *all* multiple-choice questions on the CFA, the following questions also apply:

- Are the answer positions randomly used in approximately equal numbers? (H, P)
- Are the answer choices formatted vertically? (H)
- Are *math* answer choices formatted in numerical order from least to greatest? (H)

Sources: *Developing and Validating Multiple-Choice Test Items,* by T. M. Haladyna, 2012, 3rd ed., Mahwah, NJ: Erlbaum; *Writing Test Items to Evaluate Higher-Order Thinking,* by T. M. Haladyna, 1997, Boston: Allyn & Bacon; and *Test Better, Teach Better: The Instructional Role of Assessment,* by W. J. Popham, 2003, Alexandria, VA: Association for Supervision and Curriculum Development.

Readers interested in seeing the guidelines for the other types of selected-response questions (true/false, matching, and selecting a response from a provided word bank) are encouraged to reference the same publications.

EXAMPLES OF CRITIQUED MULTIPLE-CHOICE QUESTIONS

Let's look now at three examples of multiple-choice questions (the second one appeared in previous chapters). Referring to the list of twelve guidelines, practice evaluating each question by checking either yes or no to indicate whether you think the question meets the numbered guideline. Then compare your critique with the one provided to see how closely they match.

Example 1

(In the actual CFA, a full story precedes the following question. A short summary of that story appears here for you to refer to while evaluating the related question):

Two fifth-grade girls had been best friends since kindergarten. One of the girls met a new friend who had just moved into the neighborhood. She pretended not to see her best friend when they passed on the street and then made fun of her to the new girl. This hurt her best friend's feelings. A few days later the new girl lost interest and found another friend. The girl asked her best friend to forgive her for the way she had behaved, and the two became best friends again.

RL.4.2 **DETERMINE** <u>theme of story</u>, drama, or poem from details in the text; summarize the text.

1. *Which answer choice BEST describes the theme of the story?*

   a. Good friends spend a lot of time together.
   b. Treat others the way you want to be treated.
   c. A friend would never do anything bad to you.
   d. It's too hard for anyone to be a good friend all of the time.

Does this question need revision? ___ If yes, what specifically?

Criteria Met	1	2	3	4	5	6	7	8	9	10	11	12
Yes												
No												

Critique:

All twelve guidelines are met. (Note: If Guideline 1 is yes, Guideline 2 will be no, and vice versa.) The best answer is d. Three distracters are plausible, requiring students to think. Use of the superlative *best* bumps up the thinking skill rigor of the question. An accompanying short constructed-response question could ask for evidence from the story to support the answer choice. Guideline 12 is directly targeted at the skill in bold type and the underlined concept pair, "DETERMINE theme of story," and thus would yield a valid inference of student understanding. No revision needed.

Example 2

Students will read two informational text passages (not included here due to length) about Rosa Parks and then answer the related questions.

(Priority Standard) RI.5.6 ANALYZE multiple accounts of the same event or topic, NOTING important similarities and differences in the point of view they represent.

(Supporting Standard) RI.5.8 Explain how an author uses reasons and evidence to support particular points in a text, **identifying which reasons and evidence support which point(s).**

1. *What evidence best supports Rosa Parks being called the "mother of the civil rights movement"?*

a. Rosa Parks rode a segregated bus and was arrested.
b. Her arrest started nonviolent protests to support civil rights in the United States.
c. Rosa Parks was awarded the Congressional Gold Medal.
d. Rosa Parks refused to give up her bus seat to a white man.

Does this question need revision? ___ If yes, what specifically?

Criteria Met	1	2	3	4	5	6	7	8	9	10	11	12
Yes												
No												

Critique:

All 12 guidelines are met. (Again, if Guideline 1 is yes, Guideline 2 will be no, and vice versa.) The best answer is b. Three distracters are plausible, requiring students to think. Distracter analysis confirms this:

  a. This is an accurate detail from the two texts but not enough to support the claim.
  c. This is an accurate detail from the first reading passage but not enough to support the claim.
  d. Her action was a catalyst for the boycott moving the Civil Rights Movement forward but this is not the *best* response.

Use of the superlative *best* increases the cognitive rigor of the question. Guideline 12 directly targets the skills in bold type and concepts in the Priority Standard and the supporting standard (with the exception of "*Explain* how an author uses reasons and evidence to support particular points in a text," which would be assessed in short- and extended-response questions). No revision needed.

Example 3

This example is excerpted from a different math CFA than the one being used to illustrate the various design steps in this book. The assessment question targets only the bolded elements in the following "unwrapped" geometry standard, 6.G.A.2:

Solve real-world and mathematical problems involving area, surface area, and volume.

6.G.A.2 Find the volume of a right rectangular prism with fractional edge lengths by packing it with unit cubes of the appropriate unit fraction edge lengths, and show that the volume is the same as would be found by multiplying the edge lengths of the prism. **APPLY the formulas $V = l\,w\,h$ and $V = b\,h$ to FIND volumes of right rectangular prisms with fractional edge lengths in the context of SOLVING real-world and mathematical problems.**

How much water would it take to fill the pool completely? (See next page.)

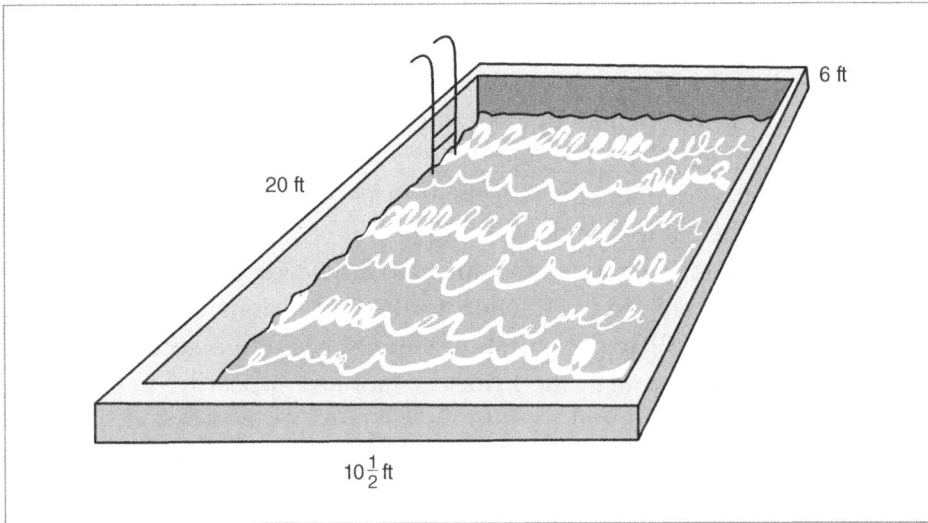

a. 36½ ft³ of water
b. 73 ft³ of water
c. 1,200 ft³ of water
d. 1,260 ft³ of water

Does this question need revision? ___ If yes, what specifically?

Criteria Met	1	2	3	4	5	6	7	8	9	10	11	12
Yes												
No												

Critique:

Correct answer: d

All three distracters are plausible, representing common student errors. Distracter analysis confirms this:

a. Student incorrectly adds the three dimensions together.
b. Student incorrectly adds the three dimensions together and doubles that sum.
c. Student correctly applies formula of length × width × height but only with the whole number values of 20 × 10 × 6, instead of using the correct width measurement of 10½.

Revision needed? Yes! All guidelines are met except Guideline 12. The question needs to more closely match these elements of the Priority Standard: **APPLY the <u>formulas V = l w h and V = b h</u> to FIND <u>volumes of right rectangular prisms with</u> <u>fractional edge lengths</u> in the context of SOLVING <u>real-world and mathematical problems</u>.** Only one of the three dimensions includes fractional edge lengths (width 10 ½ feet). The length of the pool (20 feet) and/or the height (6-foot depth) should also be mixed numbers.

Thus, two other revisions to the question are needed: (1) On the graphic of the swimming pool, add a fraction to the dimensions of length and/or height (depth), and (2) revise question stem to include a second question that matches the elements of the Priority Standard appearing in bold type. Here is an example. Original question: *How much water would it take to fill the pool completely?* New second part of question: *Apply the correct formula for finding the volume of a right rectangular prism with fractional edge lengths.*

SHORT CONSTRUCTED-RESPONSE EVALUATION GUIDELINES

The published guidelines for evaluating short constructed-response questions are fewer and more generally worded than those for the selected-response format. However, they are equally valuable in terms of evaluating and revising open-ended questions for quality. Note that two of the guidelines refer to questions with answer blanks, which are not always applicable to CFAs in certain units or grade levels.

The seven item-writing guidelines used to critique short constructed-response questions are synthesized here from these three publications (authors' initials noted parenthetically):

- *Test Better, Teach Better: The Instructional Role of Assessment* (Popham, 2003)
- *Educational Assessment of Students* (3rd ed., Nitko, 2001)
- *Classroom Applications of Educational Measurement* (3rd ed., Oosterhof, 2001)

Short Constructed-Response Guidelines for Quality

1. Is this item a recommended direct question instead of an incomplete statement? (P)

2. Does this question measure an important aspect of the unit's instructional targets? (O, N)

3. Is the wording in this question clear enough to elicit a brief but distinctive response? (P, O, N)

4. If this is a completion item, is the response blank at the end? (P, N, O)

5. If there are two (maximum) response blanks in this question, are they uniform in length to prevent unintended clues? (O, P)

6. Is there sufficient answer space for a complete student response? (P)

7. Does the format of the item allow for efficient scoring? (O)

EXAMPLES OF CRITIQUED SHORT CONSTRUCTED-RESPONSE QUESTIONS

The two examples of short constructed-response questions that follow are excerpted from the English language arts and math CFAs shown in previous chapters. Referring to the list of seven guidelines, practice evaluating each question by checking either *yes* or *no* to indicate whether you think the question meets the numbered guideline. Then compare your critique with the one provided to see how closely they match.

Example 1

(Priority Standard) RI.5.6 ANALYZE <u>multiple accounts of the same event or topic</u>, NOTING important <u>similarities and differences</u> in the <u>point of view they represent</u>.

> **(Supporting Standard) RI.5.8 Explain how an author uses reasons and evidence to support particular points in a text, <u>identifying which reasons and evidence support which point(s).</u>**

What are two differences in how the author of the first passage portrays Rosa Parks compared to how she is portrayed by the author of the second passage? Use evidence from both passages to support your response. Your response will be scored with the accompanying scoring guide [not shown here].

(Sufficient answer space provided)

Does this question need revision? ___ If yes, what specifically?

Criteria Met	1	2	3	4	5	6	7
Yes							
No							

Critique:

Five of the seven guidelines are met; Guidelines 4 and 5 are not applicable. Guideline 2 is met by the Priority Standard in all bold type and the bolded phrase in the supporting standard. No revision needed.

Example 2

6.RP.3 <u>Use ratio and rate reasoning to solve real-world mathematical problems, e.g.</u> **by reasoning about tables of equivalent ratios,** tape diagrams, double number line diagrams, or equations.

The ratio of cats to dogs in a local neighborhood is 2:3.

If there are 36 dogs in the neighborhood, how many cats will there be?

Use the table of equivalent ratios and the ordered pairs on the coordinate plane (provided in previous question) to make a prediction. Your response will be scored with the accompanying scoring guide [not included here].

Number of cats _____

Explain your prediction:

_____

_____

_____

_____

Does this question need revision? ___ If yes, what specifically?

Criteria Met	1	2	3	4	5	6	7
Yes							
No							

Critique:

All seven guidelines are met. Guideline 2 is met by the match between the question and the phrase in bold type within the Priority Standard. No revision needed.

EXTENDED-RESPONSE EVALUATION GUIDELINES

The seven item-writing guidelines (including one referring to the scoring guide) used to critique *extended-response* questions (often referred to as "essay writing" in the cited works) are synthesized here from these four publications (authors' initials noted parenthetically):

- *Test Better, Teach Better: The Instructional Role of Assessment* (Popham, 2003)
- *Educational Assessment of Students* (3rd ed., Nitko, 2001)
- *Classroom Applications of Educational Measurement* (3rd ed., Oosterhof, 2001)
- *Classroom Assessment for Student Learning: Doing It Right—Using It Well* (Stiggins et al., 2004)

Extended-Response Quality Guidelines

1. Does this extended-response question explicitly describe what students are to do? (P)

2. Will this question lead all students to interpret the task in the way intended? (N)

3. Did we add sufficient details to remove any possible ambiguity or misinterpretation? (P, N, O)

4. Does this question clearly measure important aspects of the unit's instructional targets? (O, N, S)

5. Did we specify an acceptable response length and a recommended time in which to finish? (P, N)

6. Is there anything in the question that might put a group of students at a disadvantage regardless of their knowledge or reasoning level? (S)

7. Does the scoring plan describe a correct and complete response (O) without giving it away? (S)

Popham (2003) also recommends determining "a question's quality by creating a trial response to that item" (p. 95).

Stiggins et al. (2004) recommend not offering students choices of questions. "When students select their own sample of performance, it can be a biased one." (p. 176). Popham (2003) agrees: "When students can choose from several options, you really end up with different tests, unsuitable for comparison" (p. 95).

EXAMPLES OF CRITIQUED EXTENDED-RESPONSE QUESTIONS

The following two examples of extended-response questions appeared in the previous two chapters. Once more, while referring to the list of seven guidelines, practice evaluating the questions by checking either *yes* or *no* to indicate whether you think the question meets the numbered guideline. Then compare your critique with the one provided to see how closely they match.

English Language Arts Extended-Response Question Critique

W.5.1 WRITE <u>opinion pieces</u> on topics or texts. SUPPORT <u>a point of view with reasons and information</u>.

W.5.1a INTRODUCE a <u>topic</u> or text clearly, STATE an <u>opinion</u>, and CREATE an <u>organizational structure</u> in which <u>ideas are logically grouped to support the writer's purpose</u>.

W.5.1b PROVIDE <u>logically ordered reasons</u> that are <u>supported by facts and details</u>.

W.5.1d PROVIDE a <u>concluding statement</u> or <u>section related to the opinion presented</u>.

Using information from both reading passages, write a three- to five-paragraph opinion piece that explains whether or not you agree that Rosa Parks should be considered the "mother of the Civil Rights Movement." In your response, be sure to

- *State your point of view*
- *Support your point of view with reasons and information from passages 1 and 2*
- *Include a clear introduction*
- *Organize your ideas logically to support your opinion*
- *Use unit vocabulary terms in your writing*
- *Include a concluding statement related to your opinion*

Does this question need revision? ___ If yes, what specifically?

Criteria Met	1	2	3	4	5	6	7
Yes							
No							

Critique:

All seven guidelines are met. Regarding Guideline 4, this one extended-response question directly targets all of the "unwrapped" concepts and skills in the main Priority Standard (W.5.1) and the three related Priority Standards (W.5.1a, b, and d). The scoring guide that accompanies this prompt (not shown here but presented in the previous chapter) meets Guideline 7. No revision needed.

Math Extended-Response Problem-Solving Critique

The following extended-response problem-solving question for this unit includes multiple parts. Taken as a whole, this one question aligns to nearly all of the underlined concepts and CAPITALIZED skills in the four "unwrapped" Priority Standards and their associated levels of cognitive rigor.

6.RP.A.3 <u>USE</u> ratio and <u>rate reasoning</u> to <u>SOLVE</u> <u>real-world</u> and <u>mathematical problems</u>, e.g., by reasoning about tables of equivalent ratios, tape diagrams, double number line diagrams, or equations.

a. MAKE <u>tables of equivalent ratios</u> RELATING <u>quantities</u> with <u>whole number measurements</u>, FIND <u>missing values in the tables</u>, and PLOT the <u>pairs of values</u> on the <u>coordinate plane</u>. USE <u>tables</u> to COMPARE <u>ratios</u>.

b. SOLVE <u>unit rate problems</u> including those involving <u>unit pricing</u> and <u>constant speed</u>.

For example, if it took 7 hours to mow 4 lawns, then at that rate, how many lawns could be mowed in 35 hours? At what rate were lawns being mowed?

c. FIND a <u>percent of a quantity</u> as a <u>rate per 100</u> *(e.g., 30% of a quantity means 30/100 times the quantity)*; SOLVE <u>problems</u> involving <u>finding the whole, given a part and the percent.</u>

d. USE <u>ratio reasoning</u> to CONVERT <u>measurement units</u>; MANIPULATE and TRANSFORM <u>units</u> appropriately when <u>multiplying or dividing quantities</u>.

Thunder and Lightning

Thunder and lightning have a relationship that can be used to determine your distance from a lightning strike.

When you see the flash of a lightning bolt you can start counting by seconds until you hear thunder. If it takes 10 seconds to hear the thunder, the lightning struck 2 miles away.

a. *John is standing in the middle of a field and sees the flash of a lightning bolt. He counts to 15 seconds. How far away from John is the lightning strike? Show your work.*

b. *Identify the unit rate for thunder and lightning strikes. What does the unit rate mean?*

c. *Create a table that shows equivalent ratios for the relationship between thunder and lightning strikes from 0 seconds to 25 seconds.*

d. *Use the values in the table in Part C to graph the relationship between thunder and lightning on the coordinate plane.*

e. *Determine the number of seconds that John counted before he heard the thunder if he was 10 miles away from the lightning strike. Explain your answer using ratio ideas.*

f. *Sound travels at the speed of 1,087 feet per second.*

 How far would a sound travel in 5 seconds?

 Write a ratio for the speed of sound.

 Use the ratio to answer the question.

g. *If the lightning strike was 3 miles from John, how many feet away was John?*

 How many yards away was John?

 Use ratio ideas to find your answers. Show your work.

h. *John lives in Oklahoma where there are numerous lightning strikes in a month. One day there were 84 lightning strikes where John lived. If the 84 lightning strikes represented 12% of the total lightning strikes for the month, how many lightning strikes were there for the month?*

 Show that your answer is correct. Show all of your work.

Extended-Response Quality Guidelines (reprinted here for easy reference)

1. Does this extended-response question explicitly describe what students are to do? (P)

2. Will this question lead all students to interpret the task in the way intended? (N)

3. Did we add sufficient details to remove any possible ambiguity or misinterpretation? (P, N, O)

4. Does this question clearly measure important aspects of the unit's instructional targets? (O, N, S)

5. Did we specify an acceptable response length and a recommended time in which to finish? (P, N)

6. Is there anything in the question that might put a group of students at a disadvantage regardless of their knowledge or reasoning level? (S)

7. Does the scoring plan describe a correct and complete response (O) without giving it away? (S)

Does this question need revision? ___ If yes, what specifically?

Criteria Met	1	2	3	4	5	6	7
Yes							
No							

Critique:

All seven guidelines are met. Regarding Guideline 4, this one extended-response question directly targets all of the bolded concepts and skills in the main Priority Standard (6.RP.A.3) *and* its four related Priority Standards (6.RP.A.3a, b, c, and d). The individual scoring guides (not included here) that are specific to each part of this multiple-part extended-response question collectively meet Guideline 7. No revision needed.

PLAN FOR REVISION OF ASSESSMENT QUESTIONS

After evaluating post-CFA questions for quality using the guidelines presented in this chapter, it does happen that educators are happy to discover that many of their assessment items meet the established criteria!

This tends to be the exception, however, rather than the rule. More often, teams find significant gaps between the quality guidelines and the items they have written. Reminding everyone that the purpose of the entire authoring-critiquing-revision process is one of continuous improvement, discussion next turns to the issue of when to schedule the revision work. Often teams want to revise each question as soon as they critique it. But if this is not possible due to time constraints, they create a follow-up action plan.

Guided by the following three questions, the team members record their responses in an action plan to be shared with their administrators.

1. When will we revise our assessments, using the revision notes we have made today? (Record suggestions: late-start days; substitute teachers during school day; contract pay for after-school, weekend, or summer work; and so on.)

2. What information, assistance, and/or resources do we need to accomplish this?

3. When can we reasonably expect these revisions to be completed?

THE SUPPORTIVE ROLE OF ADMINISTRATORS

Administrators play a vital role in helping collaborative teams schedule the time needed to make the necessary improvements to their CFA questions that they have now identified. The administrators must schedule meetings with each course- or grade-level team to discuss that team's action plan and to provide assistance as needed.

This is the most effective way to safeguard and promote the ongoing improvements in the quality of team-created common formative assessments. After all sections of the post-CFA (multiple choice, short constructed response, extended response, and Essential Questions) are critiqued and revised for quality, the teacher team will have produced a first-rate end-of-unit assessment that aligns with all of the unit's learning intentions and student success criteria. They will now have the means to accurately interpret student understanding and make valid and reliable inferences to inform their instructional next steps.

CHAPTER SUCCESS CRITERIA

In the next chapter, you will learn how to plan out the *learning progressions* to help students achieve the overall unit learning intentions. These progressions coincide with *quick progress* checks to help educators interpret what students need next instructionally *and* what adjustments students need to make in their learning strategies.

But first, please, once again take a few moments and write your responses to the success criteria for this chapter, or simply evaluate your understanding of each mastery statement on a scale of one (low) to five (high). Reread any sections necessary to improve your comprehension of the content. As suggested at the conclusion of prior chapters, if you are reading this book as part of a professional study group, share your thoughts and ideas with colleagues.

Success Criteria:

- Summarize the following types of guidelines for ensuring that CFA questions are of quality

  - Fairness
  - Validity
  - Reliability
  - Alignment
  - Multiple-choice questions
  - Short constructed-response questions
  - Extended-response questions

- Describe how to use the assessment quality guidelines to refine or revise assessment questions after they are first written.

10

Learning Progressions and Quick Progress Checks

In This Chapter You Will Learn:

- How to determine learning progressions to help students achieve the unit learning intentions.
- How to plan quick progress checks to coincide with the learning progressions.
- The important role of reciprocal feedback in the instruction-assessment-adjustment cycle.

In these final two steps of the CFA process, the key message is Teach-Assess-Interpret-Adjust. Teacher teams now determine the *learning progressions—* the instructional pathways—that will enable their students to fully understand and achieve the unit learning intentions. The teams then plan *quick progress checks* to coincide with the identified learning progressions. Student responses to these quick checks yield high-quality feedback that educators use to correctly interpret student understanding and adjust instruction. Students use the same feedback to self-regulate their learning strategies. These "en route" instructional corrections enable students to continually move toward the goal of achieving the unit learning intentions and success criteria, as measured by the post-CFA.

Figure 10.1   CFA 2.0 Design Steps 9 and 10

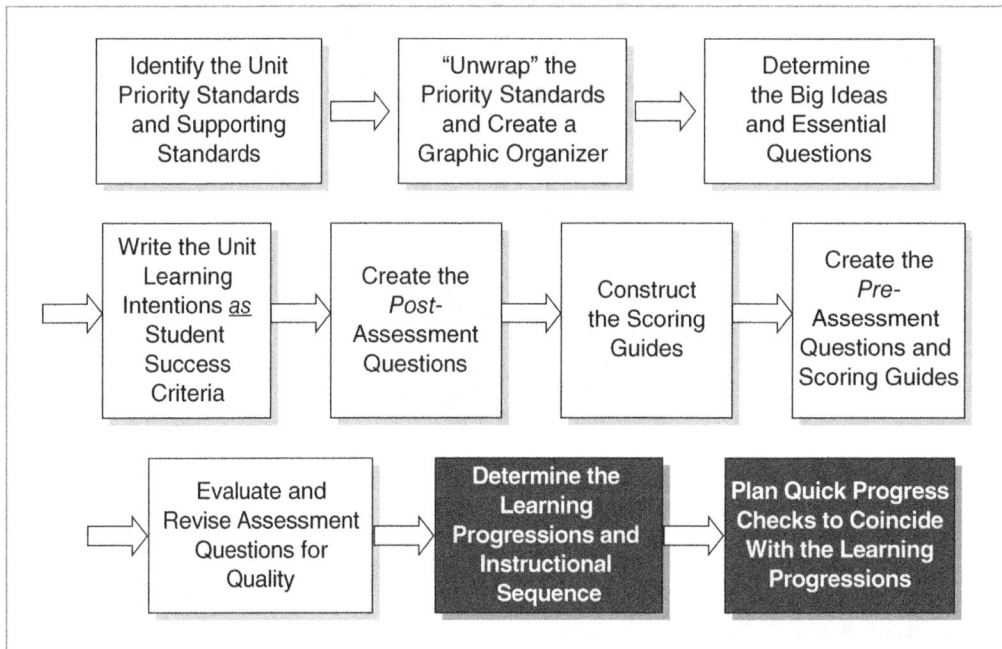

CFA Design Step 9: Determine the Learning Progressions and Instructional Sequence. Learning progressions are the sequenced "building blocks" of instruction that lead students to understand the unit learning intentions. Look at each unit learning intention to decide what increments of instruction students will need to fully understand that learning intention. Then sequence these instructional building blocks in the order they will occur during the unit.

UNDERSTANDING LEARNING PROGRESSIONS

Learning progressions represent prerequisite knowledge and skills that students must acquire incrementally before they are able to understand and apply more complex or advanced concepts and skills.

W. James Popham and Margaret Heritage have written extensively on the purpose, function, and effective use of learning progressions and their critical connections to formative assessment and instruction. Their valuable contributions to this important subject, one that may be fairly new to many educators, are showcased in this chapter. I highly recommend their respective publications as must-read information for teacher teams wanting further details on how to construct their own learning progressions.

In *Transformative Assessment* (2008), Popham uses specific terminology to describe learning progressions as "a set of building blocks—subskills and bodies of enabling knowledge—to be achieved by students on their way to mastering a target curricular aim" (p. 25).

In *Formative Assessment* (2010), Margaret Heritage defines learning progressions as the "pathways along which students are expected to progress" (p. 38). Describing their key purpose, she writes,

> Explicit learning progressions can provide the clarity that teachers need. By describing a pathway of learning, they can assist teachers in planning instruction. . . . When teachers understand the continuum of learning in a domain and have information [through formative assessment] about [students'] current status relative to the learning goals, they are better able to make decisions about what the next steps in learning should be. (p. 39)

In *Formative Assessment in Practice* (2013), Heritage elaborates on her definition of learning progressions and reaffirms their value to educators:

> Learning progressions are also called progress variables, progress maps, and learning trajectories. Progressions invite a developmental view of learning because they lay out how expertise develops over a more or less extended period of time, beginning with rudimentary forms of learning and moving through progressively more sophisticated states. When teachers' instruction and formative assessment practices are undergirded by learning progressions, teachers can better use formative assessment to map where an individual student's learning currently stands and take steps to move him or her forward. (Chapter 2, para. 2)

There is, at the present time, a limited research base with regard to learning progressions:

> Ideally, learning progressions should be developed from a strong research base about the structure of knowledge in a discipline and about how learning occurs. Yet the research base in many areas is not as robust as it might be (citing Herman, 2006): 'Current research

only defines how a limited number of areas can be divided into learning progressions.' (Heritage, 2010, p. 40)

The fact that this is a still-emerging field of research certainly does not minimize the importance of teacher teams identifying learning progressions as part of the CFA design process. It simply means they may not find a lot of outside guidance, examples, and research support for doing so. Instead, they can begin by referring to the examples provided in this chapter and the cited publications. This is a great opportunity for teacher teams to rely upon their own professional judgment and collaboratively plan out these building blocks of instruction. The benefits of doing so will likely become highly evident when they experience firsthand the corresponding improvements in both instruction and student learning.

COLLABORATIVELY DETERMINE THE LEARNING PROGRESSIONS

Experienced educators are usually well-grounded in their content areas and accustomed to informally identifying learning progressions as a natural part of their instructional planning, even if they do not refer to them as such. From their years in the classroom, they know what to teach, when to teach it, and how to get their students to the learning targets for a unit of study. However, their internalized understanding of instructional steps is often only visible in their daily or weekly lesson planners, where each day's instructional plan is written down.

Often the deep thinking required for solid instructional planning takes place in isolation, at teachers' individual classroom desks, rather than in an environment of collegial support. Because the determination of learning progressions and their instructional sequence is too important to leave to chance, CFA team members need to make these determinations collaboratively, intentionally, and in advance of unit instruction. While they are deliberately mapping out the instructional pathways for a unit of study together, teachers are able to tap into the team's collective expertise to better determine the specific instructional components necessary for getting students from point A to point Z in their learning.

Deciding the learning progressions together makes crystal-clear the instructional sequence for the entire unit. Often, less-experienced educators who do not know a particular content area as well as their experienced colleagues may inadvertently leave key learning progressions out of their instructional sequence. Even experienced educators admit to not always knowing exactly how to "chunk" the unit incrementally so that students will attain the unit learning intentions. And yet, if one of those important chunks is left out of the instructional sequence, it will create a gap in student learning that may go undetected. When team members identify all of those chunks through collaboration, students will have a far better chance of succeeding on the post-CFA because they have followed a predetermined instructional pathway through the unit.

PRELIMINARY CONSIDERATIONS

In Chapter 2 of *Transformative Assessment* (2008), Popham provides two important preliminary issues to consider before educators plan out their learning progressions. The first issue has to do with the number of building blocks: "To keep a learning progression sufficiently lean so that it is likely to be used, the only building blocks to include are those for which you plan to collect assessment evidence" (Popham, 2008, p. 33).

The second issue concerns the "grain size" of the building blocks:

The "grain size" of a building block reflects the nature of the content it comprises. Is it small, specific, or simple, or is it large, ambiguous, or complex? . . . . One useful way to think about the grain size of building blocks is to focus on the amount of instructional time it will take to get students to master them. Large building blocks are those requiring substantial amounts of instructional time; small building blocks are those requiring far less instructional time. (Popham, 2008, p. 33)

STEPS TO DETERMINE THE LEARNING PROGRESSIONS

In that same chapter, Popham presents four sequential steps (2008, pp. 35–42) to determine the learning progressions. Presented here in italics are his steps, along with my commentary regarding how they connect to the CFA process:

Step 1: Acquire a thorough understanding of the target curricular aim. In other words, know exactly what each of the unit learning intentions represents—the knowledge and skills students must acquire by the end of the unit. The "unwrapping" of the Priority Standards and the subsequent creation of the graphic organizer of concepts, skills, and levels of cognitive rigor will make this "thorough understanding" clear.

Step 2: Identify all requisite precursory subskills and bodies of enabling knowledge. This means that each learning progression must be essential to students' attaining the unit learning intentions. To determine this, teacher teams work backwards to identify the prerequisite knowledge and skills students must gain en route to those learning outcomes. These will become the assessable building blocks of unit instruction, so important that reteach-ing would be necessary for any students who could not successfully show they understood them.

Step 3: Determine whether it's possible to measure students' status with respect to each preliminarily identified building block. The quick progress checks, described later in this chapter, must be planned as definite ways to assess student understanding of the learning progressions. If a quick progress check can't do what it's supposed to do (provide credible evidence of student learning related to the learning progression in focus), it must be revised so that it can. If the team members decide that the learning progression can't be assessed effectively, they discuss whether or not it's really essential to students' understanding. If it isn't, the team makes the decision to drop it from the sequence and puts in its place a different learning progression that is assessible.

Step 4: Arrange all building blocks in an instructionally defensible sequence. As teacher teams work backwards from a learning intention and generate the various chunks of in-process instruction needed for students to attain it, they often write those chunks on sticky notes or index cards. Team members then place them in a vertical or horizontal format and rearrange the individual notes/cards as needed until everyone agrees that the sequence makes sense instructionally.

Identifying an instructional sequence for the identified learning progressions is never going to be perfect or "set in stone." Popham (2008) states encouragingly,

> Any learning progression you develop, however well thought out and carefully constructed, is incapable of being anything but your best-guess hypothesis of the sequenced precursors that lead, step by step, to students' mastery of an important curricular aim. First-version learning progressions frequently need some serious reworking. (p. 41)

So just experiment and know that your team's expertise in doing this will improve as you become increasingly familiar with the practice.

Examples of ELA Learning Progressions

In the ELA examples that follow, the unit learning intentions in reading and writing are the "unwrapped" Priority Standards listed in the center column of the Unit Learning Intentions <u>as</u> Student Success Criteria document created in Step 4. The learning intentions are followed by the related learning progressions, written in verb phrases and labeled with Popham's terminology, "subskills" and "enabling knowledge." The italicized learning progressions, three in Reading and five in Writing, are numbered to indicate the sequence for instruction.

READING

Learning Intention:

RI.5.6 ANALYZE <u>multiple accounts of the same event or topic</u>, NOTING important <u>similarities and differences</u> in the <u>point of view they represent</u>.

Learning Progressions in Instructional Sequence

Subskill	Enabling Knowledge
1. *Identify*	*main purpose of a text*
2. *Identify and compare*	*points of view of at least two authors on same topic*
3. *Identify*	*similarities and differences between points of view on same topic or event*

WRITING

Learning Intention:

W.5.1a INTRODUCE a <u>topic</u> or text clearly, STATE an <u>opinion</u>, and CREATE an <u>organizational structure</u> in which <u>ideas are logically grouped to support the writer's purpose</u>.

Learning Progressions in Instructional Sequence

Subskill	Enabling Knowledge
1. *Identify*	*difference between fact and opinion*
2. *Use*	*organizational structures for different purposes of writing*

(Continued)

(Continued)

Subskill	Enabling Knowledge
3. *Name*	*different techniques to use when writing an introductory sentence, statement, paragraph, quotation, provoking question, story, or anecdote, etc.*
4. *Identify*	*evidence in a text to support an opinion*
5. *Write*	*cohesive paragraph with a beginning, middle, and end*

Example of Math Learning Progressions

In the math example, five "unwrapped" Priority Standards—one main Priority Standard (6.RP.3) and four related Priority Standards (a, b, c, and d)—represent the unit learning intentions. They are listed in the center column of the Unit Learning Intentions *as* Student Success Criteria document created in Step 4. For illustration purposes, only the first of the related learning intentions (6.RP.3a) is presented here. Its nine italicized learning progressions are numbered to indicate the sequence for instruction.

Main Learning Intention:

6.RP.A.3 USE ratio and rate reasoning to SOLVE real-world and mathematical problems, e.g., by reasoning about tables of equivalent ratios, tape diagrams, double number line diagrams, or equations.

Related Learning Intention:

6.RP.3a. MAKE tables of equivalent ratios RELATING quantities with whole number measurements, FIND missing values in the tables, and PLOT the pairs of values on the coordinate plane. USE tables to COMPARE ratios.

Learning Progressions in Instructional Sequence

1. *Teach students how to build a table of equivalent ratios based on a given context.*

2. *Practice building tables of equivalent ratios based on given contexts.*

3. *Teach students various methods to find missing values in a table of equivalent ratios.*

4. *Practice finding missing values in a table of equivalent ratios.*

5. *Review with students ordered pairs and the coordinate plane in the first quadrant.*

6. *Teach students how to use values on the table of equivalent ratios to make ordered pairs.*

7. *Teach students how to plot ordered pairs on a coordinate plane in the first quadrant.*

8. *Practice making ordered pairs from a table of equivalent ratios.*

9. *Practice plotting ordered pairs on a coordinate plane in the first quadrant.*

CFA Design Step 10: Plan Quick Progress Checks to Coincide With the Learning Progressions. A quick, informal, ungraded check for student understanding needs to occur immediately after each learning progression. Quick progress checks provide immediate feedback to educators and students about students' understanding of the learning progression and where to go next instructionally. The most effective formative progress checks are planned in advance by the teacher team to coincide with the various learning progressions.

QUICK PROGRESS CHECKS

It is almost always necessary for teachers to employ learning progressions as the frameworks by which they can identify *appropriate occasions for assessment-informed adjustment decisions.* Learning progressions, in an almost literal sense, become the maps that provide guidance on how best to carry out formative assessment. (Popham, 2008, p. 29; italics added)

After teacher teams finish their initial determination of learning progressions leading to the learning intentions, they next need to plan the formative "checks for student understanding" that coincide with those progressions. In the CFA process, these are called **quick progress checks,** which students respond to independently. They help educators know whether all, many, few, or only individual students need reteaching of the subskills and enabling knowledge within the learning progression. These checks, aligned to the post-CFA questions, preview how students are likely to perform on the post-CFA well in advance so that any misconceptions and lack of understanding can be corrected.

When educators share the feedback from quick progress checks with their students, asking probing questions and suggesting strategies to help them move forward, these checks for understanding become, for students, assessments *as* learning that show them *how* to improve.

QUICK PROGRESS CHECKS CONTAIN SUCCESS CRITERIA

A quick progress check contains the success criteria for that mini-assessment in the form of one or more verbs (skills) stating what students are to do. For example, in the quick progress check for an ELA learning progression, *"Identify* and *compare* the points of view of at least two authors," the two verbs spell out what students need to *do*—identify and compare. Student responses will provide the evidence of learning. If students are correctly able to demonstrate both skills on their own, they have achieved the success criteria.

Here are two sequenced math learning progressions followed by a quick progress check that assesses student understanding of both:

1. Teach students how to build a table of equivalent ratios based on a given context.

2. Practice building tables of equivalent ratios based on given contexts.

Quick Progress Check:

The ratio of boys to girls in a local school is 2:3.
Fill in the table below with equivalent ratios.

Boys	Girls

The directions, *"Fill in the table below with equivalent ratios,"* indicate what students are to do (even though in the related standard, the verb used is *"FIND" missing values in the tables*). If students are correctly able to demonstrate that skill independently, they have provided evidence of their learning that meets the success criteria.

ELA Quick Progress Checks

Here again are the reading and writing unit learning intentions and related learning progressions that will span the multi-week unit of study. Quick progress checks, in italicized print, have been inserted after each progression. The italicized verbs simultaneously convey to students the assessment directions *and* the success criteria.

READING

Learning Intention:

RI.5.6 ANALYZE multiple accounts of the same event or topic, NOTING important similarities and differences in the point of view they represent.

Learning Progressions in Instructional Sequence

Subskill	Enabling Knowledge
1. Identify	main purpose of a text

Quick Progress Check: *Students read two brief nonfiction passages (1–2 paragraphs each) on a similar topic or event and identify in writing the main purpose of each passage.*

2. Identify and compare	points of view of at least two authors on same topic on same topic

Quick Progress Check: *Students reread the two nonfiction passages on the same topic and respond to the following directions: Identify the author's point of view in the first reading passage. Identify the author's point of view in the second reading passage. Compare the two authors' points of view.*

3. Identify	similarities and differences between points of view on same topic or event

Quick Progress Check: *Students read two brief nonfiction passages on a similar topic written by different authors and then use a Venn diagram to identify the similarities and differences in the points of view of the two authors.*

WRITING

Learning Intention:

W.5.1a INTRODUCE a <u>topic</u> or text clearly, STATE an <u>opinion</u>, and CREATE an <u>organizational structure</u> in which <u>ideas are logically grouped to support the writer's purpose</u>. Learning Progressions in Instructional Sequence

Subskill	Enabling Knowledge
1. Identify	the difference between fact and opinion

Quick Progress Check: *Students read several brief statements (2–3 sentences each) and identify whether those statements are facts or opinions.*

2. Use	organizational structures for different purposes of writing

Quick Progress Check: *Referring to the different organizational structures presented, students read and complete a matching task that requires them to identify the organizational structure presented in each passage. Students will then select two of the organizational structures with accompanying topics and write a paragraph for each (i.e., create organizational structures for different purposes of writing).*

For example, if there are four organizational structures to choose from—compare/contrast, time order, cause and effect, and sequencing—the teacher provides accompanying topics such as these: oceans and lakes for compare and contrast; major holidays of the year for time order; smoking and diseases for cause and effect; and making a peanut butter and jelly sandwich for sequencing. Teachers can provide other topics for students to choose from, or students can choose their own.

3. Name	different techniques to use when writing an introductory sentence, statement, paragraph, quotation, provoking question, story, or anecdote, etc.

Quick Progress Check: *Students read several introductions to short reading passages and then identify the writing technique used.*

4. Identify	evidence in a text to support an opinion

Quick Progress Check: *Students read 3–5 different paragraphs on different topics and identify in writing the opinion <u>and</u> evidence that supports the opinion in each passage.*

5. Write	cohesive paragraph with a beginning, middle, and end

Quick Progress Check: *Students respond to a nonfiction writing prompt and write a cohesive paragraph that includes a beginning, middle, and end.*

A recommended resource filled with excellent ideas for planning quick progress checks in English language arts is *Checking for Understanding: Formative Assessment Techniques for Your Classroom* (2007). In it, coauthors Douglas Fisher and Nancy Frey offer numerous practical ways to use oral language strategies, questioning techniques, and a variety of writing methods to check for student understanding.

Math Quick Progress Checks

Here again is the math learning intention and its related learning progressions shown earlier. Now three quick progress checks have been inserted where appropriate.

Note how the three quick progress checks, in italics, do not occur in a one-to-one ratio with the learning progressions as they do in the ELA example, but rather as follows:

- The first quick progress check assesses student understanding of *the first two* learning progressions.
- The second quick progress check assesses student understanding of *the next two* learning progressions.
- The third quick progress check assesses student understanding of *the last five* learning progressions.

Learning Intention:

6.RP.3a. MAKE <u>tables of equivalent ratios</u> RELATING <u>quantities</u> with <u>whole number measurements</u>, FIND <u>missing values in the tables</u>, and PLOT the <u>pairs of values</u> on the <u>coordinate plane</u>. USE <u>tables</u> to COMPARE <u>ratios</u>.

Learning Progressions in Instructional Sequence

1. Teach students how to build a table of equivalent ratios based on a given context.

2. Practice building tables of equivalent ratios based on given contexts.

Quick Progress Check (to assess student understanding of Learning Progressions 1–2):

The ratio of boys to girls in a local school is 2:3.

Fill in the table below with equivalent ratios.

Boys	Girls

Next Learning Progressions in Instructional Sequence

3. Teach students various methods to find missing values in a table of equivalent ratios.

4. Practice finding missing values in a table of equivalent ratios.

Quick Progress Check (to assess student understanding of Learning Progressions 3–4):

The table below shows equivalent ratios to 4:5.

Fill in the missing values.

4	5
12	
	20
20	
	30
28	

Remaining Learning Progressions in Instructional Sequence

5. Review ordered pairs and the coordinate plane (first quadrant) with students.

6. Teach students how to use values on the table of equivalent ratios to make ordered pairs.

7. Teach students how to plot ordered pairs on a coordinate plane in the first quadrant.

8. Practice making ordered pairs from a table of equivalent ratios.

9. Practice plotting ordered pairs on a coordinate plane in the first quadrant.

Quick Progress Check (to assess student understanding of Learning Progressions 5–9):

Use the table of equivalent ratios below to list ordered pairs.

Plot the ordered pairs on a coordinate plane.

Yards	Feet
1	3
2	6
3	9
4	12
5	15

MAKING ADJUSTMENTS IN INSTRUCTION AND LEARNING

In *Embedded Formative Assessment* (2011), Dylan Wiliam provides a spot-on, comprehensive description of the function of **formative assessment:**

> An assessment functions formatively to the extent that evidence about student achievement is elicited, interpreted, and used by teachers, learners, or their peers to *make decisions about the next steps in instruction* that are likely to be better, or better founded, than the decisions they would have made in the absence of that evidence. (p. 43; italics added)

"Feedback is a 'consequence' of performance" (Hattie, 2009, p. 174). The primary reason educators administer quick progress checks is to gain credible evidence—feedback—about students' current degree of understanding relative to the learning progressions in focus so they can make instructional adjustments. Assessment evidence provides feedback for students to help them know what learning adjustments they need to carry out. When used in this dual way, feedback is used reciprocally.

UNDERSTANDING THE MEANING AND PURPOSE OF FEEDBACK

In *Visible Learning* (2009) and *Visible Learning for Teachers* (2012), John Hattie provides research-based evidence about the vital importance of feedback for educators *and* for students:

> To make feedback effective, teachers must have a good understanding of where the students are, and where they are meant to be—and the more transparent they make this status for the students, the more students can help to get themselves from the points at which they are to the success points, and thus enjoy the fruits of feedback.
>
> Feedback serves various purposes in reducing this gap: it can provide cues that capture a person's attention and helps him or her to focus on succeeding with the task; it can direct attention toward the processes needed to accomplish the task; it can provide information about ideas that have been misunderstood; and it can be motivational so that students invest more effort or skill in the task.
>
> Acknowledging errors allows for opportunities. Error is the difference between what we know and can do, and what we aim to know and do—and this applies to all (struggling and talented; students and teachers). Knowing this error is fundamental to moving towards success. This is the purpose of feedback. (Hattie, 2012, p. 115)

What makes Hattie's advocacy for feedback doubly compelling is his supporting evidence, deduced from the voluminous research he and others conducted:

> The evidence about its effectiveness is documented in *Visible Learning*. In brief, the average effect size is 0.79, which is twice the average effect of all other schooling effects. This places feedback in the top ten influences on achievement, even though there is considerable variability. (Hattie, 2012, p. 116)

FEEDBACK-INFORMED INSTRUCTIONAL ADJUSTMENTS

After educators administer their quick progress checks, they need to *respond instructionally* to what the feedback indicates students need next in their learning. This is the whole purpose of formative assessment—to inform instruction so that there is a positive change in student understanding. In Hattie's words, "The act of teaching requires deliberate interventions to ensure that there is a cognitive change in the student." (2012, p. 19)

Here is the completed ELA example that includes the learning intentions in focus, their related learning progressions, and the quick progress checks—now accompanied by suggestions in italics of what the teacher can do instructionally with the student feedback from each of those quick checks for understanding.

READING

Learning Intention:

RI.5.6 ANALYZE <u>multiple accounts of the same event or topic</u>, NOTING important <u>similarities and differences</u> in the <u>point of view they represent</u>.

Learning Progressions in Instructional Sequence

Subskill	Enabling Knowledge
1. Identify	main purpose of a text

Quick Progress Check: Students read two brief nonfiction passages (1–2 paragraphs each) on a similar topic or event and identify in writing the main purpose of each passage.

Suggested Instructional Adjustments Based on Assessment Results:

- *Depending on number of students in need of corrective instruction, provide individual or small flexible group support.*
- *Conduct a Think Aloud to model how to identify the main purpose of two new passages that teacher and students read together.*
- *Reassess to determine if students are now able to correctly identify the main purpose of a text in the original two reading passages used in the quick progress check.*

2. Identify and compare	points of view of at least two authors on same topic

Quick Progress Check: Students reread the two nonfiction passages on the same topic and respond to the following directions: Identify the author's point of view in the first reading passage. Identify the author's point of view in the second reading passage. Compare the two authors' points of view.

Suggested Instructional Adjustments Based on Assessment Results:

- *Depending on number of students in need of corrective instruction, provide individual or small flexible group support.*
- *Define point of view and then reread the two new passages.*
- *Conduct a Think Aloud to model how to identify the author's point of view in each of the two new passages.*
- *Reassess to determine if students are now able to correctly identify the author's point of view in the original two reading passages used in the quick progress check.*

3. Identify	similarities and differences between points of view on same topic or event

Quick Progress Check: Students read two brief nonfiction passages on a similar topic written by different authors and then use a Venn diagram to identify the similarities and differences in the points of view of the two authors.

Suggested Instructional Adjustments Based on Assessment Results:

- *Depending on number of students in need of corrective instruction, provide individual or small flexible group support.*
- *Define similarities and differences and then once again reread with students the two new passages.*
- *Using a Venn diagram, model how to identify the similarities and differences between the two authors' points of view.*
- *Reassess to determine if students can now correctly create their own Venn diagram with the original two reading passages used in the quick progress check.*

WRITING

Learning Intention:

W.5.1a INTRODUCE a topic or text clearly, STATE an opinion, and CREATE an organizational structure in which ideas are logically grouped to support the writer's purpose. Learning Progressions in Instructional Sequence

Subskill	Enabling Knowledge
1. Identify	the difference between fact and opinion

Quick Progress Check: Students read several brief statements (2–3 sentences each) and then identify whether those statements are facts or opinions.

Suggested Instructional Adjustments Based on Assessment Results:

- *Depending on the number of students in need of corrective instruction, provide individual or small flexible group support.*
- *Conduct a Think Aloud to model how to identify facts and opinions and why this distinction is important to understand.*
- *Provide a list of factual statements and opinion statements for students to practice identifying.*
- *Reassess students' understanding to determine if they can now correctly distinguish between fact and opinion.*

2. Use	organizational structures for different purposes of writing

Quick Progress Check: Referring to the different organizational structures presented, students read and complete a matching task that requires them to identify the organizational structure presented in each passage. Students will then select two of the organizational structures with accompanying topics and write a paragraph for each (i.e., create organizational structures for different purposes of writing).

For example, if there are four organizational structures to choose from—compare/contrast, time order, cause and effect, and sequencing—the teacher provides accompanying topics such as these: oceans and lakes for compare and contrast; major holidays of the year for time order; smoking and diseases for cause and effect; and making a peanut butter and jelly sandwich for sequencing. Teachers can provide other topics for students to choose from or students can choose their own.

Suggested Instructional Adjustments Based on Assessment Results:

- *Depending on number of students in need of corrective instruction, provide individual or small, flexible group support.*
- *Review key trigger words and the types of organizational patterns associated with them.*

* *Select the organizational structures to present to students and find accompanying topics for students to choose from.*

- *Explain to students that each type of organizational structure includes "trigger words" associated with that structure.*
- *Students read each of the structures and try to identify the organizational structure and the trigger words that helped them identify it.*
- *Generate with students other trigger words for each of the structures that they can reference when they write.*
- *Reassessment: Students will select two of the organizational structures with accompanying topics and write a paragraph for each.*

3. Name	different techniques to use when writing an introductory sentence, statement, paragraph, *quotation, provoking question, story, or anecdote, etc.*

Quick Progress Check: Students read several introductions to short passages and then identify the writing technique used.

Suggested Instructional Adjustments Based on Assessment Results:

- *Depending on the number of students in need of corrective instruction, provide individual or small flexible group support.*
- *Review the different techniques to use in an introduction.*
- *Read aloud several introductory sentences or paragraphs, and for additional practice have students use whiteboards to identify the technique.*
- *Use students' whiteboard responses as evidence of improved learning.*

4. Identify	evidence in a text to support an opinion

Quick Progress Check: Students read 3–5 different paragraphs on different topics and identify in writing the opinion <u>and</u> evidence that supports the opinion in each passage.

Suggested Instructional Adjustments Based on Assessment Results:

- *Depending on number of students in need of corrective instruction, provide individual or small, flexible group support.*
- *Conduct a guided practice in identifying an opinion and its supporting evidence. Ask students to explain why the identified evidence supports the*

opinion and other pieces of evidence do not. Students practice with one or two more examples.

- *Reassessment: Provide students with a few short reading passages with the opinion and supporting evidence correctly and incorrectly identified. Students determine which evidence correctly supports the opinion and which does not.*

5. Write	cohesive paragraph with a beginning, middle, and end

Quick Progress Check: Students respond to a nonfiction writing prompt and write a cohesive paragraph that includes a beginning, middle, and end.

Suggested Instructional Adjustments Based on Assessment Results:

- *Depending on the number of students in need of corrective instruction, provide individual or small, flexible group support.*
- *Provide samples of paragraphs that need to be improved. Ask students to identify needed improvements and then rewrite the paragraph to improve it. Students' individual paragraph responses will be the reassessment of their learning.*

Math Example of Quick Progress Checks and Suggested Instructional Adjustments

Here is the culmination of the math example that includes the learning intention in focus, its related learning progressions, and quick progress checks—now accompanied by suggestions of what the teacher can do instructionally with that evidence.

Learning Intention:

6.RP.3a. MAKE <u>tables of equivalent ratios</u> RELATING <u>quantities</u> with <u>whole number measurements</u>, FIND <u>missing values in the tables</u>, and PLOT the <u>pairs of values</u> on the <u>coordinate plane</u>. USE <u>tables</u> to COMPARE <u>ratios</u>.

Learning Progressions in Instructional Sequence

1. Teach students how to build a table of equivalent ratios based on a given context.

2. Practice building tables of equivalent ratios based on given contexts.

198

Quick Progress Check (to assess student understanding of Learning Progressions 1–2):

The ratio of boys to girls in a local school is 2:3.

Fill in the table below with equivalent ratios.

Boys	Girls

Suggested Instructional Adjustments (individual student or small flex group):

- *Use concrete objects to build and record equivalent ratios.*
- *Reassess students with the same quick progress check using different num-ber values.*

Next Learning Progressions in Instructional Sequence

3. Teach students various methods to find missing values in a table of equivalent ratios.

4. Practice finding missing values in a table of equivalent ratios.

Quick Progress Check (to assess student understanding of Learning Progressions 3–4):

The table below shows equivalent ratios to 4:5.

Fill in the missing values.

4	5
12	
	20
20	
	30
28	

Suggested Instructional Adjustments (individual student or small flex group):

- *Determine reasoning process each student used to fill in the missing values.*
- *Build equivalent ratios with concrete objects to find missing values.*
- *Practice multiplication and division relationships to find missing values.*
- *Reassess students with the same quick progress check using different num-ber values.*

Remaining Learning Progressions in Instructional Sequence

5. Review ordered pairs and the coordinate plane (first quadrant) with students.

6. Teach students how to use values on the table of equivalent ratios to make ordered pairs.

7. Teach students how to plot ordered pairs on a coordinate plane in the first quadrant.

8. Practice making ordered pairs from a table of equivalent ratios.

9. Practice plotting ordered pairs on a coordinate plane in the first quadrant.

Quick Progress Check (to assess student understanding of Learning Progressions 5–9):

Use the table of equivalent ratios below to list ordered pairs.

Plot the ordered pairs on a coordinate plane.

YARDS	FEET
1	3
2	6
3	9
4	12
5	15

Suggested Instructional Adjustments (individual student or small flex group):

- *Review basics of coordinate plane (axis, origin, ordered pairs).*

- *Practice plotting ordered pairs.*
- *Reassess students with the same quick progress check using different num-ber values.*

USE OF FEEDBACK BY STUDENTS

Educators need to help students understand that making mistakes is an unavoidable part of learning—not only in school but also in everyday life. A mistake is anything that didn't work out the way we thought it would. A mistake is also helpful feedback that enables us to adjust what we are doing and learning. Our continual message to students must be, "Feedback is our friend."

> Mistakes are potent learning tools when viewed diagnostically rather than evaluatively. In school, teachers can build on mistakes to increase learning when we frame them as part of the instruction process rather than as an indicator of failure. (Mendler, 2000, p. 10)

In *High Impact Instruction: A Framework for Great Teaching* (2013), author Jim Knight concurs: "Students learn more when teachers identify categories of error in student work and provide elaborated feedback and modeling to ensure students learn how to move forward" (p. 77).

Feedback is a reciprocal exchange between educator and student. It is a communication loop or cycle that repeats itself continually: The educator provides the quick progress check, the student provides the response. The educator analyzes the feedback to correctly interpret student understanding and shares that feedback with the student. The student identifies next learning steps. The educator then makes instructional adjustments while the student adjusts his or her learning strategies.

Feedback always addresses three questions: *Where am I going? How am I going? Where to next?* Note the pronoun "I" in the first two questions. The underlying message communicated by that pronoun is that feedback is primarily directed *to and from* the learner. In *Visible Learning* (2009), Hattie shares both his "mistake" in seeing feedback (only) as something educators provide to students and his later realization:

> It was only when I discovered that feedback was most powerful when it is from the *student to the teacher* that I started to understand it better. When teachers seek, or at least are open to, feedback from students as to what students know, what they understand, where they make errors, when they have misconceptions, when they are

not engaged—then teaching and learning can be synchronized and powerful. Feedback to teachers helps make learning visible. (p. 173)

The more students can be involved in their own learning—setting appropriate goals, selecting appropriate strategies to achieve those goals, monitoring and adjusting their learning approaches and strategies based on feedback, sharing their thinking with teachers, and frequently reflecting on their progress in order to improve—the more *student-directed* the entire assessment process can become.

In *How to Give Effective Feedback to Your Students* (2008), author Susan Brookhart describes the kinds of feedback that work best in various content areas and how to adjust feedback for different kinds of learners. Brookhart identifies three characteristics of effective feedback, given to students in the form of comments that are about the task, are descriptive, affect both performance and motivation, and "foster interest in the task for its own sake, an orientation found in successful, self-regulated learners" (p. 8).

CONNECTED PRACTICES: "TEACH-ASSESS-INTERPRET-ADJUST"

Learning progressions, success criteria, quick progress checks, and teaching-learning adjustments are closely linked and in continual use throughout each unit of study. This series of connected practices, expressed in the phrase Teach-Assess-Interpret-Adjust, can be summarized as follows:

- Educators *teach*, in a preplanned sequence, the learning progressions essential for students to attain the end-of-unit learning intentions.
- A quick progress check, embedded with success criteria, is administered after each learning progression, or two or more related learning progressions, to *assess* student understanding.
- Assessment evidence provides credible feedback about what students have or have not learned as a result of instruction within that learning progression.
- Educators use the feedback to correctly *interpret* student understanding and *adjust* their instruction.
- Students use the feedback to *adjust* their learning strategies.
- Educators confirm that students understand each learning progression (through reassessment) before moving on to the next learning progression in the instructional sequence.

Educators have enthusiastically endorsed the inclusion of collabora-tively designed learning progressions and quick progress checks in the CFA 2.0 process, referring to these as the missing key elements absent from the original CFA model. Certainly it will require teacher teams a greater investment of time to include these new additions. But in doing so, each teacher on that team will be able to implement a unit of study with all of its components intentionally aligned—standards, instruction, assessment, and data analysis. One powerful result may be that fewer students will need to be retaught and reassessed on the Bridge because they have already closed their learning gaps throughout the unit by means of the quick progress checks and the resulting adjustments to both teaching and learning.

CHAPTER SUCCESS CRITERIA

In Chapter 11, you will learn how teacher teams can maximize their learning together by collaboratively scoring their CFAs and analyzing the student results together.

Before turning the page, however, please take a few moments and write your responses to the success criteria for this chapter, or simply evaluate your understanding of each mastery statement on a scale of one (low) to five (high). Again, close any learning gaps you may have by rereading related sections or through discussion. As suggested at the conclusion of prior chapters, if you are reading this book as part of a professional study group, share your thoughts and ideas with colleagues.

Success Criteria:

- Define learning progressions and describe their function in relation to the unit learning intentions.
- Define quick progress checks and how teacher teams use them.
- Summarize the important role of reciprocal feedback in the instruction-assessment-adjustment cycle.

11

Collaborative Scoring and Analysis of CFA 2.0 Results

In This Chapter You Will Learn:

- The true purpose and function of a collaborative learning team.
- How teams collaboratively score the short- and extended-response questions on the CFAs.
- How teams can use a selected data analysis protocol to process post-CFA student results and effectively prepare for the Bridge.

The CFA 2.0 design process culminates in the completion of the ten steps by the teacher team. However, teams can extend their work together through the collaborative scoring of student responses and the collaborative analysis of student results. This will help team members quickly and effectively prepare for their time on the Bridge at the end of the unit when they provide remediation for students who did not achieve all of the unit success criteria and enrichment for those who did. As shown in Figure 11.1, these three collaborative practices are sequential yet connected.

204

Figure 11.1 The Connected Practices of Professional Learning Teams

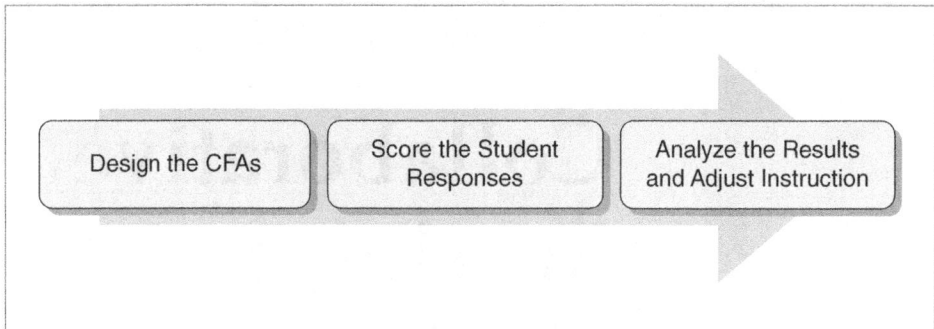

Design the CFAs → Score the Student Responses → Analyze the Results and Adjust Instruction

Professional learning teams provide the perfect structure for these interdependent practices to take place. However, without effective collaboration skills and a commitment to honoring agreed-upon professional norms, these connected practices can become greatly compromised. Establishing these skills and professional norms to ensure productive collaboration is the essential function of PLCs.

THE "L" IN PLCs

Educators and leaders have been using the phrase *professional learning communities* (PLCs) for more than a decade as a way of referring to almost any type of meeting that takes place among a group of teachers. Rick DuFour cautioned against this in 2004, saying, "The term has been used so ubiquitously that it is in danger of losing all meaning" (para. 2). It is therefore important for educators and leaders to reassess and clarify their understanding of what a PLC is and does.

A professional learning community exists for one primary purpose: to improve student learning by improving the teaching practices of educators. To improve educators' practice requires not just students' learning but *educators'* learning as well. DuFour (2004) emphasizes this essential purpose as being "not simply to ensure that students are taught but to ensure that they learn. This simple shift—from a focus on teaching to a focus on learning—has profound implications" (para. 5).

In the CFA 2.0 context, a teacher learning team meets to *learn* what they can from their students' assessment results so that each member can more effectively adjust his or her own classroom instruction as needed for individual students. This often necessitates a *change* in teaching practices. The degree to which an instructional change proves effective is apparent in the resulting student data and the visible improvements in student learning.

PROTOCOLS ESSENTIAL

In 2008 education researchers Vescio, Ross, and Adams conducted a systematic review of the literature on PLCs. They included only peer-reviewed studies and empirical evidence related to the impact of PLCs on student learning. Among their findings were these: the core elements of a PLC—sharing values, setting goals, and building a positive adult culture—contributed to as much as an 85 percent variance in teacher pedagogy and 36 percent variance in student achievement (p. 83).

Yet not all PLCs achieve such desirable results, even when these core elements are present. Why?

One of the critical factors necessary for PLCs to have a positive impact on student learning is to *follow protocols consistently.* "Stable settings, job-alike teams, peer facilitators, and protocols create 'intensive, focused opportunities to experiment with aspects of practice'" (Grossman & McDonald as cited in Gallimore, Ermeling, Saunders, & Goldenberg, 2009, p. 551). Teacher teams that faithfully follow specific protocols, processes, and procedures while analyzing evidence of student learning—in order to make instructional decisions based on that evidence—have a greater likelihood of achieving this positive impact.

HORIZONTAL AND VERTICAL LEARNING TEAMS

Grade- or course-level educators who all teach the same unit of study at the same time are referred to as horizontal learning teams. Vertical learning teams comprise educators who teach *different* grades or courses, but within the same department or subject area.

School leaders need to ensure that educators from special education, English language acquisition, visual and performing arts, career and technical education, library and media technology, physical education, and all other content areas are also included as members of horizontal or vertical learning teams. They can serve in a dual capacity by (1) helping to improve professional practices in their own content area while (2) simultaneously assisting learning team colleagues in improving theirs.

These valued educators become part of different learning teams based on a variety of factors that include identified school improvement goals, academic focus, logistical issues, and the positive contributions they can make to the knowledge base of colleagues. To prevent them from being spread too thin, however, special area educators should not serve on more than one learning team at a time.

Whether organized horizontally or vertically, learning teams must meet consistently and regularly if they are to truly benefit from one another's insights. Ideally they should meet once a week every month throughout the school year. For a month-long unit of study, the first meeting should be used to analyze the pre-CFA results, set a learning team SMART goal, and select instructional strategies to meet that goal by the end of the unit. The second and third weekly meetings should be devoted to reviewing student work from the quick progress checks, making accurate inferences about student learning, discussing the effectiveness of the targeted teaching strategies, and deciding how best to adjust instruction to better meet the learning needs of all students. The fourth week requires two or even three meetings—one meeting to collaboratively score the post-CFAs and one or two meetings to process the student results and plan for remediation and enrichment of students while they are on the Bridge. (A description of these meetings appears later in the chapter.)

COLLECTIVE WISDOM

A true professional learning community establishes a safe environment that recognizes and respects the needs of each educator to be able to learn from and with colleagues without fear of judgment or reprisal from anyone. The synergy of experience and expertise among the team members generates powerful insights into solving the professional challenges they face. When one teacher achieves excellent student results on the common formative assessment and another does not, a supportive learning environment makes it possible for the second teacher to ask the first how he or she achieved those results. Often these conversations occur spontaneously during team meetings and result in paradigm shifts that have a significant and lasting impact on professional practice. This kind of job-embedded professional development is a powerful expression of "collective wisdom."

INDIVIDUAL VERSUS COLLABORATIVE SCORING OF CFAs

Individual grade- and course-level educators typically score their students' pre- and post-CFAs on their own. By personally scoring their own students' assessments, they gain valuable insights into their students' understanding and can better gauge the impact of their instruction.

Scoring the multiple-choice questions with an answer key on either a pre- or post-CFA is fairly quick and easy. However, accurately scoring each of the constructed-response questions (short and extended) with scoring guides requires more time and thought.

The detailed success criteria for each constructed-response question state in specific, objective wording what students need to include in their responses. An educator reads a student's response and checks the corresponding box for each of the success criteria that the student achieves. The educator then assigns a numerical score or performance level to the response based on how many of the criteria the student has met.

But will teachers who score student responses on their own gain the same depth of insight into student understanding as those who score those same papers with colleagues in a collaborative setting? To help you reflect on this question, here is how learning team members collaboratively score their post-CFAs—in particular, the short and extended constructed-response questions.

Even with an objectively worded scoring guide, the *interpretation* of whether or not those criteria are present in a student's response can still be quite subjective. This is when it is helpful for an educator to have "another set of eyes" looking at a student response to make sure that both evaluators score the student response in the same way. Collaborative scoring ensures the *objective* evaluation of each student's constructed responses.

As soon as grade- and course-level students complete the post-CFA, learning team members meet to collaboratively score the papers. First they individually score at least three of the same student papers. Then they compare their results to make sure they are all scoring those papers the same. The goal is to **calibrate** with one another, meaning, "to arrive at the same scoring result."

To achieve this, the team first selects three student papers at random and numbers them 1, 2, and 3. They next review the scoring guide success criteria and make sure they all have the same understanding of what those criteria mean. Each member then scores one of the three papers, writes the performance level on a sticky note, attaches it to the back of the paper, and passes it to another team member. The process repeats until all three student papers have been scored by all team members. Then the sticky notes on the back of each student paper are transferred to the front.

Team members now discuss and resolve any score discrepancies and reach a scoring agreement. These resolutions must be based on the *scoring criteria* and not on personal opinions or interpretations. When several educators can consistently calibrate the score for a student response, they achieve **inter-rater reliability.** At this point they can, time permitting, continue scoring the remainder of student papers collaboratively, or they can score the rest of the student papers on their own. Either way, because all learning team members are now on the same page of what to look for in each student's constructed responses, they have learned what it means to consistently score student responses using the scoring guide's detailed success criteria.

Collaborative scoring is a powerful professional practice. While teachers are scoring student papers together, they are discussing with one another the diverse quality of student responses. They are spontaneously sharing their frustrations, insights, and expertise with one another. During this deep examination of student work, they are able to ask themselves and each other if they are truly assessing what they thought they were assessing. They are able to pinpoint the challenges of reaching students who are not yet achieving the success criteria and may require intervention. They are recognizing the need to provide enrichment or acceleration for students who are demonstrating advanced or exemplary levels of understanding. The power of these kinds of collaborative discussions to bring about improvements in teaching and learning cannot be overstated.

> As a result of the insights and skills gained through this [collaborative scoring] system, teachers become much more purposeful about selecting instructional and curriculum approaches, moving students ever closer to the appropriate learning outcomes. (Langor, Colton, & Goff, 2003, p. 11)

IMPLICATIONS FOR GRADING

The issue of how to fairly correlate levels of student performance represented on a scoring guide with the assignment of letter grades continues to spark lively debate among educators. Here is a scenario that occurs frequently in schools today. A parent arrives at the classroom door and asks to see how his or her child is doing in school. The teacher opens the grade book or the computer grading program and replies, "Quite well! She has two 'exemplary' scores, three 'proficient' marks, and one or two 'progressing' papers." The parent looks puzzled and replies, "But what does that mean in terms of a letter grade?"

The challenge of assigning grades is a formidable one, given the simple fact that there is such a diverse understanding and philosophy with regard to grading, not only among educators and leaders but also among parents and students. When computing grades, individual educators will often weight various assignments and assessments differently from the way their colleagues might. The misinterpretation of single scores is particularly problematic. Educators will often "use a single score to represent student performance on a wide array of skills and abilities" (Marzano, 2000, p. 6).

Tom Guskey and Jane Bailey (2001) examine the grading issue from a student's point of view:

> Around the middle school years and sometimes earlier, students' perceptions of grades begin to change. Although the reasons for this change are uncertain, it seems likely due to teachers' shifting emphasis from the formative aspects of grades to their summative functions. As a result, students no longer see grades as a source of feedback to guide improvements in their learning. Instead, they regard grades as the major commodity teachers and schools have to offer in exchange for their performance. This change brings a slow but steady shift in students' focus away from learning and toward what they must do to obtain the grade commodity. (p. 18)

Despite the general agreement that grades are imperfect measures of student progress, they appear to be firmly fixed in the culture of American education. So how to resolve the lack of consensus among professional educators and leaders as to whether or not to grade common formative assessments *for* learning? The operative word here is *formative.* If an assessment of current understanding is intentionally formative—meaning that the student is *in progress* toward attainment of the learning goals—then assigning a letter grade to that student's progress is premature and difficult to justify.

Grades should reflect student performance only on *summative* assessments or, stated more correctly, on assessments that are used to generate *summative evaluations* of student performance. In fairness to students, grades should represent the degree to which they have achieved the learning intentions by the conclusion of the unit, not before.

After a review of almost eight thousand classroom studies focused on determining the impact of feedback on student improvement, John Hattie (1992) declared, "The most powerful single modification that enhances achievement is feedback. The simplest prescription for improving education must be 'dollops of feedback'" (p. 9).

The quick progress checks that educators administer after learning progressions throughout the unit are the instruction-learning adjustment points, for themselves and for their students. In direct response to the assessment results or "dollops of feedback," teachers adjust their instruction and students adjust their learning strategies. Because the quick progress checks are aligned to the post-CFA, they enable students to practice for the post-CFA in "bite-size" chunks. Students are then equipped to sit for the on-demand, end-of-unit assessment that is an independent summative measure of their learning because they have been preparing for success all along the way. Educators can then justifiably assign a grade based on each student's independent performance.

EFFECTIVE USE OF THE "BRIDGE"

Educators use the Bridge that immediately follows the analysis of post-CFA results at the end of the unit to facilitate greater student learning. They provide enrichment activities for students who achieved and/or exceeded the student success criteria and earned a proficient grade. For students who did not, educators use the post-CFA results formatively to customize subsequent instruction. During their time on the Bridge, those students can successfully close whatever learning gaps they may still have and then be ready to begin the next unit of study.

Here is a grading idea for your professional consideration that may invite pushback but nevertheless supports the effective use of the Bridge from a *formative* assessment perspective: After reteaching, educators reassess students by asking them to revise their answers to the post-CFA questions they originally missed. If a student can now respond to those questions correctly, the teacher can decide to change the student's initial low grade to a higher one that reflects the improvements shown. Since the ultimate goal of the post-CFA is to gain evidence of what students have learned by the *end* of the unit, rather than merely to assign a summative letter grade that is "set in stone," this is a fair and equitable consequence of teacher and student effort worth considering.

RECOMMENDED GRADING RESOURCES

Because the issue of grading continues to set off polarizing discussions, consider the possibility that everyone involved may simply need new information in order to make a more informed decision. The following publications are highly recommended resources to assist you and your colleagues in this decision-making process:

How to Grade for Learning (O'Connor, 2nd ed., 2009)

Developing Standards-Based Report Cards (Guskey & Bailey, 2009)

Grading Exceptional and Struggling Learners (Jung & Guskey, 2012)

Practical Solutions for Serious Problems in Standards-Based Grading (Guskey, 2009)

Fair Isn't Always Equal: Assessing & Grading in the Differentiated Classroom (Wormelli, 2006)

Meaningful Grading Practices for Secondary Teachers (Nagel, 2015)

SHARING POST-CFA RESULTS WITH STUDENTS

As soon as the post-CFAs are scored and recorded by the teacher team, students receive their results along with their own personal Pre-Post Assessment Results grid. This is the same bar graph on which, weeks earlier, students had shaded in the number of pre-CFA items they answered correctly and a goal score to achieve on the post-CFA. (Reminder: The number 10 on the graph is used for illustration only. It is not a recommendation of how many assessment questions to include on either the pre- or post-CFA.)

Pre-Post Assessment Results			
10			
9			
8			
7			
6			
5			
4			
3			
2			
1			
Student Name	**Pre-CFA Score**	**Goal** **Post-CFA Score**	**Actual** **Post-CFA Score**

Now students shade in the *post*-CFA results column to correspond with their actual number of correct answers. They then compare the three columns to see the progress they have made in achieving the unit learning intentions from the beginning to the end of the unit. They re-read their personal SMART goal (Specific-Measurable-*Ambitious*-Relevant-Timely) to determine for themselves whether or not they achieved their goal.

Students then complete a post-unit self-reflection, noting where they did well, what strategies they feel are working best for them, where they need to go next in their learning, and what plan they have to improve while they are on the Bridge.

The learning team members are now ready to meet again to *analyze* the post-CFA results, interpret student learning needs, and plan for follow-up instruction based on their inferences. Educators need a predetermined instructional plan during the days on the Bridge to maximize learning for all students. The remainder of this chapter describes how teacher teams working in a collaborative learning setting can select the right data analysis procedure and effectively use it for this purpose.

COLLABORATIVE ANALYSIS OF ASSESSMENT RESULTS

Today, schools and school districts continue to be inundated with data. Yet with all the data, schools are still reporting that they are, as Richard DuFour puts it, "data rich and information poor" (DuFour, DuFour, & Eaker, 2005, p. 40). If educators do not effectively use the wealth of available assessment data to gauge the impact of their instruction on student learning *in order to improve it*, they are "information poor."

Various data analysis procedures and protocols are in use today. Regardless of the particular procedure a school or district chooses, it needs to include these key components:

- Charting of the student data by performance levels (exceeding, achieving, progressing, beginning);
- Analyzing the data to make accurate and reliable inferences about student learning;
- Setting a learning team SMART goal (Specific, Measurable, *Ambitious*, Relevant, and Timely) at the beginning of the unit to achieve by the end of the unit;
- Selecting effective research- and evidence-based teaching strategies to meet the SMART goal; and
- Formulating an action plan to guide the team's next steps.

Here is a representative sampling of effective data analysis procedures and protocols. School and district leadership teams should investigate several different options before deciding on the one that best fits the needs of their learning teams—and then ensure that everyone is "speaking" the same language particular to that selected procedure or set of protocols.

1. The Four Critical Questions of PLCs (Rick DuFour, Solution Tree, www.solution-tree.com/presenters/plc-at-work)

2. The Data Team process (The Leadership and Learning Center, www.lead-andlearn.com)

3. Success Analysis Protocol (National School Reform Faculty, http://www.nsrf-harmony.org/)

4. The 8-Step Continuous Improvement Process (Peggy Hinckley, http://www.peggyhinckley.com/8_step_process)

5. Impact PLCs (B. R. Jones, *The Focus Model*, 2014, www.brjonesphd.com)

By following with fidelity a selected data analysis procedure, learning teams will receive these key benefits:

1. Using the common formative *pre*-assessment results, teachers can plan unit instruction that includes differentiation for individual students needing intervention or acceleration.

2. Using the common formative *post*-assessment results, teachers will gain credible evidence of student achievement in relation to the unit learning intentions and student success criteria.

3. Comparing the student results from the pre- and post-assessments, teachers will gain an accurate measure of improvement in student learning achieved by individual students, individual classes, and the entire grade level or course. Popham (2003) offers a related key benefit: "A pretest/post-test evaluative approach can contribute meaningfully to how teachers determine their own instructional impact" (p. 14).

4. Collaborating with colleagues from different areas of specialization, educators will contribute to and benefit from the collective wisdom of everyone involved.

IMPLICATIONS FOR INTERVENTION AND ACCELERATION

Differentiated instruction is "providing teaching that is tailored to the learning needs of each student in a classroom" (Yatvin, 2004, p. 5). To differentiate instruction effectively, educators must have access to a wide repertoire of instructional techniques. "Only teachers who utilize a variety of instructional models will be successful in maximizing the achievement of all students. ... Teachers need to 'play to' students' strengths and to mitigate students' learning weaknesses. This can be done only through the use of instructional variety" (Tomlinson, 1999, p. 61).

Carefully planned and timely remediation and intervention for students at risk are vital to closing the student achievement gap. Thoughtfully planned accelerations for students capable of going "above and beyond" are equally vital to enriching the educational experience of high-performing students.

During the **collaborative analysis** of student results, learning teams must discuss and decide *how* they will appropriately intervene for at-risk students, *how* they will differentiate instruction for students who almost achieved the unit learning intentions, and *how* they will accelerate learning for those who did meet or exceed them.

To accomplish these instructional adjustments, educators need effective instructional strategies. They need to know what to do when students, despite their best efforts, do not meet the targeted learning intentions. Collaborative data analysis meetings provide the perfect context for these important discussions and resulting decisions to take place.

PLANNING FOR THE BRIDGE

The key components of any effective data analysis procedure (charting the student data by performance levels, analyzing the data to determine students' learning needs, setting a team SMART goal, selecting effective teaching strategies, and writing an action plan to guide implementation) have been in use by PLCs for many years. These components are particularly effective in working with the pre-CFA data because the unit of study is just beginning and there is plenty of time to implement the pre-CFA action plan. But applying these same components to the post-CFA data presents a different challenge.

What often happens after teacher teams administer the post-CFA to their students is a mad rush to score the papers and analyze the results before the next unit of study begins. If the assessment is well written, the collaborative analysis of the post-CFA data will plainly reveal the learning needs of each student in the grade level or course. Yet usually there is little if any time for teams to effectively plan how they will respond instructionally to these identified needs. If there is no time intentionally built into the curriculum pacing calendar for reteaching and reassessing of student understanding, then how and when can teacher teams use the data to improve student learning?

The purpose of the Bridge between units is to provide students with three-to-five periods of additional class time to improve or extend their learning. It is the designated time for teachers to adjust instruction specific to students' needs, whether in the form of remediation, intervention, or acceleration.

However, just scheduling the Bridge is not enough. Many schools and districts have built into their pacing guides a "buffer" between units. But unless teacher teams can meet again after the post-CFAs are scored to plan next steps, they will not have the time required to thoughtfully determine how to best use this intermission between units.

Here is a practical plan teacher teams can follow to instructionally respond to the post-CFA data. It will enable teams to complete the preliminary preparations needed before students enter the Bridge:

1. Administer the post-CFA on Wednesday and meet as a team to collaboratively score the student papers later that day or immediately after school.

2. Using the charts presented in the next section, begin processing the student results on Thursday during common planning time or immediately after school.

3. Finalize the charts on Friday so that all team members are prepared to enter the Bridge the following Monday.

Because the students will have completed the post-CFA on Wednesday, and teachers will not be ready to begin the Bridge activities until next Monday, students will need to be purposefully engaged on Thursday and Friday. Here is a two-day lesson plan for doing so:

1. Return scored assessments to students on Thursday. In each classroom, students complete their individual Pre-Post Assessment Results graph and unit self-reflection. In cooperative groups of three or four, they then begin an end-of-unit performance task matched to the unit learning intentions (described in Chapter 3). This will give students an opportunity to apply what they have been learning to a real-world situation.

2. On Friday, students complete the performance task in their cooperative groups. Teachers announce that the Bridge activities will begin Monday.

The key to making all of this work is the creative and flexible scheduling of common planning time. School leaders can be of great help by finding innovative and resourceful ways to make certain that these collaborative team meetings happen immediately after the post-CFAs are administered.

THE LEARNING TEAM CHARTS

Note: The information that follows is specific to the processing of *post-CFA* student results in preparation for the Bridge. Learning teams can adapt this information as needed when processing pre-CFA results.

During the meeting to analyze students' responses, learning team members refer to the following five questions to guide their discussions and Bridge planning:

1. *How should we chart our data?* Here is a sample chart that learning teams can use to record the post-CFA performance levels of students. The team must first decide a "cut" score that represents the number of questions students must answer correctly to achieve the unit learning intentions. Next they determine a numerical range for each of the four performance levels (exceeding, achieving, progressing, and beginning). They then tally how many students scored in each of the levels and record their individual classroom totals on the team chart.

Teacher	Student Scores by Performance Level				Class Total
	Exceeding Learning Intention	**Achieving** Learning Intention	**Progressing** Toward Learning Intention	**Beginning** Understanding of Learning Intention	
A	4	15	6	3	28
B	2	18	5	5	30
C	5	20	4	2	31
D	1	13	20	5	39
Grade-Level Total	12	66	35	15	128

Source: Dave Nagel, 2014; adapted with permission.

2. *What inferences can we make about student learning?* The learning team now conducts an item analysis to determine which questions students answered correctly and incorrectly. To help them infer why certain questions in particular may be proving more difficult for students than others, the team refers to the distracter analyses they created when writing their multiple-choice questions and the scoring guides they created for the

short- and extended-response questions. This information assists them in pinpointing student misconceptions.

The team members then list the various learning challenges students are having and prioritize those challenges in descending order of importance. They target the top priority (or top two priorities at most) to keep a sharp focus on students' most pressing learning need(s). They then record on the following chart their inferences in relation to those specific learning challenges.

For illustration purposes, this chart and the ones that follow refer to a high-priority reading challenge that is common to the majority of students in the grade level. These charts are designed not only to plan instructional corrections for underachieving students, but also include inferences and next instructional steps (for the same reading priority) for students who met and exceeded the unit learning intentions.

Performance Level	Inference
Exceeding Learning Intentions	Students can make connections and summarize more succinctly between texts in *different genres* at the same reading levels.
Achieving Learning Intentions	Students can make connections between the text and previous ones we have read in the *same genre*.
Progressing Toward Learning Intentions	Students are struggling with making connections between this text and previous ones.
Beginning Understanding of Learning Intentions	Students struggled with the reading level of the text. Those who were able to comprehend the text could not make connections between this text and other texts.

Source: Dave Nagel, 2014; adapted with permission.

3. *What are the students' next learning steps?* Now the learning team discusses and records the next learning steps students need to take based on their inferences. Educators will share this feedback with their students to help them understand where they need to go next in their learning. Students will use this information to adjust their learning strategies while on the Bridge.

The following chart shows the match-up between the educators' inferences and their identified next learning steps for each student group. Note how the information from the first chart carries over to this one in order to show the connections between them. This same transfer of information will continue in subsequent charts.

Performance Level	Inference	Next Learning Step
Exceeding Learning Intentions	Students can make connections and summarize more succinctly between texts *in different genres* at the same reading levels.	Students learn how to make connections and summarize more succinctly between texts in different genres *at more challenging reading levels.*
Achieving Learning Intentions	Students can make connections between the text and previous ones we have read in the *same genre.*	Students learn how to make the same connections and summarize more succinctly between texts in *different genres at the same reading levels.*
Progressing Toward Learning Intentions	Students are struggling with making connections between this text and previous ones.	Students first decide if the vocabulary is getting in the way of their making connections, and if it is, what help they need to correct that. Next, students identify the setting, character development, and impact of plot on character actions in the first and second texts *separately.* Then they look for the connections of those literary elements *between* the two texts.
Beginning Understanding of Learning Intentions	Students struggled with the reading level of the text. Those who were able to comprehend the text could not make connections between this text and other texts.	Students make connections between texts using a *lower level of vocabulary.* Less challenging vocabulary will help them see and make connections between the two texts more easily. If students cannot make connections between texts with easier vocabulary, teacher and students determine if a deeper reading comprehension issue is the cause. This will indicate the need for different next learning steps for students.

Source: Dave Nagel, 2014; adapted with permission.

As reiterated throughout this book, accurately identifying next learning steps for students is only possible if the inferences educators derive from the CFA results are accurate. This again underscores the critical need for the assessment questions to be of high quality and intentionally aligned to the unit learning intentions.

For example, when the team's discussion turns to those students who are currently at the "beginning understanding" performance level, is the team certain that the next learning steps listed on the chart are the most appropriate? If not, team members may inadvertently make ineffective instructional adjustments in response. If the inferences are correct, then the identified next learning steps will allow the teachers to see whether the difficult vocabulary was indeed the problem or whether the students simply do not yet have the comprehension mastery needed to make connections across different texts.

4. *What instructional strategies can we use to meet students' next learning steps?* Regardless of the different data analysis protocols and procedures in use today, the importance of selecting appropriate instructional strategies to meet the learning team's SMART goal is common to them all. Two peer-reviewed, empirical studies found that measurable improvement in student learning only occurred in PLCs that focused on changing the instructional practices of their teachers (Supovitz, 2002; Supovitz & Christman, 2003).

After the learning team records its inferences and next learning steps for students on the related chart, the team needs to identify specific instructional strategies directly matched to those steps. To accomplish this, team members review and select research- and evidence-based instructional strategies. In many instances, different strategies will be used with different performance-level groups. At other times, the same or similar strategies will be used with multiple groups.

For an instructional strategy to produce an increase in student understanding, members of the learning team need to know the intended effect the strategy should have. They then need to make sure that each educator understands how to effectively implement that strategy in the classroom.

The following chart shows the connections between the planned next steps for student learning and the team-selected instructional strategies.

Performance Level	Next Learning Step	Instructional Strategies
Exceeding Learning Intentions	Students learn how to make connections and summarize more succinctly between texts in different genres *at more challenging reading levels.*	Guided practice modeled by teacher showing how to make connections between *above grade level reading passages* in different genres. Teacher monitors students' independent practice of the same. Teacher then models how to rewrite summaries more succinctly. Students practice doing so independently.

(Continued)

220

(Continued)

Performance Level	Next Learning Step	Instructional Strategies
Achieving Learning Intentions	Students learn how to make the same connections and summarize more succinctly between texts in different genres *at the same reading levels*.	Guided practice modeled by teacher making connections between *texts in different genres at the same reading level* followed by students' independent practice of the same. Teacher then models how to rewrite summaries more succinctly. Students practice doing the same, first in pairs or cooperative groups and then independently.
Progressing Toward Learning Intentions	Students first decide if the vocabulary is getting in the way of their making connections, and if it is, what help they need to correct that. Next they identify the setting, character development, and impact of plot on character actions in the first and second texts *separately*. Then they look for the connections of those literary elements *between* the two texts.	Teacher daily models small-group guided practices and reflective questioning while increasing students' comprehension of grade-level *Tier 2* (high frequency/multiple meaning) vocabulary and *Tier 3* (low frequency/context specific) vocabulary. Teacher includes more intentional use of classroom word walls and *semantic word mapping* (connecting words or concepts using a graphic organizer), 15–20 minutes three times per week. Teacher models two guided practices: identifying literary elements in two texts *separately* and making connections between them. Students then practice in pairs and independently to accomplish the same.
Beginning Understanding of Learning Intentions	Students make connections between texts using a *lower level of vocabulary*. If students cannot make connections between texts with easier vocabulary, teacher and students determine if a deeper reading comprehension issue is the cause. This will indicate the need for different next learning steps for students.	Teacher models small-group guided practices and reflective questioning daily while increasing intentional use of the classroom word walls and *semantic word mapping* (connecting words or concepts using a graphic organizer), 15–20 minutes daily. Teacher models two guided practices: identifying literary elements in two texts *separately* and making connections between them. Students then practice in pairs and independently to accomplish the same.

Source: Dave Nagel, 2014; adapted with permission.

5. *What evidence will we look for to know if our actions are working?* Finally, the team must know how to determine if their strategies are having the desired effect on student learning. Here is where teams make decisions about how they will monitor a strategy's impact. What will be the positive evidence that the strategy is successful? What will be the negative evidence that it is not having its intended effect on student learning? During the unit, the most effective way to determine the effectiveness of the strategies selected is by administering quick progress checks following instruction that incorporates those strategies. Because these strategies here will be in use while students are on the Bridge, the degree of their effectiveness will be apparent as soon as students are reassessed.

The learning team members describe and chart what they expect to see in student achievement if the strategies and actions they are putting in place are working. Certain strategies will prove equally effective with progressing-level *and* beginning-level student groups.

Performance Level	Instructional Strategy	Evidence of Positive Impact	Evidence of Negative Impact
Exceeding Learning Intentions	Guided practice modeled by teacher showing how to make connections between *above grade level reading passages in different genres.* Teacher monitors students' independent practice of the same. Teacher then models how to rewrite summaries more succinctly. Students practice doing so independently.	Students are able to read above grade level passages in different genres and make connections between them with little help from the teacher; specific students (Tony and Taryn) are able to do so without any help; (James and David) are able to do so independently by the end of the first modeled example.	Two students (Marcus and Ariel) are not able to independently make connections between above grade level passages due to increased difficulty of reading level or the challenge of doing so in different genres. Need more guided practice and support to do so independently.
Achieving Learning Intentions	Guided practice modeled by teacher making connections between texts *in different genres at same reading level* followed by	Students are able to successfully make connections between texts. Following cooperative group practices of writing	Guided practice is not leading students to being able to make connections between texts in different genres on

(Continued)

222

(Continued)

Performance Level	Instructional Strategy	Evidence of Positive Impact	Evidence of Negative Impact
	students' independent practice of the same. Teacher then models how to rewrite summaries more succinctly. Students practice doing the same, first in pairs or cooperative groups and then independently.	summaries more succinctly, students (specifically Karin, Juan, and Stefan) are able to do so independently or with little guidance and input from the teacher.	their own (specifically Marta and Damien). Students are not able to rewrite the summary more succinctly on their own without a great deal of additional support (specifically John and Tanisha).
Progressing Toward Learning Intentions	Teacher models small-group guided practices and reflective questioning daily while increasing students' comprehension of grade-level *Tier 2* (high frequency/ multiple meaning) vocabulary and *Tier 3* (low frequency/ context specific) vocabulary. Teacher includes more intentional use of classroom word walls and *semantic word mapping* (connecting words or concepts using a graphic organizer), 15–20 minutes three times per week. Teacher models two guided practices: identifying literary elements in two texts *separately* and	Students are showing greater independency, developing confidence and competence during the guided practice sessions. They are moving to independent practice sooner than expected. Students are using the word wall when appropriate and are completing the semantic word maps with less support over time (specifically Kristen and Michael). Everyone in the group is able to independently identify literary elements and make connections in two texts after guided practice.	Specific students (Manny and Rebecca) miss connections due to difficulty with *Tier 3* vocabulary and/ or are still unable to make the connections on their own. Other students (Riley and Alex) need more support than expected. Strategies not working due to need for more vocabulary work first.

Performance Level	Instructional Strategy	Evidence of Positive Impact	Evidence of Negative Impact
	making connections between them. Students then practice in pairs and independently to accomplish the same.		
Beginning Understanding of Learning Intentions	Teacher models small-group guided practices and reflective questioning daily while increasing intentional use of the classroom word walls and *semantic word mapping* (connecting words or concepts using a graphic organizer), 15–20 minutes daily. Teacher models two guided practices: identifying literary elements in two texts *separately* and making connections between them. Students then practice in pairs and independently to accomplish the same.	Same as "Progressing" but with more guided and small-group practice needed. Monitor specific students (Marco and Felipe) as indicators that the strategies are working.	Same as "Progressing." Monitor specific students (Taylor and Maria) as indicators that the strategies are *not* working. Need to regroup with teacher team to either improve use of targeted strategies or select different ones.

Source: Dave Nagel, 2014; adapted with permission.

THE ACTION PLAN

To conclude the data analysis process, the learning team now prepares a brief action plan to help each member carry out the instructional adjustments while on the Bridge. Important questions to guide the discussion include

* What are the immediate learning needs of our team members? This is a critical question to ask *first*. If there are adult learning gaps related to the corrective instructional strategies the team has selected to use, team members must be able to voice their concerns, be heard in a supportive way, and receive needed assistance.

- What needs to be done by each teacher first, second, third, and so on, to effectively implement the selected instructional strategies?
- What resources and/or instructional materials are needed?
- Who do we go to for help if we encounter problems while implementing the identified instructional strategies?
- What additional help or support, if any, do we need from our administrator(s)?

LEARNING TEAM REFLECTION

After the Bridge instructional activities are concluded and the unit is officially over, the learning team engages in a wrap-up group reflection:

1. While on the Bridge, did our planning charts help us close student learning gaps and move all students forward? What changes, if any, should we make next time?

2. Did we use the identified instructional strategies as planned to improve student learning for each group of students?

3. Did we monitor student learning and make needed adjustments to our instruction early enough?

4. Do we need further assistance or practice in how to use the targeted instructional strategies effectively? Looking back over the entire unit, what worked? What didn't? What should we continue doing? What should we discontinue?

6. What have we learned about our instructional impact on student learning?

7. As a learning team, what are our next learning steps?

THE END GOAL: IMPROVED LEARNING FOR ALL

The entire CFA 2.0 process engages horizontal and vertical learning teams in designing their unit assessments, collaboratively scoring their students' responses, analyzing feedback results and making accurate inferences together, sharing inferential feedback with students, and planning instructional adjustments for use during the unit and again on the Bridge. Collectively, these professional practices are all aimed at achieving one end goal—improving learning for all students.

Chapter 12 presents success criteria that learning teams can use to determine if they are carrying out the CFA 2.0 design steps correctly. Similar to a scoring guide for students, this comprehensive list of criteria—specific to each step in the process—will provide learning teams with the assurance that they have indeed created a high-quality CFA.

And now, for the final time, please take a few minutes to respond to this chapter's success criteria, self-assess your understanding of the chapter content, and/or debrief with colleagues.

Success Criteria:

- State the true purpose and function of a collaborative learning team.
- Describe how learning teams collaboratively score constructed-response questions using the scoring guide success criteria.
- Summarize how teams can use a selected data analysis protocol to process post-CFA student results and effectively prepare for the Bridge.

12 Success Criteria for CFA 2.0 Design Teams

This chapter is presented in two parts: The first part focuses on the specific success criteria teacher teams need to achieve to create high-quality pre- and post-CFAs. The second part addresses the effective implementation of CFAs, Priority Standards, and "unwrapping" Priority Standards in schools and school districts.

PART 1: SUCCESS CRITERIA FOR CFA 2.0 DESIGN TEAMS

To create a quality set of matched pre- and post-CFAs for each unit of study, CFA design teams must invest a significant amount of time, thought, and energy. When assessment design is rightly viewed as an "ongoing process, not a singular event," team members gain confidence and expertise through continual practice and perseverance. This firsthand engagement is what promotes true ownership of the entire CFA 2.0 process until it becomes an indispensable part of professional practice.

Teacher teams need success criteria specific to each of the ten CFA 2.0 design steps that they can reference while creating their own CFAs and again after completing their first drafts. In the sections that follow, these criteria reflect the key points pertaining to those steps. Teacher teams are encouraged to refer back to the related chapters in this book for clarification as needed.

The success criteria, written as verb phrases, are preceded by a check box. Teams can check the criteria that are already included and highlight any that are missing and need to be added. When team members can confirm that all success criteria are represented in their CFAs, they will know they have created a quality assessment.

The following alphabetized key presents abbreviations for the specific components in the CFA 2.0 process. These abbreviations appear throughout the success criteria below:

BI/EQ: Big Idea/Essential Question

LP: Learning Progression

QPC: Quick Progress Check

PS: Priority Standards

SS: Supporting Standards

SSC: Student Success Criteria

ULI: Unit Learning Intention

UPS: "Unwrapped" Priority Standards

Teams will benefit from a review of the following success criteria each time they create, critique, and revise a CFA.

Design Team Success Criteria

Step 1: Identify the Unit Priority Standards and Supporting Standards

- ❏ List full text of PS in bold type preceded by proper coding
- ❏ List full text of SS in regular type preceded by proper coding
- ❏ Limit total number of standards to sharply focus unit instruction and assessment

Step 2: "Unwrap" the Priority Standards and Create a Graphic Organizer

- ❏ Underline teachable concepts (nouns, noun phrases) and capitalize skills (verbs)
- ❏ Create graphic organizer for "unwrapped" concepts, skills, and levels of cognitive rigor:
- ❏ Make connections explicit between skills and concepts (e.g., ANALYZE author's point of view; SOLVE real-world mathematical problem)

❒ Assign approximate level of the revised Bloom's Taxonomy (1–6) <u>and</u> Webb's Depth of Knowledge (1–4) to each concept-skill pair

❒ Include *all* "unwrapped" concepts and skills from PS only

Step 3: Determine the Big Ideas and Essential Questions

❒ Big Ideas:

  ❒ Three to four key understandings students discover on their own
  ❒ Topical statements specific to unit UPS, not broad generalizations
  ❒ Derived from UPS, not curriculum materials
  ❒ Written as sentences, not phrases
  ❒ Convey long-term benefit for learning
  ❒ Represent desired student responses to teacher's EQs

❒ Essential Questions:

  ❒ Represent comprehensive list of ULIs and SSC for unit of study
  ❒ Require higher-level thinking skills to answer
  ❒ Written as "one-two punch" questions when appropriate
  ❒ Engaging for students
  ❒ Will lead students to discover corresponding BIs

Step 4: Write the Unit Learning Intentions <u>as</u> Student Success Criteria

❒ Organize UPS, BIs, EQs, and SS into comprehensive list of ULIs
❒ Write the ULIs <u>as</u> SSC
❒ Create three-column SSC chart, one each for EQ, UPS, and unit vocabulary
❒ Head each column with performance statement that begins with verb(s) indicating what students are to do
❒ Confirm SSC represent all ULIs to be assessed on CFAs

Step 5: Create the Post-Assessment Questions

❒ Include blend of selected-response questions (multiple choice) and constructed-response questions (short response, extended response, Big Idea responses)
❒ Directly align all questions to UPS and levels of cognitive rigor on graphic organizer
❒ Include proper academic vocabulary, not simplified terms
❒ Reflect formats, language, vocabulary of external, large-scale assessments
❒ Write multiple-choice questions to include stem, correct/best answer, and three distracters

❏ Provide distracter analysis for each multiple-choice question
❏ Write appropriate number of short-response questions
❏ Provide commentary or solution statement for each question
❏ Create one extended-response question that aligns to most, or all, SSC
❏ Write directions for students to provide BIs in response to EQs
❏ Double check: make sure all questions collectively address all SSC

Step 6: Construct the Scoring Guides

❏ Prepare answer key for selected-response questions
❏ Decide number and names of performance levels
❏ Write criteria for "achieving" and "exceeding" performance levels
❏ Use objective wording only; no vague, subjective terms open to multiple interpretations
❏ Include combination of quantitative and qualitative criteria
❏ Write criteria directly matched to directions in assessment question
❏ Create *task-specific* scoring guides for short-response questions
❏ Create *task-specific* scoring guide for the extended-response question
❏ Create *generic* scoring guide for BI responses to EQs

Step 7: Create the Pre-Assessment Questions and Scoring Guides

❏ Decide whether pre-CFA will be aligned or "mirrored"
❏ Select/copy questions from post-CFA or create new ones
❏ Decide whether to use same or different reading passage
❏ Decide whether to use same or different math problems
❏ Copy/create answer key for selected-response questions
❏ Copy/create scoring guides for constructed-response questions

Step 8: Evaluate and Revise Assessment Questions for Quality

❏ Confirm direct alignment of questions to all unit SSC
❏ Confirm direct alignment of questions to UPS and levels of cognitive rigor
❏ Check questions for validity, reliability, and absence of bias
❏ Ensure all questions meet established criteria for quality; revise as needed
❏ Check questions for clear, concise language
❏ Confirm questions will provide credible evidence of student learning
❏ Confirm student feedback will yield accurate inferences about student learning

❏ Ensure proper academic vocabulary, not simplified terms
❏ Confirm alignment to formats, language, vocabulary of external, large-scale assessments

Step 9: Determine the Learning Progressions and Instructional Sequence

❏ Confirm that LPs reflect Popham's four steps for determining learning progressions (Chapter 10):

  ❏ *Step 1: Acquire a thorough understanding of the target curricular aim.*
  ❏ *Step 2: Identify all requisite precursory subskills and bodies of enabling knowledge.*
  ❏ *Step 3: Determine whether it's possible to measure students' status with respect to each preliminarily identified building block.*
  ❏ *Step 4: Arrange all building blocks in an instructionally defensible sequence.*

❏ Review each series of LPs leading to a specific ULI; revise as needed
❏ Review the *number and size* of LP "building blocks" planned for each ULI; revise as needed

Step 10: Plan Quick Progress Checks to Coincide With Learning Progressions

❏ Review each QPC to ensure it matches related LP; revise as needed
❏ Reconfirm insertion points of QPCs within each set of LPs
❏ Make sure each QPC clearly states what students are to do
❏ Confirm that student responses to QPCs will make accurate inferences possible and inform instructional next steps

PART 2: A FRAMEWORK FOR EFFECTIVELY IMPLEMENTING CFA 2.0 PRACTICES

The original edition of *Common Formative Assessments* (Ainsworth & Viegut, 2006) included a Framework for Implementing Powerful Practices. The purpose of this framework was to assist educators and leaders in implementing, with fidelity, several connected standards-based practices. The resource appeared in a three-column format with the following column headings: Current State, Action Steps, and Desired State. Each standards-based practice was accompanied by specific descriptors of what that practice should look like when it was being effectively implemented in a school and/or school district.

The same three-column template appears in this chapter, although the focus is now exclusively on the foundational practices of Priority Standards, "Unwrapping" the Standards, and CFAs. These three powerful practices work in tandem to support the effective implementation of the CFA 2.0 process within a school and school district.

The updated descriptors, written as specific success criteria in the Desired State column, are key indicators of effective implementation related to each practice. School and district teams are encouraged to copy these indicators (along with others of their own choosing) into the Desired State column of a duplicate template. This will serve as a customized blueprint of success criteria for their school or district to follow.

After the descriptors in the Desired State column are decided, teams must conduct an honest evaluation of where they are in relation to these descriptors. Very few learning teams already have every one of these success criteria in place, so teams should feel no discouragement when they record a candid assessment of where they currently are.

The Action Steps in the middle column is where school and district teams determine the specific steps they need to take in order to progress from where they currently are (Current State criteria recorded as a result of their self-assessment) to where they want to be (Desired State criteria).

The following alphabetized key represents CFA 2.0 practices in abbreviated form. These abbreviations appear as follows:

BI/EQ: Big Idea/Essential Question

CFA: Common Formative Assessment

PLT: Professional Learning Team

PS: Priority Standards

SSC: Student Success Criteria

ULI: Unit Learning Intention

UPS: "Unwrapped" Priority Standards

Priority Standards (PS)

Current State	Action Steps	Desired State
• Elementary math and language arts PS only • High school: certain departments have identified PS • Most teaching aligned to PS • PS connected to school improvement	• PS workshop for all teachers, administrators, board representative • PS *rationale* understood by all • PS *process* understood by all • Drafts of PS distributed to sites for feedback	• K–12 vertical articulation of PS • Using PS as clear learning targets from grade to grade, course to course • PS used to focus instruction and

Current State	Action Steps	Desired State
plans in certain schools	• Design multiple-week unit directly aligned to PS • Vertical conversations within grade spans and across grade spans (elementary with middle schools, middle with high schools) • Interdisciplinary conversations and planning sessions between general education teachers and special area teachers • Administration: school administrators direct the implementation of PS • On-site PS coaches provide ongoing assistance • Tie actions to accountability plans	assessment in all classrooms • Publication of district PS documents that are teacher, student, parent friendly • PS implementation by every teacher, in every grade/content area, across the school/district • Determine interdisciplinary PS

"Unwrapping" Priority Standards (UPS)

Current State	Action Steps	Desired State
• Varied understanding of UPS purpose and process • Limited understanding of its direct application to teaching • Limited understanding of PS and UPS linked to CFAs • PS "unwrapped" only in certain grades and content areas	• UPS workshop for all teachers, leaders, and board representative • Interdisciplinary conversations and planning sessions between general education teachers and special area teachers • Elementary: provide time for teachers to meet in grade-level PLTs to "unwrap"	• UPS in use across all grades and content areas throughout the district • All teachers understand rationale and use process regularly • Identify instructional resources to support UPS

(Continued)

(Continued)

Current State	Action Steps	Desired State
• BIs and EQs sporadically in use	• Middle and high school: create additional common planning time for PLTs to "unwrap" • Include UPS as foundation for curricular units of study • Phase out textbook-driven instruction; replace with ULIs and SSC that focus classroom instruction and assessment	• Use of EQs to focus instruction and assessment • BIs represent student learning goals for every unit • Use of UPS, BIs, and EQs as basis for deciding ULIs and SSC • SSC include EQs, UPS, and unit vocabulary posted in every classroom

Common Formative Assessments (CFAs)

Current State	Action Steps	Desired State
• Grade levels and departments experimenting with CFA design • Varied understanding of CFA purpose and process • Limited agreement on assessment terms • Varying degrees of assessment literacy • Lack of understanding of how CFAs link to district benchmarks and large-scale assessments	• CFA 2.0 design workshops for all teachers, leaders, and board representative • Deliberately align with PS and UPS • Collaboratively design pre-/post-assessments in grade- or course-level PLTs • All team members administer pre-CFA prior to unit instruction and post-CFA at end of unit • PLTs begin scoring CFAs collaboratively • Use assessment results as feedback to share with students and to adjust instruction on the Bridge between units	• PLTs design CFAs directly aligned to ULIs and SSC • Include multiple formats (selected response, short constructed response, extended response) • Reflective of district and large-scale assessments in terms of format, rigor, and type • Designed as matching pre- and post-assessments to measure actual student learning gains • CFAs used as true assessments *for* learning; not to assign grades but to inform instruction

Current State	Action Steps	Desired State
	• Start small, build slowly—one unit CFA per quarter or trimester in year one, increasing to two units per quarter or trimester in year two	• CFAs used with each unit in all grades and content areas, particularly four "core" content areas • All teachers understand and are involved in CFA process • Special educators and special area teachers assist regular education teachers in preparing students for success on CFAs • Collaboratively designed, scored, and analyzed in PLTs • Establish school and district "bank" of PLT-created CFAs

IMPLEMENTATION SEQUENCE AND TIME FRAME

Educators and leaders often request a suggested implementation sequence for Priority Standards, "Unwrapping" Priority Standards, and creating CFAs. The chart below represents the recommended order for introducing these practices in a school and school district. The time frame for doing so needs to be determined locally, keeping in mind that a "good idea, poorly implemented, is a bad idea." This means that it is best to roll out these practices at a pace the organization can effectively manage, not trying to do too much too quickly.

Time Frame (Specific to School and District)	Recommended Implementation Sequence
	• PS workshop to explain rationale and apply process to targeted content area standards; attended by all educators, district and school leaders, board representative
	• K–12 vertically aligned PS determined and published for elementary, middle, and high school in targeted content areas
	• All teachers begin focusing on grade- or course-level PS in their units of study

(Continued)

(Continued)

Time Frame (Specific to School and District)	Recommended Implementation Sequence
	• UPS workshop to explain rationale and apply process to content area PS; attended by all educators, district and school leaders, board representative
	• All teachers begin using grade- or course-level UPS in their units of study
	• CFA 2.0 workshops to explain rationale and apply process to content area PS; attended by all educators, district and school leaders, board representative
	• Select and establish particular PLT process and related protocols for collaboration
	• *All* teachers are part of grade- or course-level PLTs; collaboratively design first pre- and post-CFAs
	• PLTs collaboratively *score* pre- and post-CFAs
	• PLTs collaboratively *analyze* pre- and post-CFA feedback results, make accurate inferences of student understanding, share feedback with students, and plan instructional next steps to improve learning for all

ENCOURAGING WORDS

Building the *highway to aligned assessments,* described and illustrated in Chapter 1 and detailed throughout this book, represents a grand vision. And like all grand visions, it comes "dressed in work clothes." Learning and applying each of the ten CFA 2.0 design process steps will call for teacher teams to devote their time, thought, and energy in a collaborative effort to produce a set of aligned unit assessments with the potential to make a powerful impact on student learning. As you and your colleagues work through the process, one step at a time, hold to that grand vision there before you. In the end, I think you will agree that it was more than worth the effort.

LEADERSHIP CHAPTERS

In the final two chapters, Donald Viegut presents important ideas for leaders who are striving to effectively implement CFAs in schools and school districts while simultaneously creating a culture of improvement that makes it possible to *sustain* those implementation efforts for years to come.

13 Effective Implementation of Common Formative Assessments

Donald Viegut

Ensuring common formative assessments are rolled out effectively throughout a school or district requires strategic leadership. To successfully implement common formative assessments, leaders must have high expectations that teachers will do the work and do it well. It's been said, "no one ever rose to lower expectations" (attributed to Carl Boyd).

At the same time, however, leaders must couple their high expectations with support for the educators implementing the assessments. To expect high levels of work *without* providing the needed support frustrates educators and causes them to distrust leaders and to slow or even stop working altogether on common formative assessments.

Effective instructional leaders narrow the scope of change, prioritize resources, and create a conducive climate to give common formative assessments the support they require for successful implementation.

Michael Fullan (2001) discusses the need to avoid "disturbance" when engaged in change to create positive results. "Right away we know that taking on all the innovations that come along is not the kind of disturbance that is going to approximate any desired outcome" (p. 109). Leaders must believe in and commit to the goal, and that commitment requires choices. The district or school cannot commit to a dozen school improvement goals at one time or teachers will not be able to implement the new practice in front of them. As Mike Schmoker said, "Overload and fragmentation are the result of having too many simultaneous goals" (personal communication, 1999).

Focusing resources on fewer changes provides the level of support needed to accomplish meaningful change and signals the essential value of those changes. To make any significant change, educators need time, targeted professional learning, and sustained support for the work.

Leaders must grow a culture and climate where new practices aimed at improving student learning can thrive and prosper over time. The administrator who recognizes the value of a professional practice helps educators embrace that practice. As Phillip Schlechty (2002) notes, "The primary function of a leader is to inspire others to do things they might otherwise not do and encourage others to go in directions they might not otherwise pursue" (p. xxx). When leaders create the climate in which teachers see genuine value in implementing common formative assessments to improve student learning, see themselves as the primary owners of and stakeholders in that process, and can proceed in a climate of trust, then teachers asked to implement the work are more likely to commit to it.

Leaders identify and focus on positive strategies to work toward successfully implementing common formative assessments. They set high expectations for educators and for students, and they address at least these key areas:

- Assess the local context before beginning to avoid initiative fatigue.
- Build energy for change by helping faculty understand how the initiative is nested in the bigger picture.
- Carefully plan the timeline and framework.
- Lead collaboratively.
- Anticipate hurdles and avoid them. Ensure that teachers have routine opportunities to collaborate in grade-level and content-area work sessions during the school day to work on common formative assessments.
- Support educators' work by providing ongoing, timely professional development related to each of the interdependent practices (Priority Standards; "unwrapping" the standards; assessment literacy; collaborative design, scoring, and analysis of common formative assessments; data teams; and effective teaching strategies).
- Sustain the initiative by making available clerical support that faculty can use as needed, providing opportunities for coaching, and ensuring follow-up conversation when needed.

Each of these strategies will now be discussed in turn.

ASSESS LOCAL CONTEXT

The leaders in one school district we worked with saw the value of common formative assessments and enthusiastically embraced the idea. They immediately began planning a full-scale implementation. This district had implemented a string of initiatives over a few years, and when faculty faced yet another new plan, they resisted. They had begun to resent what they saw as disconnected initiatives without an overall implementation plan. This district is an example of well-intended leaders who did not consider the local context.

Too often leaders try to meet their improvement goals by adding the next solution or the newest initiative. That practice has a significant impact on those closest to implementing the work. As Thomas Guskey said, "A good idea—poorly implemented—is a bad idea" (personal communication, 2002).

To appropriately create the conditions for success, leaders assess local context and then make informed choices as to what needs to happen next. They are intentional about how that work should be carried out. They are careful not to add to initiative fatigue and strive to sustain a healthy culture.

To help assess local context and position an initiative to succeed, leaders must first answer these questions:

- What initiatives have we implemented recently?
- What went well in those implementations? What could have been done better?
- What is the faculty mindset toward change?
- How is our instructional leadership progressing?
- Have stakeholders been included in planning our next actions?
- Do staff feel a sense of common purpose?
- Have we communicated the calendar of work so that all staff clearly understand the next steps and the end goal?
- Have we assessed our last implementation so that staff can see the effects of their efforts?

BUILD ENERGY TO BACK SUCCESS

The next step in setting the stage for effective school- and districtwide planning is to create the conditions for success. Creating energy is important. The value of energy in improvement work cannot be overstated. By meeting people where they are rather than where we may want to begin, we build energy and create the conditions for success.

Recently I was asked to kick off the work on a new initiative by intro-ducing the concept and then building the component parts without con-sidering individual motivation. I had a series of critical conversations with district leaders about where we needed to begin. I had to ask: How engaged and successful would the participants be with the new work in that circumstance? What confidence would the group have in me when I brought forward the next important thing for their attention? We were able to agree on starting with *why*, as recommended by Sinek (2009).

In a relatively short, 90-minute session we discussed with the faculty the following questions:

- What is happening to the education profession on a nationwide basis?
- Why is the new link between education and the economy so politi-cally charged?
- What do communities, parents, and students need from us right now?
- What danger lies ahead?
- Why is this our problem to solve?
- Why must we view our contributions as essential?

After the session, nearly everyone in the room understood the *why* behind the plan. We could say that more than 90% of the faculty present were ready to roll up their sleeves and begin on the important work.

Teachers also must understand the bigger picture of how individual instructional practices fit within the overall initiative if they are to invest in the process. Effective leaders are careful to help educators make strong con-nections between common formative assessments and other components within the instruction and assessment model (as described in Chapter 1). Faculty then are more likely to become engaged in adopting the new prac-tice. If educators see common formative assessments as occurring separately or in isolation from their other efforts to improve student achievement, however, they are less likely to engage either individually or collectively.

Teachers embrace new professional practices when leaders communi-cate their overall designs for improving student achievement and offer specific strategies to support those efforts long term. Leaders help teachers understand how the parts connect with the whole. Discussing these links through the lens of a quest for continuous improvement allows partici-pants to see the whole improvement plan. The links that leaders need to be explicit about include

- The link between common formative assessment, core standards, and priority learning targets;

- The link between learning target and the type of assessment used;
- The link between student results on common formative assessments and how those results inform decisions about which instructional strategies to use next;
- The link between teacher and student feedback loops and motivational grading practices;
- The link between common formative assessment and student engagement, and between common formative assessment and educator effectiveness; and
- The links between student ownership of learning, quality instructional design, and the skills students need in order to navigate life and work.

Understanding these links helps educators see that what we teach, how we teach, how we assess learning, how we use data to inform instruction and our plan for intervention are integral to the overall design. Presenting common formative assessments this way creates a deeper understanding of how different aspects of teachers' overall work are connected.

Starting the conversation with context positions people to listen with an open mind, to fully engage, and, in fact, to be the solution. Adding tasks onto busy people's workload without context and connection dooms an initiative. When leaders consider individuals' motivations and connect with them at the emotional level about the importance of the work, educators will own the process and take on the work.

Strategies for Implementation

A series of defined strategies will help all participants implement the work. These strategies help create the conditions that foster a mindset and understanding that result in improved actions:

- Have high expectations with accompanying support
- Create whole-to-part understanding
- Create an implementation framework for planning
- Implement specific high-support strategies
- Create time to meet the challenge
- Offer ongoing professional development
- Hold to intention despite hurdles
- Lead collaboratively to create energy
- Foster trust
- Progress at an acceptable pace

PLAN FOR CHANGE

To ensure that common formative assessments are implemented properly, school leaders and leadership teams create an implementation framework for planning. Figure 13.1 is a partially completed example of a simple blueprint adapted from work by education consultant Laura Besser. The first column asks participants to assess their *current reality* as to how well the new practice is being implemented. The second column has participants describe the *desired state* they wish to see once the practice is fully implemented. The last column then lists the *action steps* needed to achieve the desired results.

Figure 13.1 Plan for Implementing Common Formative Assessments

Current Reality	Desired State	Action Steps
• Varied understanding of common formative assessments • Varied understanding of the process • Varied understanding of how common formative assessments apply to teaching • Varied understanding of the application to existing assessments • Varied understanding of the direct relationship to state assessments	• Complete alignment of Priority Standards with common formative and summative assessments across all grades, content areas, schools, and districts • All teachers and administrators understand the rationale for common formative assessments and the process for creating them • Resources have been identified to support implementation of the new practice	• Professional development will occur for all administrators and all K–12 teachers about common formative and summative assessments • Teachers in all grade levels and departments in all schools will have shared time to plan collaboratively • Schedules will be restructured to promote collaboration, including special area teachers • Priority Standards will be identified and aligned with common formative assessments

Schools, districts, and leadership teams will want to map out a projected timeline for the first *full* year of implementation and then—when appropriate—develop a timeline for the second, third, fourth years, and so on. Having a preliminary timeline that can be modified as implementation progresses will help everyone keep the big picture in mind. Figure 13.2 is a chart showing a projected timeline for implementation. It is partially completed as an illustration.

Figure 13.2 Sample Implementation Timeline

Time Frame	Implementation Goal	Personnel and Resources
June 2014	• First presentation on the big picture of common formative assessments and initial planning for implementation	• District leadership • School leadership teams (administrator and selected teacher representatives)
August 2014	• First design and administration of common formative assessments	• All grade levels and departments, all schools
September 2014	• Professional development on assessment literacy and refining common formative assessments	• All staff (administrators and educators) • All-day seminar on same
October 2014	• Revision and second administration of common formative assessments	• All grade levels and departments, all schools

The figures refer only to implementing common formative assessments. Refer to Chapter 12 to see similar tables that include other practices for readers to reference when completing their own implementation plans and time frames.

Finally, leaders must narrow the scope, focus attention, and prioritize resources to give common formative assessments the support they require for successful implementation. Leaders need to be able to stand before their boards of education, administrations, and faculty and clearly state

1. What common formative assessments are

2. How they intend to use them

3. The resources that will be needed to implement them

4. The realistic time it will take to achieve full implementation

5. The realistic time it may take to see corresponding results on state assessments

COLLABORATE TO CREATE CHANGE

A wonderful planning strategy is to involve a collaborative leadership team to plan implementation. Rather than appointing one person to make all decisions regarding implementation, select a representative group of faculty to work with the school or district leader(s) in charge. Planning with their leader, faculty can anticipate and problem-solve potential roadblocks and decide the best ways to articulate next steps to all those involved.

Giving faculty members a real voice in determining direction builds genuine trust within and among the educators charged with the day-to-day implementation of the initiative and leads to better outcomes. "People will strive to do high-quality work where trust exists," writes Deming (as cited in Schmoker & Wilson, 1993, p. 12).

Leaders who involve educators in every aspect of an initiative's implementation ultimately produce a critical mass of people who fully "own" the process and are willing to continue implementation. The work then does not depend upon the continuing presence and commitment of any one individual. Too often when a leader leaves his or her position, any initiative that leader instituted comes to a screeching halt. This kind of disruption fosters inevitable disappointment, frustration, and cynicism among those who have invested long hours and intensive effort to implement the initiative.

By creating a collaborative leadership team of dedicated leaders and educators, leaders can facilitate progress and will be able to continue the initiative until it becomes fully embedded in the culture of the school or district.

The leadership team motivates other educators by arranging numerous face-to-face conversations with individuals and actively listening to them, particularly just after educators have attended a professional development session. Leaders then *take action* on what others say, gaining credibility and trust. Checking the "collective pulse" may be the most important thing a collaborative leadership team can do to ensure that people continue investing their professional time, energy, and talent in implementing the initiative.

Create Collaborative Leadership

These strategies help support a culture of collaborative leadership:

- Include school and district opinion leaders on planning teams.
- Communicate to faculty that they will not be held accountable for the things they have not been trained in.
- Communicate a schedule of training so that 100 percent of faculty know when they will learn more about the new practice.

- Create a culture of innovation by having all leaders seen talking about the learning and new direction.
- Provide feedback that is specific about where people are in their learning and application of the practice, and more important, what they need to do next to improve and the support that will help them to do so.
- Continually invite people in for discussion.
- Continually ask what help and support people need next.

Richard DuFour and Robert Eaker (1998) write, "most (leaders) have not been trained in initiating, implementing, and sustaining change" (p. 14). Creating a collaborative setting is an informed choice leaders make and does not require extensive resources or training. Involving a broad group in making decisions is one easy method to help sustain change.

FACE THE HURDLES

Schools and districts striving to implement an initiative may face challenging circumstances. Schools and districts that have not been deeply involved in school improvement planning can feel that implementing the work described in this book is too formidable.

Some schools and districts have more staff, stronger leadership, a longer history of providing professional development, or school schedules that support effective implementation. Others have few or none of those advantages. Yet schools and districts that want to improve and plan for that goal *do* improve. Results depend upon intention. Action requires focusing on what *can* be done despite the hurdles that must be faced and overcome.

Schools and districts that have experience implementing initiatives acknowledge that the challenges continue. They know, however, that the challenges are surmountable and that their sustained efforts are producing improved student achievement.

Giving faculty the opportunity to proactively brainstorm possible hurdles and to think through solutions will create a culture of collaboration, trust, and success. The chart below can be used with staff as an opportunity for reflection on typical hurdles and doable solutions.

Challenges We Anticipate	Our Plan to Address Those Challenges

Educators will most likely answer that one of the most important things they need to effectively implement common formative assessments is the time to do the work well.

To be successful, educators must have time for professional dialogue, collaboration, and reflection. Finding time for this work is no small challenge given that the average teacher's workday begins at approximately 7:30 in the morning and concludes at about 4:00 in the afternoon, followed by time spent in the evening correcting student work, planning and preparing for the next instructional day, completing extracurricular assignments, engaging in his or her own learning, and managing graduate coursework. Teachers often attend school functions held in the evenings and complete school-related work on weekends, during school holidays, and over the summer. To ask for more of their free time is unreasonable.

Those planning professional development must prioritize and choose the work wisely. Planners must ask: With the limited actual time available for faculty to work on improvement, what will we choose to spend our time on?

Next, leaders must create time for educators to do the additional work that such a comprehensive initiative requires by changing school and district schedules. Without such changes to support the implementation of any change initiative, improvements in student achievement will be limited.

Successful schools and districts use an array of strategies to create time for educators to collaboratively design common formative assessments:

- "Weed the garden." This phrase, attributed to Douglas Reeves, means deciding what practices educators can *stop* doing without harming student learning in order to allow time for best practices.
- Schedule early release days and late start days for students, and make common formative assessments priority work for those days.
- Hire substitute teachers to enable teachers from a grade level or department to meet together.
- Make common formative assessments a standing agenda item for all administrative leadership team meetings.
- Troubleshoot related issues that may threaten or stall progress and consume time.
- Pay teachers a stipend for work beyond the contracted school day, such as meeting in grade-level or department teams, during summer workshops, or working independently.
- Dedicate time during grade-level and department meetings for creating common formative assessments and related practices.
- Reduce the number of all-faculty meetings to once a month or less;

allocate that time for grade-level and department meetings to create common formative assessments.

- Consider the school schedule to find creative ways to enable teachers to collaborate. For example, some elementary schools schedule the music, art, and physical-education specialists' times back-to-back at each grade level, which allows teachers who teach the same grade level to have a common planning time to meet.

IMPLEMENT THE INITIATIVE

How leaders frame professional development for administrators and faculty is critical. Professional development that not only informs and motivates administrators and faculty but also continues to advance the important work taking place will produce optimal results. Well-planned professional development enables teachers to return to their instructional settings energized and ready to continue implementing the new practice more effectively.

Creating a *series* of professional development experiences will deliver new information and move forward the work of implementation. The most effective professional development is that which allows and expects participants to *apply* what they have learned in their own programs and then discuss that application during a follow-up session. In this way, participants bring to the next session firsthand experience of the practice and can participate in meaningful discussions concerning its effectiveness. They are able to ask colleagues and the presenter specific questions, receive new information, and plan for the next phase of implementation.

The presenter or facilitator strives to directly meet the needs of those who are implementing common formative assessments by setting up the conditions for interactive dialogue and support. In this way, faculty members are encouraged to share with each other successes or challenges regarding how they give specific feedback to students or how they are flexibly regrouping students for instruction based on the assessment results. They may also share specific techniques for differentiating instruction or employing the effective teaching strategies the data team selected during its last meeting. They may bring with them work products from the classroom and request feedback on the quality of those items.

The professional development presenter or facilitator—working closely with the leaders—will do well to create follow-up agendas that include

- revisiting the big picture to remind everyone of the place the particular new practice holds in the larger comprehensive instruction and assessment initiative;

- encouraging participants to share their progress with the new practice since the prior or initial professional development session;
- responding effectively to any questions or needs for clarification;
- providing feedback on work products the participants created and used independently;
- allowing participants the routine opportunity—by pausing the meeting every twenty minutes or so—to apply the new information in a simulated way;
- modeling a mindset as the staff development leader that intentionally gives energy to participants; and
- structuring planning time for next steps and agreeing that this planning time will remain focused on developing a calendar of work that meets faculty needs and appropriately advances the work.

The session leader encourages participants to ask questions throughout the session to promote active engagement, interaction, and dialogue. Open dialogue creates the conditions in which faculty engagement is seen as valued and participants see their contributions as essential.

At the same time, staff developers must be mindful of their own and others' words and actions. In each professional development setting participants can choose to be multipliers, who amplify the capabilities of people around them, or diminishers, who see limited capabilities in others, according to Liz Wiseman, Lois Allen, and Elise Foster in their book *The Multiplier Effect: Tapping the Genius Inside Our Schools* (2013). Staff developers must portray the face of a multiplier and when faced with the words and actions of a diminisher, model by sharing strengths of individuals and allowing time to self-assess leadership style.

SUSTAIN THE PROGRESS

Some individuals, whether leaders or educators, may feel threatened by a new initiative. It is critical to try to understand what might be causing them to feel a sense of threat. Ignoring concerns increases the likelihood that long-term implementation goals will not be realized, and issues not properly addressed tend to multiply.

Individuals may need greater clerical support or opportunities for coaching. Honest and open dialogue can greatly alleviate both real and imagined problems. People feel supported when their concerns are acknowledged and receive sincere attention.

When a few educators in a Midwestern school district expressed their concern over the amount of work the implementation of common formative assessments was sure to require, district leaders wisely responded,

"We will only progress at a pace that is acceptable to our organization," which did much to defuse anxieties. The important message of the district leadership was this: "As we progress, we will continue to listen, respond, and be supportive."

Structures for Sustainability

When a school or district reaches the point in its implementation efforts that discussions turn to sustainability, it is a sure indicator that progress is under way. At this point, the collaborative leadership team will likely be asking questions related to existing structures. Those striving to sustain the new initiative need to invest time individually and collegially to discuss their responses to the following questions:

- Have we built early release days for students into our school calendar to give teachers time to collaborate and refine their work with common formative assessments?
- Are teacher teams collaborating successfully? Are we redefining what successful collaboration looks like?
- Have we identified instructional coaches to support teacher growth?
- What other support or professional development do teachers need?
- What are our expectations for *teachers* in this initiative?
- What are our expectations for *administrators* in this initiative?
- Do our induction and mentoring programs introduce new employees to this initiative?
- Is our instructional design affecting teachers' and students' roles and changing the instructional setting?
- Do we regularly monitor progress using the data we collect? Are we using that data to improve our process?
- Is the initial work with common assessment having a significant effect on daily classroom practice, specifically daily formative feedback to students?
- Are we making clear connections between student–teacher feedback loops and the effect on student engagement?
- Has the work led educators to talk about aligning resources to school and district priorities?
- Are we seeing predictable trends across grade levels and subject areas that provide insights about what work we might undertake next?
- Do we have an overall district professional development plan that supports sustained implementation of the initiative?
- Are we putting that plan into systematic operation?
- Is there a current practice or initiative that should be abandoned or de-emphasized in order for common formative assessments to succeed?

One of the greatest supports that leaders can provide faculties as they strive to implement any new practice is the opportunity for regular collegial conversations. When educators encounter challenges or uncertainties, or when they need coaching, they need to be able to dialogue with colleagues, mentors, and leaders to work through the particular "knot points" they may be experiencing. Relational leadership is about the meaning and identity that are created when people work together (Wenger, 1998). Relational leaders recognize the need for a support system or network and provide it.

Leaders commit to maintaining support educators need and to keeping the initiative as a priority over several years, until it becomes part of the instructional culture of the school and district. To inculcate a practice, leaders make celebrations of progress a routine part of the work. Recognizing the accomplishment of small steps is key to maintaining staff members' energy.

"Celebrations reignite the human spirit and propel staff toward even greater accomplishments," write Hirsh, Psencik, and Brown (2014, p. 212). "Celebrations can touch hearts and fire imaginations, bonding people together and connecting them to the organization's goals, vision, and values."

Creating these conditions helps ensure that progress made will not be eroded. Fullan (2005) states, "When the conditions of sustainability are put in place, the work is more efficient, effective, and rewarding" (p. 104).

CONCLUSION

"Although school culture is deeply embedded in the hearts and minds of staff, students, and parents, it can be shaped by the work of the leaders," Kent Peterson and Terrence Deal write (2002, p. 12). If leaders hold to high expectations, provide educators with the necessary support to implement the change, and prioritize an initiative over several years, then common formative assessments will become part of the district and school instructional culture.

Leaders must contain the static, the white noise, and pet agendas, as well as the negativity that individually or collectively can suck the energy from a well-intended group. Leaders create *sustained, high-level support within an atmosphere of genuine trust* to ensure a promising practice that may have a significant effect on student learning is allowed to take hold.

"Leaders must shape and nourish cultures where every teacher can make a difference and every child can learn, and where there are passion and a commitment to designing and promoting the absolute best that is possible," according to Peterson and Deal (2003, p. 8).

In this chapter, the reader has been presented with recommendations for the initial implementation of common formative assessments that are important for any school or district to consider. In the 14th and final chapter, you will find guidelines for *sustaining* districtwide implementation once it is under way.

14 Creating a Culture of Improvement

Donald Viegut

F ew educators have written about change as insightfully as Gene Hall
and Shirley Hord. For more than 30 years, their observations have
influenced educators and noneducators alike. To summarize their findings: Change is a *process*, not an *event* (Hall & Hord, 2001).

Implementing each of the instruction and assessment practices we
have described throughout this book takes effort and perseverance. The
toughest work leaders have to do is to sustain the growth of what they
have begun. This is not meant to discourage readers but to prepare them
for the realistic challenges of firmly establishing a new practice within the
organization's existing culture.

Hall and Hord (2001) find that adaptive change leading to higher-level
performance requires three to five years—and occurs then only when the
change is managed and led well. They assert that change is not clean, linear, or assured of success, regardless of the conditions, and advise change
leaders to dig in for the long haul.

Athletes, for example, recognize that perseverance has a payoff.
Weight trainers, sprinters, and dancers often experience wonderful spurts
of growth and then plateau. Eventually, they reach a stage where it is much
harder to lift more, run faster, or reach the next level of technique. The
same is true in implementing school improvements. After noticeable initial
growth, progress can slow or even stall as the result of a variety of factors
or a convergence of variables.

Establishing appropriate structures to sustain the implementation of common formative assessments is essential to safeguarding a new practice and propelling it forward. Fullan (2005) states that "setting up and maintaining an effective structure involves much more than the typical organization chart. It means identifying and cultivating a coalition of leaders" (p. 69). This coalition includes those within the district as well as those who support it from the outside: parents, local business leaders, key community leaders, elected officials, leaders in other area schools, and local university faculty.

In this final chapter, we present our recommendations for sustaining the implementation of common formative assessments. These recommendations address what is necessary to grow an internal culture of focused and continuous long-term improvement and also how to develop the external culture.

GROWING THE INTERNAL CULTURE

Creating an internal culture of innovation and improvement is essential to beginning and sustaining schools' key work. To improve the likelihood of common formative assessment becoming an established practice, successful district leaders nest the work within that culture of improvement. They prioritize improvement initiatives, reduce or remove the "noise" of outside distractions, and nest the assessment work within a clearly articulated instructional design. They are intentional about *placing common formative assessment center stage* in the culture of improvement. Doing so heightens the importance of the work and immediately creates a deeper meaning for faculty. As a result, leaders are more likely to garner support from early adopters—and leverage the change with that small percentage of people who may lag in implementation.

Leaders need to continually motivate people to take on the complexities and anxieties of difficult change. As Stephen Neill writes, "The good teacher . . . discoversthe natural gifts of his pupils and liberates them by the stimulating influence of the inspiration that he can impart. The true leader makes his followers twice the men and women they were before."

The most successful leaders use restructuring tools to help the school or district learn to function as a professional community. They find a way to channel staff and student efforts toward a clear, commonly shared purpose for student learning; they create opportunities for teachers to collaborate and help one another achieve the purpose; and teachers in these schools take collective—not just individual—responsibility for student learning. Schools with strong professional communities are better able to offer authentic pedagogy and are more effective in promoting student achievement (Lambert, 1998).

Hall and Hord's (2001) research led them to create tools that help leaders along the path of change. Leaders can use their tools to guide and encourage the change process: the Concerns-Based Adoption Model, description of Levels of Use of a new practice, Stages of Concern that teachers may exhibit during change, and Innovation Configurations that describe what one might see at different levels of implementation all help leaders gauge progress and discern teachers' energy for continuing the hard work of change.

When implementing change, leaders, too, can become complacent. Sustainability requires constantly refreshing leaders' approach to change through new leadership, feedback from students, or a faculty listening session. Leaders recognize four key strategies that can help ensure they create an internal culture conducive to supporting sustained change: self-reflection, choosing the right moment, maintaining focus, and building relationships.

Self-Reflect

As a first step toward managing the educational system to make sustainability possible, leaders charged with this responsibility take an inventory of the current context in which the work is taking place. By asking and answering tough questions, leaders begin to understand their particular context for sustaining the work of implementation and what they yet need to do. The start of an initiative may be too early for leaders to be able to respond to each of these self-reflection questions. Yet at some point on the continuum of implementation, leaders will need to arrive at an answer for each question and develop a corresponding action plan where appropriate. Only then can true sustainability have the likelihood of becoming a reality.

Individuals may wish to set aside an hour free of distractions to reflect and write down brief responses to each of the following questions. Then, as you come together as a leadership team, you will likely benefit from self-reflection questions. Taken together as a leadership team, the group's responses help define a vision for sustaining implementation.

Self-Reflection Questions

Vision

- Do I have a clear vision of what long-term implementation looks like?
- Do I have a well-conceived strategy to guide faculty from initial information into active involvement and on to full implementation?

(Continued)

(Continued)

Self

- What are my strengths and weaknesses relative to leading and sustaining implementation?
- What are my "information gaps," and what must I do in order to close them?
- What must I do differently to achieve more desirable results?
- What do those to whom I am accountable expect of me?

Faculty

- Are other school improvement initiatives already under way? If so, how are faculty members managing these initiatives? Are they doing well, or are they already overwhelmed?
- How well are we growing our cadre of faculty leaders?
- What percentage of faculty is fully engaged in current school improvement issues? What will I do about those who are not? What is my strategy to support top implementers?
- What is my strategy to address the bottom 10% of performers?
- What motivates my faculty?
- What is the faculty's learning curve for this initiative?
- Does the faculty trust me?

Board of Education

- Do I have the board of education's support for our plans?
- Will I have board support when implementation efforts meet with difficulties, conflicting agendas, or community pressures?
- Will I have continuing board support if anticipated improvements in state assessment results are not immediate?
- What can I do to anticipate these challenges and prepare for them proactively?
- How often do I provide progress reports to the board? What metrics will I use for this reporting?

Teachers' Union

- Do I have the teachers' union support for this initiative?
- Are union leaders actively promoting common formative assessments to improve student learning?
- Are there factions of dissent among union members that need to be addressed?
- Am I building coalitions of mixed employee groups to continually break down barriers?

Time and Resources

- Do I have budget dedicated to staff and curriculum development?
- Is funding adequate?

- Am I aware of and do I have access to additional resources to support the work?
- Do I have appropriate time built into the school year to enable a sustained approach to this school improvement effort?

Hurdles

- Have I identified our hurdles? What (or who) are they?
- Do I have strategies to address those hurdles? Are those strategies manageable?

Instruction

- Are we moving beyond building the assessment system and making significant inroads into instructional change?
- Have the majority of conversations within professional learning communities shifted to focus on instructional effectiveness?

Intervention

- Are faculty routinely and freely sharing intervention strategies?
- Are classroom teachers' mindsets shifting to see intervention as their primary obligation?

Choose the Right Moment

Effective leaders are agents of educational change and become experts at recognizing the importance of timing. They ask

- When do leaders announce a change?
- Who should make the announcement?
- What needs to be said, and how?

The collaborative leadership team needs to answer these questions before making a formal announcement about a new initiative within the school or district. The right moment to address staff typically comes just after educators have had sufficient opportunity to learn, apply, and evaluate the new practice. If the practice satisfies their professional judgment, and shows the potential for improving instruction and student learning, they will be ready to commit to it.

One strategy that has an uncommon cost/benefit ratio is a simple year-end communication. With many educational institutions experiencing greater turbulence than ever before, it is easy for leaders to be so fatigued by the end of the school year that they forget how much has gone well or how much the staff have accomplished.

I have worked with superintendents to craft this effective, one-page memo to employees:

> Memo: To all employees
>
> From: Superintendent
>
> Re: Progress and plans
>
> Date: May 2015
>
> As we near the end of the school year, I wanted to share some final thoughts. We all have witnessed many stresses on our immense obligation to educate the children of our community. Resources are scarcer, scrutiny of the profession has grown, and the mandates for change just keep coming. We could look at this situation with despair; however, let's reflect on those things we did accomplish in 2014–2015:
>
> - We finalized common assessments in the middle school;
> - We supported PLC development at the high school; and
> - We scaffolded our priority content in math and language arts in the primary/ intermediate grades.
>
> We need to leave this year holding our heads high for our contributions to these efforts!
>
> We have exciting plans for the 2014–2015 school year that we want to share now so that you are able to help gear up for your next contribution and so that we are transparent in our work with you. Our plans for 2014–2015 are for professional development focused on
>
> - enhancing instructional strategies;
> - grading practices that motivate students;
> - giving feedback that improves student engagement.

Framing and sending a communication such as this helps leaders introduce the next effort. This simple letter shows empathy for what educators face today, reinforces their accomplishments, and articulates where the school or district is headed so that everyone knows what to expect.

Maintain Focus

Leaders need to continually remind all those involved in the change how important the initiative is and keep it at the forefront of all discussions and actions pertaining to improved student achievement. This work requires *sustained focus.*

Common formative assessment, when implemented well, has proven to be an important and viable remedy to lagging student achievement. However, for the work to serve as a sustainable solution over time, leaders need to address the reality of competing agendas. Every organization has a few people who can juggle multiple agendas equally well. The majority of people, however, work more effectively by prioritizing their work and then concentrating their time on tasks that advance those priorities. It is nearly impossible to give equal, sustained attention to multiple priorities and achieve wonders with each one.

Fullan writes about the importance of attending to the tasks that matter most rather than simply the tasks at hand "so that the normal 'distractors'—managerial issues, crises, and so on—are handled in a way that do not take school and system leaders constantly away from the focus on students and learning" (2005, pp. 68–69).

If the local context is one in which common formative assessment is one of many initiatives competing for faculty time, training resources, and instructional leaders' attention, the well-intended effort will fall short of implementation expectations. To sustain the work of implementing common formative assessments, leaders must make sure that the practice remains a top priority in everyone's mind over an extended period of time.

One elementary school administrator, for example, shared the wisdom he had gleaned from his experience sustaining a school improvement initiative over four years. "When working with any new initiative," the administrator said, "leaders must remember that most people are going to need to hear your message seven or eight times before they will really make a personal commitment to it. And until that happens, you need to keep everyone's attention constantly focused on that message."

In addition, as the work progresses, part of the challenge of sustaining the initiative can come from increased expectation. Often the further an initiative progresses, the more closely everyone scrutinizes its quality. For example, there is a vast difference between occasionally using common formative assessments in a school or district and *frequently* using high-quality common formative assessments across grade levels and content areas. The higher the quality of the assessments, the more meaningful the analysis of data from those assessments will be. The more teachers use the data to inform their instruction, the greater the improvements will be in student learning.

As implementation continues, some questions arise and should be carefully considered:

- Are we measuring the content we want to measure?
- Are our assessments really the right measures for this content?
- Are these assessments of sufficiently high quality and rigor to meet the established criteria for well-written assessments?

* Do we have adequate classroom interventions in place for students who are not successful initially? For those students who need acceleration?

- What skill sets and staff development do teachers need relative to intervention and acceleration?
- What resources and personnel support do teachers need to effectively use intervention and acceleration techniques?
- Is academic intervention a standing agenda item at faculty meetings and administrative meetings? Do we have a goal for academic interventions in our school improvement plans?
- How is this initiative influencing our grading instruments and reporting processes?
- Does our school calendar support ongoing professional development for this initiative?
- Are district resources committed to our efforts sufficient to produce the change we want?

These questions and others are the natural outgrowth of the sustained and concerted effort to institute a new practice. Routine reflection enables all participants to consider progress and make midcourse corrections. Those who continue to ask and answer the tough questions will stand the greatest chance of achieving sustained implementation.

Build Relationships

A new style of leadership is emerging in successful companies—one that focuses on people and relationships as essential to getting sustained results (Fullan, 2001). Relationships matter. As Senge, Scharmer, Jaworski, and Flowers (2004) write, "When people in leadership positions begin to serve a vision infused with a larger purpose, their work shifts naturally from producing results to encouraging the growth of people who produce results" (p. 145).

Those selected to lead a districtwide initiative through the unpredictable waters of implementation need excellent people skills and experience. A first-year administrator can gather and distribute pertinent information to faculty, study current research related to the initiative, and encourage teachers to experiment with common formative assessments. The question, however, is whether the person has the expertise needed to work well with people and lead sustained implementation of the initiative.

Effective leaders are able to build and nurture relationships, oversee the implementation process without micromanaging it, and offer timely guidance rooted in deep content knowledge of curriculum, instruction, and assessment. The ability to foster and maintain good relationships while navigating "the rapids" of change may be one of the most difficult challenges a leader faces.

Effective change agents need to continually strengthen relationships with the educators doing the actual work of implementation year in and year out. They connect relationship building with the calendar of work. They are able to step back from busy work and increase their attention to the human factor.

Districts I have worked with vary widely in their attention to this factor. Some are strong on relationship but weak in planning. Others have binders full of plans and are driving hard, yet relationships do not appear to be a priority.

The most successful settings have leaders who intentionally connect relationship building to the work, who build important relationships *while* doing the work. One caution: Some people focus on being well liked but actually gain less respect because people perceive them as lacking substance. Leaders understand that connecting with people personally within the work is the best approach, demonstrating how to balance being human with the credibility of advancing the work.

Leaders self-reflect on their ability to sustain relationships. They ask themselves questions such as these:

- How adept am I at fostering and maintaining relationships based on mutual trust and respect?
- Have the changes I have made in the past damaged or strengthened professional relationships?
- Am I the most qualified person to lead this initiative?
- What success have I really had in bringing about significant educational change?
- Am I willing to do everything it will take to implement this effort successfully?
- What strategy can I use to connect people and progress?
- Am I emphasizing the human element of our work strongly enough?
- How could I better monitor my efforts joining relationship building to the work calendar? What metric might I use?
- Who can be my confidante?

Leaders should keep in mind that it is time "to alter our perspective: to pay as much attention to how we treat people—co-workers, subordinates, customers—as we now typically pay attention to structures, strategies, and statistics" (Lewin and Regine as cited in Fullan, 2001, p. 53). Fullan states that change requires systems of people willing to go the extra mile.

That system also must include those outside of education, another area that insightful leaders know they must address.

DEVELOPING THE EXTERNAL CULTURE

One educational setting can be vastly different from another. One setting may appear much as it did 30 years ago, while a more progressive setting is filled with adult learners and leaders who are so confident about their work that the leader or role authority is difficult to identify. All stakeholders in this system appear to have leadership roles, including those outside the school walls.

Educators' best work in the next 10 years will come from partnerships yet to be defined. Schools have worked in isolation for too long and, in many cases, in we/they environments. As an education community, we must concede that those outdated beliefs and isolated structures need to be vanquished. Leaders, faculty, and well-intended community members want change and improvement, and most important, they are willing to roll up their sleeves to co-create a new culture.

To create a new culture requires understanding what exists, a picture of a preferred state, and a deep internal belief that we can do far better together in the future than what we have done alone in the past. When educators invite new players into the discussion, the intention must be authentic and the focus must be on the important work that matters to schools' future.

Four priority areas help create a new culture:

- Developing community leaders;
- Expanding your network and associating with the best;
- Collaborating with institutions of higher education; and
- Advocating for schools through stories of incredible progress.

Develop Community Leaders

When influential leaders outside the school or district understand, discuss, and openly support an initiative to improve student learning, that initiative will gain momentum. Conversely, if those leaders are uninformed or have limited understanding as they discuss the initiative, or if they are actively working to sabotage and undermine implementation efforts, progress will suffer.

Seven strategies have worked to successfully influence external stakeholders' support of a school improvement initiative:

1. Include influential leaders in planning team meetings.

2. Visit leaders' workplaces to discuss the initiative with them.

3. Share information on the current context, what the improvement work is about, why you feel it matters to them, the community, and the schools, and then ask for their help.

4. Share information about the initiative with area school and district leaders to develop a broader, more regional partnership agreement that can help promote the new practice.

5. Establish regional councils to collectively share in developing and advancing the work.

6. Communicate often and with great transparency the initiative's goals, challenges, and progress, as well as individuals' contributions.

7. Monitor progress as a group, and have the group plan adjustments.

Applying these seven high-impact strategies will help school and district leaders develop an external culture of key community members who are informed, supportive, and willing to "go the distance" to sustain the initiative.

Expand Your Network

Our social networks influence us. They influence how we think, our attitudes, and our actions (Christakis & Fowler, 2009). Successful people understand that to become the very best, regardless of the undertaking, requires the proper environment and the right company.

What does this mean for educators and leaders? It means placing ourselves alongside those working to accomplish the same ends in every aspect of the school improvement process. Leaders and educators who associate with community leaders, educators, schools, and districts wrestling with the same issues will benefit from colleagues' attitude, advice, and experience. Associating with those who have the motivation and commitment to succeed in a particular endeavor or those who have already achieved success can help those striving toward ever-higher levels of performance.

Partnering with others doing the same or similar work to improve student learning benefits both organizations. Those who have already blazed the trail can provide a genuine service to the school or district seeking guidance. Leaders beginning the implementation of a new initiative can ask those who have already progressed successfully:

- What strategies were the most effective?
- What were your greatest challenges? How did you meet those challenges?

- What adjustments did you need to make as you moved forward?
- Who guided the implementation? What made these leaders successful?
- What actions did you take to keep the positive momentum going?
- How can we best learn from what you have done?

Inevitably, both the giver and the receiver will gain valuable insights and experiences as they continue their dialogue. As Michael Fullan (2005) writes,

> As these leaders pursue the depth of change, they must build a coalition of leaders. Creating a movement around the work where area school districts are talking with a common language and agenda carries huge support. This differs greatly from the old days of being the lone ranger school district trying to continually outshine your neighboring district. There is huge safety in numbers in creating a movement. Like distributed leadership at the school level, large-scale reform requires pluralized leadership, with teams of people creating and driving a clear, coherent strategy. (p. 67)

If other schools or districts in the area have not undertaken the same initiative, educators can cast a wider net throughout the state or in other regions of the country and arrange visits. Having the benefit of others' experience invariably saves time, money, and stakeholder morale and is well worth the time, energy, and resources invested in seeking it.

And as a district begins to effectively implement common formative assessments, other area schools and districts likely will learn of the work and will seek guidance. Developing local "partnerships of excellence" can expand the district, serving ever more schools and districts.

Collaborate With Higher Education Institutions

Developing external relationships with higher education institutions may prove an unexpected boon to long-term implementation of common formative assessments. Little effort has been made in the past in education reform to coordinate across educational sectors to ensure students' academic success throughout their education. Educational reform and change historically have been isolated within either the PreK–12 or higher education sectors. This lack of coordination may make students' transitions between the systems more difficult and diminish their educational opportunities (Venezia & Kirst, 2001, p. 1).

When PreK–12 districts and higher education institutions collaborate and invest in mutual problem solving, pre-service programs are strengthened and lead to more effective beginning teachers, PreK–12 districts benefit from the outside perspective and expertise, and the organizations can heighten mutual respect.

Local individual schools and PreK–12 districts can form alliances with local four-year universities and two-year technical colleges/community colleges. In one example, area districts forged an alliance with the University of Wisconsin-Stevens Point and co-created an on-site master's degree program based on the national Interstate New Teacher Assessment and Support Consortium (INTASC) Standards for Educators (1992). Two years after the program's inception, the university graduated 28 classroom teachers with master's degrees. The participating teachers gained a level of professional development they otherwise might not have had and learning that will benefit them for the remainder of their educational careers. During that same period, the PreK–24 partnership also supported school and district leaders' ongoing work with Priority Standards and common formative assessments. The program has continued, building on its successes.

One of the most promising efforts to influence external culture is the creation of regional PreK–24 (prekindergarten through Grade 12 school districts and institutions of higher education) councils. Nationally, the PreK–24 initiative has gained tremendous momentum as a force for school improvement with leadership from Kati Haycock of the Education Trust in Washington, D.C. Establishing formal, regional PreK–24 councils benefits partners as they support each other in implementing best practices. As all those within the PreK–24 councils contribute to the collaborative work and share information that is relevant and useful to all, valuable ideas wash back onto the shores of individual member schools and districts.

A well-organized, well-informed PreK–24 council has the potential to be a valuable resource for local school leaders as they implement common formative assessments. For example, PreK–24 council members can learn about and advertise grant opportunities available to schools and districts. As school budgets tighten, grants can supplement funding to support district teachers with ongoing professional development needed to fully implement common formative assessments and provide other interdependent practices associated with the initiative.

Advocate Through Stories of Incredible Progress

All members of the education community must keep the improvement process and quality of results on their radar screen.

How is the education community doing in the midst of partisan politics? Most admit that times could be better. Being aware of the context in which public schools operate today affects our energy and willingness to advocate. Just as our education context is evolving, so must our willingness to advocate—building relationships with elected officials, write letters, create elevator speeches, and conduct door-to-door campaigns. Each strategy can be appropriate in a local context.

However, stakeholders no longer respond to anything that looks or feels like hollow advocacy. Placing the substance of an improvement process at the heart of advocacy takes on a different and deeper meaning, even among those who were not paying attention. The next iteration of educators' work, then, is advocating for best practices such as work on common formative assessment.

For example, a fellow superintendent recently invited CEOs and chamber of commerce leaders into a session to share information with them about the district's continuous improvement process using common formative assessments. The head of the chamber phoned the superintendent the following day to praise the district's efforts and closed the phone call by promising the chamber's support for anything the district needed. By embedding the substance of the system's improvement efforts into the message, the district won greater support.

Strategies to Tell Your Improvement Story

- Meet one-on-one with key community leaders. Share the school or district's progress and explain why the change matters to them and the community.
- Work to get yourself and key district or school leaders invited into circles that educators typically have not been part of and then share your story.
- Position board members to relate your improvement story by helping them craft talking points.
- Help all staff members understand the work, the message, and why they must "manage up" the improvement efforts in the community.
- After momentum has shifted, invite media outlets into the discussion to help tell the story.
- After momentum has shifted, invite key opinion leaders from the community into the process improvement work.
- Create opportunities for focus in areas where there can be mutual effort, commitment, and benefit.

CONCLUSION

Effective leaders recognize that systems must be managed. Left to themselves, systems will become dysfunctional. If a system is not managed, the role of persons or groups within it may not be clear, and their relationships with other people and groups, as well as with the system as a whole, may not be understood (Warwick, 1992, p. 26). As Fullan (2005) states, when the conditions of sustainability are put in place, the work is more efficient, effective, and rewarding.

Having a keen eye on systemwide sustainability from the beginning and throughout implementation is critical in staying the course on the quality work required of schools today. Nesting the work of common formative assessments in your culture of improvement and building internal and external cultures of change are essential strategies for systemwide sustainability.

These ideas for designing and implementing common formative assessments as part of an integrated instruction and assessment system will help readers apply the practices in their own educational settings and put in place the structures needed to sustain them over time. Through dedicated effort, educators may realize the improvement in student learning to which we all aspire.

We wish you unparalleled success as you and your colleagues continue working to enrich the lives of children and young adults!

Glossary

Assessment literacy is the ability to understand the different purposes and types of assessment in order to select the most appropriate type to meet a specific purpose. (Chapter 2)

Big Ideas represent the three or four foundational understandings specific to the unit of study that are important for students to discover on their own as they learn and apply the "unwrapped" concepts and skills from the Priority Standards. Written as full sentences to express a complete thought, Big Ideas communicate to *students* the benefit or value of learning the unit standards that endures long after instruction ends. (Chapter 5)

"Bridge" is a shortened form of the phrase, "bridge between units." Its purpose is to give teachers and students additional time at the end of a unit of study to regroup in order to close student learning gaps before beginning the next unit. During this time, students who need additional instruction (reteaching, remediation) receive it in a different way than it was initially taught during the unit and then have the opportunity to be reassessed and show improvement (i.e., achieve the student success criteria). Those students who are ready for enrichment and acceleration engage in activities that enlarge their understanding of the unit's learning intentions. (Chapter 1)

Calibrate means "to arrive at the same scoring result." When learning team members meet to collaboratively score students' constructed responses, they first individually score at least three of the same student papers. Then they compare results with each other to make sure they are all scoring those papers at the same performance level. The goal is to calibrate with one another. (Chapter 11)

Classroom formative assessments include pretests or pre-assessments given to students before unit instruction occurs, informal checks to gauge student progress during instruction, and even a comprehensive assessment at the conclusion of the unit—*if* the results are used to inform instruction. Formative assessments are typically not used to assign grades. These assessments *for* learning yield diagnostic student feedback that educators use solely to inform and adjust instruction. (Chapter 2)

Classroom summative assessments given by individual teachers can occur at the end of a unit, quarter, trimester, semester, course, or academic school year. These assessments take place after all instruction and student learning have ended. They report the final results of student learning to the educators, to their students, to students' parents, and to administrators—typically to support the assignment of letter grades and/or levels of proficiency. Thus, they serve as assessments *of* learning. (Chapter 2)

Collaborative analysis of student responses by the teacher team members includes charting of student performance data, analyzing the results, and planning next instructional steps based on the student feedback in order to help all students "close the gaps" in their understanding of the unit learning intentions. (Chapter 11)

Collaborative scoring ensures that all teacher team members are scoring student responses at the same performance level. To *calibrate* means "to arrive at the same scoring result." Team members discuss and resolve any differences of opinion to reach a scoring agreement. When several educators can consistently calibrate the score for a student response, they are achieving inter-rater reliability. (Chapter 11)

Common formative assessments (CFAs) are aligned pre- and post-assessments *for* learning that are collaboratively designed by a grade or course-level team of educators to assess student understanding of the particular learning intentions and student success criteria currently in focus within a curricular unit of study. (Chapter 2)

Common summative assessments given by teacher teams can occur at the end of a unit, quarter, trimester, semester, course, or academic school year. Similar to *classroom* summative assessments, they take place after all instruction and student learning have ended. They report the final results of student learning to the educators, to their students, to students' parents, and to administrators—typically to support the assignment of letter grades and/or levels of proficiency. Summative assessments are referred to as assessments *of* learning. (Chapter 2)

Constructed-response questions require students to produce an answer from their own minds (i.e., they are constructing a response). *Short* constructed responses include individual words, phrases, single sentences, short paragraphs, or computation work. *Extended* constructed responses include multiple sentences or paragraphs, essays, or a problem-solving process with explanation of steps and/or verification of answer. (Chapter 7)

Effect size "provides a common expression of the magnitude of study outcomes for many types of outcome variables. An effect size of d = 1.0 indicates an increase of one standard deviation on the outcome . . . typically associated with advancing children's achievement by two to three years. An effect size of 1.0 would mean that, on average, students receiving that treatment would exceed 84 percent of students not receiving that treatment" (Hattie, 2009, pp. 7–8). The effect size of 0.40 is what Hattie refers to as the hinge-point for identifying an effective practice. It equates to approximately one year of student growth in learning. Any professional practice that can produce an effect size of 0.40 or greater is worth implementing well. (Chapter 2)

Essential Questions are engaging, open-ended questions that educators use to spark student interest in learning the content of the unit about to commence. Even though plainly worded, they carry with them an underlying rigor. Presented to students at the beginning of the unit, the expectation is that they will respond to the Essential Questions with their own corresponding Big Ideas on the post-CFA at the end of the unit. (Chapter 5)

Fairness (in assessment design) means that the assessment items are not biased by factors (such as race, gender, religion, ethnicity, sexual orientation, socioeconomic status) that have nothing to do with student understanding of the standards being assessed. (Chapter 9)

Feedback is a reciprocal exchange between educator and student. It is a communication loop or cycle that repeats itself continually: The educator provides the quick progress check, the student provides the response. The educator analyzes the feedback to correctly interpret student understanding and shares that feedback with the student. The student identifies next learning steps. The educator then makes instructional adjustments while the student adjusts his or her learning strategies. (Chapter 10)

Formative assessment is a process used by teachers and students during instruction that provides feedback to adjust ongoing teaching and learning to improve students' achievement of intended instructional outcomes. (Chapter 10)

Instructional sensitivity is "the degree to which students' performances on a test accurately reflect the quality of instruction specifically provided to promote students' mastery of what is being assessed" (Popham, 2013, p. 63). (Chapter 2)

Inter-rater reliability refers to the ability of learning team members to consistently calibrate or reach agreement when scoring students' constructed responses. Scores must be based on the *scoring guide criteria* and not on personal opinions or interpretations. When several educators can consistently calibrate the score for a student response, they are achieving inter-rater reliability. (Chapter 11)

Learning intentions "describe what it is we want students to learn in terms of the skills, knowledge, attitudes, and values within any particular unit or lesson. Learning intentions should be clear, and provide guidance to the teacher about what to teach, help learners be aware of what they should learn from the lesson, and form the basis for assessing what the students have learnt and for assessing what the teachers have taught well to each student" (Hattie, 2009, pp. 162–163). (Chapter 4)

Learning progressions are the sequenced "building blocks" of instruction that lead students to understand the unit learning intentions. Look at each unit learning intention to decide what increments of instruction students will need to fully understand that learning intention. Then sequence these instructional building blocks in the order they will occur during the unit. (Chapter 10)

Performance tasks are hands-on, active learning tasks that enable students to *apply* the concepts and skills they are learning by creating a product or performance that can be evaluated with a scoring guide. Although not part of a CFA, they help students develop deep understanding of the targeted learning intentions *during* the unit so students are better prepared to demonstrate all they have learned on the post-CFA at the *end* of the unit. (Chapter 3)

Priority Standards are "a carefully selected *subset* of the total list of the grade-specific and course-specific standards within each content area that students must know and be able to do by the end of each school year in order to be prepared for the standards at the next grade level or course. Priority standards represent the *assured student competencies* that each teacher needs to help every student learn, and demonstrate proficiency in, by the end of the current grade or course" (Ainsworth, 2013, p. xv). (Chapter 4)

Professional learning teams are grade- or course-level teams of educators who follow established protocols while collaboratively designing and scoring CFAs and then analyzing and interpreting the results in order to adjust their instruction and improve student learning. (Chapter 11)

Quick progress checks are short formative assessments that educators administer to students *after* key learning progressions. Their sole purpose is to generate evidence of individual student understanding relative to the learning progression(s) in focus. If the quick progress checks are well constructed, educators are able to correctly interpret the evidence, adjust instruction appropriately, and meet students' identified learning needs. (Chapter 10)

Reliability means *consistency* of what an assessment measures over time. If an assessment is reliable, students provide similar responses to the particular assessment questions at different times and/or under different circumstances. If an assessment is "unreliable—inconsistent—it cannot contribute to accurate, score-based inferences and sound instructional decisions" (Popham, 2003, p. 54). (Chapter 9)

Scoring guides (often referred to as "rubrics") are *detailed* success criteria that make the performance expectations of the success criteria *explicit.* They communicate in specific, objective terms exactly what students need to include in their constructed responses on the CFA to show they have achieved the learning intentions upon which the assessment questions are based. (Chapter 8)

Selected-response questions include multiple choice, matching, true/false, and fill-in items with a provided answer bank. As its name signifies, students are *selecting* their answer from a set of answer choices. (Chapter 7)

Student success criteria represent the comprehensive list of what students must know and be able to do by the end of a unit of study and include the Essential Questions, the "unwrapped" concepts and skills in the unit Priority Standards, and the unit vocabulary terms. They describe for students *how* to be successful in attaining the unit learning intentions. (Chapter 6)

Supporting standards are those standards not designated "priority." As their name indicates, they support or connect to the Priority Standards. "They are 'taught' within the context of the Priority Standards, but do not receive the same degree of instruction and assessment emphasis as do the

Priority Standards. The supporting standards often become the *instructional scaffolds* to help students understand and attain the more rigorous and comprehensive Priority Standards" (Ainsworth, 2013, p. xv). (Chapter 4)

Unit of study is a "series of specific lessons, learning experiences, and related assessments based on designated Priority Standards and related supporting standards for an (instructional) focus that may last anywhere from two to six weeks" (Ainsworth, 2010, p. 324). (Chapter 1)

"Unwrapping" the standards means to analyze and deconstruct the wording of grade-level and course-specific standards within each unit of study to determine exactly what students need to know (teachable concepts) and be able to do (specific skills). When educators "unwrap" standards, they underline the concepts (important nouns and noun phrases) and circle or CAPITALIZE the skills (verbs and verb phrases). (Chapter 5)

Validity means that the inferences educators are able to draw from student responses to assessment questions are correct. The assessment questions need to measure what they are intended to measure (in the CFA context, student understanding of the predetermined unit learning intentions and student success criteria), so that educators can infer accurately what students do and do not understand. "Validity is the most important single attribute of a good test. The emphasis is on the interpretation (of student understanding by the educators)." (Visible Learning Plus) (Chapter 9)

References

Ainsworth, L. (2003). *"Unwrapping" the standards: A simple process to make standards manageable.* Oxford, OH: Advanced Learning Press.

Ainsworth, L. (2008). *Common formative assessments training manual.* Englewood, CO: Lead + Learn Press.

Ainsworth, L. (2010). *Rigorous curriculum design: How to create curricular units of study that align standards, instruction, and assessment.* Englewood, CO: Lead + Learn Press.

Ainsworth, L. (2013). *Prioritizing the common core: Identifying specific standards to emphasize the most.* Englewood, CO: Lead + Learn Press.

Ainsworth, L. (2014). *"Unwrapping" the common core: A simple process to manage rigorous standards.* Englewood, CO: Lead + Learn Press.

Ainsworth, L., & Viegut, D. (2006). *Common formative assessments: How to connect standards-based instruction and assessment.* Thousand Oaks, CA: Corwin.

Anderson, L. W., & Krathwohl, D. R. (Eds.). (2001). *A taxonomy for learning, teaching, and assessing: A revision of Bloom's taxonomy of educational objectives.* New York: Longman.

Black, P., & Wiliam, D. (1998a). Assessment and classroom learning. *Assessment in Education: Principles, Policy and Practice, 5*(1), 7–73.

Black, P., & Wiliam, D. (1998b, October). Inside the black box: Raising standards through classroom assessment. *Phi Delta Kappan, 80*(2), 130–149.

Black, P., & Wiliam, D. (2009). Developing the theory of formative assessment. *Educational Assessment, Evaluation and Accountability, 21*(1), 5–31.

Brookhart, S. M. (2008). *How to give effective feedback to your students.* Alexandria, VA: Association for Supervision and Curriculum Development.

Brookhart, S. M., & Nitko, A. J. (2007). *Assessment and grading in classrooms.* Upper Saddle River, NJ: Pearson.

Christakis, N. A., & Fowler, J. H. (2009). *Connected: How your friends' friends' friends' affect everything you feel, think, and do.* New York: Little, Brown.

Clarke, S. (2008). *Active learning through formative assessment.* London: Hodder Education.

DuFour, R. (2004). What is a professional learning community? [Electronic version]. *Educational Leadership, 61*(8), 6. Retrieved from http://www.ascd.org.

DuFour, R., DuFour, R., & Eaker, R. (Eds.). (2005). *On common ground: The power of professional learning communities.* Bloomington, IN: National Education Service.

DuFour, R., & Eaker, R. (1998). *Professional learning communities at work: Best practices for enhancing student achievement.* Bloomington, IN: National Education Service.

Erickson, H. L. (2002). *Concept-based curriculum and instruction: Teaching beyond the facts.* Thousand Oaks, CA: Corwin.

Fisher, D., & Frey, N. (2007). *Checking for understanding: Formative assessment techniques for your classroom.* Alexandria, VA: Association for Supervision and Curriculum Development.

Flach, T. K. (2011). *Engaging students through performance assessment: Creating performance tasks to monitor student learning.* Englewood, CO: Lead + Learn Press.

Fullan, M. (2001). *Leading in a culture of change.* San Francisco: Jossey-Bass.

Fullan, M. (2005). *Leadership and sustainability.* Thousand Oaks, CA: Corwin.

Gallimore, R., Ermeling, B., Saunders, W., & Goldenberg, C. (2009, May). Moving the learning of teaching closer to practice: Teacher education implications of school-based inquiry teams. *Elementary School Journal, 109*(5), 537–553.

Guskey, T. R. (Ed.). (2009). *Practical solutions for serious problems in standards-based grading.* Thousand Oaks, CA: Corwin.

Guskey, T. R., & Bailey, J. M. (2001). *Developing grading and reporting systems for student learning.* Thousand Oaks, CA: Corwin.

Guskey, T. R., & Bailey, J. M. (2009). *Developing standards-based report cards.* Thousand Oaks, CA: Corwin.

Haladyna, T. M. (1997). *Writing test items to evaluate higher-order thinking.* Boston: Allyn & Bacon.

Haladyna, T. M. (2012). *Developing and validating multiple-choice test items* (3rd ed.). New York: Routledge.

Hall, G. E., & Hord, S. M. (2001). *Implementing change: Patterns, principles, and potholes* (3rd ed.). Upper Saddle River, NJ: Pearson.

Hattie, J. (1992). Measuring the effects of schooling. *Australian Journal of Education, 36*(1), 5–13.

Hattie, J. (2009). *Visible learning: A synthesis of over 800 meta-analyses relating to achievement.* New York: Routledge.

Hattie, J. (2012). *Visible learning for teachers: Maximizing impact on learning.* New York: Routledge.

Heritage, M. (2008). *Learning progressions: Supporting instruction and formative assessment.* Washington, DC: Council of Chief State School Officers.

Heritage, M. (2010). *Formative assessment: Making it happen in the classroom.* Thousand Oaks, CA: Corwin.

Heritage, M. (2013). *Formative assessment in practice: A process of inquiry and action.* Cambridge, MA: Harvard Education Press.

Herman, J. L. (2006). Challenges in integrating standards and assessment with student learning. *Measurement: Interdisciplinary Research and Perspectives, 4,* 119–124.

Hess, K. K. (2013). *A guide for using Webb's Depth of Knowledge with Common Core State Standards.* Washington, DC: Common Core Institute. Retrieved from http://cliu21cng.wikispaces.com/file/view/WebsDepthofKnowledgeFlipChart.pdf/457670878/WebsDepthofKnowledgeFlipChart.pdf.

Hirsh, S., Psencik, K., & Brown, F. (2014). *Becoming a learning system.* Oxford, OH: Learning Forward.

Interstate New Teacher Assessment and Support Consortium. (1992). *Model standards for beginning teacher licensing, assessment and development: A resource for state dialogue.* Washington, DC: Council of Chief State School Officers.

Jones, B. R. (2014). *The focus model.* Thousand Oaks, CA: Corwin.

Jung, L. A., & Guskey, T. R. (2012). *Grading exceptional and struggling learners.* Thousand Oaks, CA: Corwin.

Knight, J. K. (2013). *High-impact instruction: A framework for great teaching.* Thousand Oaks, CA: Corwin.

Lambert, L. (1998). *Building leadership capacity in schools.* Alexandria, VA: Association for Supervision and Curriculum Development.

Langor, G. M., Colton, A. B., & Goff, L. S. (2003). *Collaborative analysis of student work: Improving teaching and learning.* Alexandria, VA: Association for Supervision and Curriculum Development.

Marzano, R. J. (2000). *Transforming classroom grading.* Alexandria, VA: Association for Supervision and Curriculum Development.

Marzano, R. J. (2003). *What works in schools.* Alexandria, VA: Association for Supervision and Curriculum Development.

Marzano, R. J. (2007). *The art and science of teaching: A comprehensive framework for effective instruction.* Alexandria, VA: Association for Supervision and Curriculum Development.

Marzano, R. J. (2010). *Formative assessment and standards-based grading: Classroom strategies that work.* Bloomington, IN: Marzano Research Laboratory and Solution Tree.

Masters, D. (2014, January). Using data to evaluate your impact. *The Inside Series.* Seminar conducted by Visible Learning Plus in Thousand Oaks, CA.

Mendler, A. N. (2000). *Motivating students who don't care: Successful techniques for educators.* Bloomington, IN: National Education Service.

Nagel, D. (2015). *Meaningful grading practices for secondary teachers: Practical strategies to prevent failure, recover credits, and ensure standards-based grading.* Thousand Oaks, CA: Corwin.

National Education Association. (2003). *Balanced assessment: The key to accountability and improved student learning.* Washington, DC: Author.

Nitko, A. J. (2001). *Educational assessment of students* (3rd ed.). Columbus, OH: Merrill Prentice Hall.

Nitko, A. J., & Brookhart, S. M. (2010). *Educational assessment of students* (6th ed.). Upper Saddle River, NJ: Pearson.

O'Connor, K. (2009). *How to grade for learning* (2nd ed.). Thousand Oaks, CA: Corwin.

Oosterhof, A. (2001). *Classroom applications of educational measurement* (3rd ed.). Upper Saddle River, NJ: Pearson Prentice Hall.

Partnership for Assessment of Readiness for College and Careers (PARCC). (2014a). *The PARCC assessment high school.* Retrieved from www.parcconline.org/high-school.

Partnership for Assessment of Readiness for College and Careers (PARCC). (2014b). *The PARCC assessment 3–8.* Retrieved from www.parcconline.org/3–8.

Peterson, K. D., & Deal, T. E. (2002). *The shaping school culture fieldbook.* San Francisco: Jossey-Bass.

Peterson, K. D., & Deal, T. E. (2003). *Shaping school culture: The heart of leadership.* San Francisco: Jossey-Bass.

Popham, W. J. (2003). *Test better, teach better: The instructional role of assessment.* Alexandria, VA: Association for Supervision and Curriculum Development.

Popham, W. J. (2008). *Transformative assessment.* Alexandria, VA: Association for Supervision and Curriculum Development.

Popham, W. J. (2013). *Evaluating America's teachers: Mission possible?* Thousand Oaks, CA: Corwin.

Sargent, J. (2004). *Data retreat workbook.* Green Bay, WI: Cooperative Educational Service Agency No. 7.

Scherer, M. (2001). How and why standards can improve student achievement: A conversation with Robert J. Marzano. *Educational Leadership, 59*(1), 14–15.

Schlechty, P. C. (2002). *Working on the work: An action plan for teachers, principals, and superintendents.* San Francisco: Jossey-Bass.

Schmoker, M. J., & Wilson, R. B. (1993). *Total quality education: Profiles of schools that demonstrate the power of Deming's management principles.* Bloomington, IN: Phi Delta Kappa.

Senge, P., Scharmer, C. O., Jaworski, J., & Flowers, B. S. (2004). *Presence: Human purpose and the field of the future.* Cambridge, MA: Society for Organizational Learning.

Sinek, S. (2009, September). *Simon Sinek: How great leaders inspire action.* [Video file]. Retrieved from http://www.ted.com/talks/simon_sinek_how_great_leaders_inspire_action.

Smarter Balanced Assessment Consortium (SBAC). (n.d.). *Sample items and performance tasks* [Web page]. Retrieved from http://www.smarterbalanced.org/sample-items-and-performance-tasks/.

Stiggins, R. J. (1997). *Student-centered classroom assessment* (2nd ed.). Upper Saddle River, NJ: Prentice Hall.

Stiggins, R. J., Arter, J. A., Chappuis, J., & Chappuis, S. (2004). *Classroom assessment for student learning: Doing it right—using it well.* Portland, OR: Educational Testing Service Assessment Training Institute.

Stiggins, R. J., Arter, J. A., Chappuis, J., & Chappuis, S. (2006). *Classroom assessment for student learning: Doing it right—using it well.* Princeton, NJ: Merrill Prentice Hall and Educational Testing Service.

Supovitz, J. A. (2002). Developing communities of instructional practice. *Teachers College Record, 104*(8), 1591–1626.

Supovitz, J. A., & Christman, J. B. (2003, November). Developing communities of instructional practice: Lessons for Cincinnati and Philadelphia. *CPRE Policy Briefs,* 1–9. Retrieved from http://files.eric.ed.gov/fulltext/ED498331.pdf.

Syrja, R. C. (2012). *Common formative assessments for English language learners.* Englewood, CO: Lead + Learn Press.

Tomlinson, C. A. (1995). *How to differentiate instruction in mixed ability classrooms.* Alexandria, VA: Association for Supervision and Curriculum Development.

Tomlinson, C. A. (1999). *The differentiated classroom: Responding to the needs of all learners.* Alexandria, VA: Association for Supervision and Curriculum Development.

Venezia, A., & Kirst, M. (2001). *The bridge project: Strengthening K–16 transition policies.* Stanford, CA: Stanford University.

Vescio, V., Ross, D., & Adams, A. (2008). A review of research on the impact of professional learning communities on teaching practice and student learning. *Teaching and Teacher Education, 24,* 80–91. Retrieved from https://www.k12.wa.us/Compensation/pubdocs/Vesci02008PLC-paper.pdf.

Wagner, T. (2008, October). Rigor redefined. *Educational Leadership, 66*(2), 20–24.

Warwick, R. (1992). *Beyond piecemeal improvements: How to transform your school using Deming's quality principles.* Bloomington, IN: National Educational Service.

Webb, N. (1997). *Criteria for alignment of expectations and assessments on mathematics and science education* (Monograph No. 6). Washington, DC: Council of Chief State School Officers.

Wenger, E. (1998). *Communities of practice: Learning, meaning, and identity.* New York: Cambridge University Press.

Wiggins, G., & McTighe, J. (1998). *Understanding by design.* Alexandria, VA: Association for Supervision and Curriculum Development.

Wiliam, D. (2007–2008). Changing classroom practice. *Educational Leadership, 65*(4), 36.

Wiliam, D. (2011). *Embedded formative assessment.* Bloomington, IN: Solution Tree.

Wiseman, L., Allen, L., & Foster, E. (2013). *The multiplier effect: Tapping the genius inside our schools.* Thousand Oaks, CA: Corwin.

Wormelli, R. (2006). *Fair isn't always equal: Assessing & grading in the differentiated classroom.* Portland, ME: National Middle School Association.

Yatvin, J. (2004). *A room with a differentiated view: How to serve ALL children as individual learners.* Portsmouth, NH: Heinemann.

Index

Made in the USA
Las Vegas, NV
27 April 2024